NEW

CUTTING EDGE

INTERMEDIATE

TEACHER'S RESOURCE BOOK

photocopiable resources by Chris Redston

helen barker

with sarah cunningham   peter moor

Longman

Contents

Introduction

New Cutting Edge Intermediate at a glance

New Cutting Edge Intermediate is aimed at young adults studying general English at an intermediate level and provides material for approximately 120 hours of teaching. It is suitable for students studying in either a monolingual or multilingual classroom situation.

STUDENTS' BOOK **CLASS CDS/CASSETTES**	*New Cutting Edge Intermediate Students' Book* is divided into twelve modules, each consisting of approximately 10 hours of classroom material. Each module contains some or all of the following: • **reading** and/or **listening** and/or **vocabulary** – an introduction to the topic of the module, including speaking • **grammar** – input/revision in two *Language focus* sections with practice activities and integrated pronunciation work • **vocabulary** – includes a *Wordspot* section which focuses on common words (*have, get, take*, etc.) • **task preparation** – a stimulus or model for the task (often listening or reading) and *Useful language* for the task • **task** – extended speaking, often with an optional writing component • a **Real life** section – language needed in more complex real-life situations, usually including listening and speaking • **writing skills** • a **Study ... Practise ... Remember!** section – to develop study skills, with practice activities and a self-assessment section for students to monitor their progress. At the back of the *Students' Book* you will find: • a **Mini-dictionary** which contains definitions, pronunciations and examples of key words and phrases from the *Students' Book* • a detailed **Language summary** covering the grammar in each module
WORKBOOK	• **Tapescripts** for material on the Class CDs/Cassettes.
STUDENTS' CD/CASSETTE	*New Cutting Edge Intermediate Workbook* is divided into twelve modules, which consist of: • **grammar** – consolidation of the main language points covered in the *Students' Book* • **vocabulary** – additional practice and input • **skills work** – *Improve your writing* and *Listen and read* sections • **pronunciation** – focus on problem sounds and word stress.
TEACHER'S RESOURCE BOOK	The optional **Student's CD/Cassette** features exercises on grammar and pronunciation. There are two versions of the *Workbook*, one with and the other without an **Answer key**.

	New Cutting Edge Intermediate Teacher's Resource Book consists of three sections:
	
	• **Introduction** and **Teacher's tips** on:
	  – Using a discovery approach in the teaching of grammar
	  – Using the *Study ... Practise ... Remember!* and *Mini-check* sections
	  – Working with lexis
	  – Responding to learners' individual language needs
	  – Making the most of the *Mini-dictionary*
	  – Making tasks work
	
	• **Step-by-step teacher's notes** for each module, including alternative suggestions for different teaching situations (particularly for tasks), detailed language notes and integrated answer keys
	
	• photocopiable **Resource bank**, including learner-training worksheets, communicative grammar practice activities and vocabulary extension activities.
	
	The teacher's notes section is **cross-referenced** to the *Resource bank* and the *Workbook*.

The thinking behind New Cutting Edge Intermediate

Overview

New Cutting Edge Intermediate has a multilayered, topic-based syllabus which includes thorough and comprehensive work on grammar, vocabulary, pronunciation and the skills of listening, reading, speaking and writing. Structured speaking tasks form a central part of each module. *New Cutting Edge Intermediate* gives special emphasis to:

*   communication
*   the use of phrases and collocation
*   active learning and study skills
*   recycling and revision.

Topics and content

We aim to motivate learners by basing modules around up-to-date topics of international interest. Students are encouraged to learn more about the world and other cultures through the medium of English, and personalisation is strongly emphasised. The differing needs of monocultural and multicultural classes have been kept in mind throughout.

Approach to grammar

Learners are encouraged to take an active, systematic approach to developing their knowledge of grammar, and the opportunity to use new language is provided in a natural, communicative way. Typically, there are two *Language focus* sections in each module, in which grammar is presented using reading or listening texts. Each *Language focus* has an *Analysis* box focusing on the main language points, in which learners are encouraged to work out rules for themselves. This is followed up thoroughly through:

*   a wide range of communicative and written practice exercises in the *Students' Book*
*   the opportunity to use new grammar naturally in the speaking tasks (see below)
*   the *Study ... Practise ... Remember!* and *Mini-check* sections, in which learners are encouraged to assess their progress and work on any remaining problems
*   the *Language summary* section at the back of the *Students' Book*
*   further practice in the *Workbook*.

(See *Teacher's tips: using a discovery approach in the teaching of grammar* on pages 6–7, and *Using the* Study ... Practise ... Remember! *and* Mini-check *sections* on page 7.)

Approach to vocabulary

A wide vocabulary is vital to communicative success, so new lexis is introduced and practised at every stage in the course. Particular attention has been paid to the selection of high-frequency, internationally useful words and phrases, drawing on information from the British National Corpus.

Vocabulary input is closely related to the topics and tasks in the modules, allowing for plenty of natural recycling. Further practice is provided in the *Study ... Practise ... Remember!* section at the end of each module and in the *Workbook*.

In order to communicate, fluent speakers make extensive use of 'prefabricated chunks' of language. For this reason, *New*

Cutting Edge Intermediate gives particular emphasis to collocations and fixed phrases. These are integrated through:

*   *Wordspot* sections, which focus on high-frequency words such as *get*, *have* and *think*
*   the *Useful language* boxes in the speaking tasks
*   *Real life* sections, which focus on phrases used in common everyday situations such as telephoning or making arrangements
*   topic-based vocabulary lessons.

(See *Teacher's tips: working with lexis* on pages 9–10.) In addition, more straightforward single-item vocabulary is also extended through the *Vocabulary booster* sections of the *Workbook*.

'Useful' vocabulary is partly individual to the learner. With this in mind, the speaking tasks in *New Cutting Edge Intermediate* provide the opportunity for students to ask the teacher for the words and phrases they need. (See *Teacher's tips: responding to learners' individual language needs* on pages 11–12.)

To encourage learner independence, *New Cutting Edge Intermediate* has a *Mini-dictionary* which includes entries for words and phrases appropriate to the level of the learner. Learners are encouraged to refer to the *Mini-dictionary* throughout the course, and there are study tips to help them to do this more effectively. (See *Teacher's tips: making the most of the* Mini-dictionary on page 12.)

The speaking tasks

New Cutting Edge Intermediate aims to integrate elements of a task-based approach into its overall methodology. There are structured speaking tasks in each module, which include interviews, mini-talks, problem-solving and story-telling. Here the primary focus is on achieving a particular outcome or product, rather than on practising specific language. Learners are encouraged to find the language they need in order to express their own ideas.

The frequent performance of such tasks is regarded in this course as a central element in learners' progress. The tasks provide the opportunity for realistic and extended communication, and because learners are striving to express what they want to say, they are more likely to absorb the language that they are learning. Much of the grammar and vocabulary input in each module is therefore integrated around these tasks, which in turn provide a valuable opportunity for the teacher to revisit and recycle what has been studied.

In order to make the tasks work effectively in the classroom:

*   they are graded carefully in terms of difficulty
*   a model/stimulus is provided for what the student is expected to do
*   useful language is provided to help students to express themselves
*   thinking and planning time is included.

(See *Teacher's tips: making tasks work* on pages 13–14, and *Responding to learners' individual language needs* on pages 11–12.)

In addition to the tasks, New Cutting Edge Intermediate offers many other opportunities for speaking, for example, through the discussion of texts, communicative practice exercises, and the wide range of games and activities in the photocopiable Resource bank in the *Teacher's Resource Book*.

Other important elements in *New Cutting Edge Intermediate*

Listening

New Cutting Edge Intermediate places strong emphasis on listening. Listening material consists of:
- short extracts and mini-dialogues to introduce and practise new language
- words and sentences for close listening and to model pronunciation
- longer texts (interviews, stories and conversations), many of which are authentic, often in the *Preparation* section as a model or stimulus for the *Task*
- regular *Listen and read* sections in the *Workbook* to further develop students' confidence in this area.

Speaking

There is also a strong emphasis on speaking, as follows:
- The tasks provide a regular opportunity for extended and prepared speaking based around realistic topics and situations (see page 6).
- Much of the practice of grammar and lexis is through oral exercises and activities.
- The topics and reading texts in each module provide opportunities for follow-up discussion.
- There is regular integrated work on pronunciation.
- Most of the photocopiable activities in the *Resource bank* are oral.

Reading

There is a wide range of reading material in the *Students' Book*, including newspaper articles, factual/scientific texts, stories, quizzes, forms, notes and letters. These texts are integrated in a number of different ways:
- extended texts specifically to develop reading skills
- texts which lead into grammar work and language analysis
- texts which provide a model or stimulus for tasks and models for writing activities.

Note: for classes who do not have a lot of time to do reading in class there are suggestions in the teacher's notes section on how to avoid this where appropriate.

Writing

Regular and systematic work on writing skills are developed in *New Cutting Edge Intermediate* through:
- regular writing sections in the *Students' Book*, which focuses on writing e-mails and letters, writing narratives and reviews, drafting and redrafting, use of linkers, etc.
- *Improve your writing* sections in the *Workbook*, which expand on the areas covered in the *Students' Book*
- written follow-up sections to many of the speaking tasks.

Pronunciation

Pronunciation work in *New Cutting Edge Intermediate* is integrated with grammar and lexis, and in the *Real life* sections in special pronunciation boxes. The focus in the *Students' Book* is mainly on stress, weak forms and intonation, while the *Workbook* focuses on problem sounds and word stress. A range of activity types are used in the *Students' Book*, including discrimination exercises and dictation, and an equal emphasis is placed on understanding and reproducing. In addition, there are *Pronunciation spots* in the *Study ... Practise ... Remember!* sections, which focus on problem sounds. These activities are intended as quick warmers and fillers, and can be omitted if not required.

Learning skills

New Cutting Edge Intermediate develops learning skills in a number of ways, as follows:
- The discovery approach to grammar encourages learners to experiment with language and to work out rules for themselves.
- The task-based approach encourages learners to take a proactive role in their learning.
- Looking words and phrases up in the *Mini-dictionary* gives students constant practice of a range of dictionary skills.
- The *Study ...* sections of the *Study ... Practise ... Remember!* focus on useful learning strategies, such as keeping notes and revision techniques. Learners are encouraged to share ideas about the most effective ways to learn.
- The *Resource bank* includes five learner-training worksheets aimed at developing students' awareness of the importance of taking an active role in the learning process.

Revision and recycling

Recycling is a key feature of *New Cutting Edge Intermediate*. New language is explicitly recycled through:
- extra practice exercises in the *Study ... Practise ... Remember!* sections. These are designed to cover all the main grammar and vocabulary areas in the module. After trying the exercises, learners are encouraged to return to any parts of the module that they still feel unsure about to assess what they have (and have not) remembered from the module.

(See *Teacher's tips: using the* Study ... Practise ... Remember! *and* Mini-check *sections* on page 7.)
- *Consolidation* spreads after Modules 4, 8 and 12. These combine grammar and vocabulary exercises with listening and speaking activities, recycling material from the previous four modules.
- three photocopiable tests in the *Resource bank* for use after Modules 4, 8 and 12.

In addition, the speaking tasks offer constant opportunities for learners to use what they have studied in a natural way, and for teachers to assess their progress and remind them of important points.

Teacher's tips

Using a discovery approach in the teaching of grammar

New Cutting Edge Intermediate often uses a 'discovery' approach to grammar input because:
* we believe that students absorb rules best if they work them out for themselves
* students of this level often have some previous knowledge of the language.

This knowledge is often difficult for the teacher to predict. The 'test-teach' exercises and *Analysis* boxes are designed so that students can utilise this knowledge, and so that teachers can adjust their approach to take account of it.

❶ Get to know the material available

Every module of *New Cutting Edge Intermediate* has two *Language focus* sections, which include:
* a short text or 'test-teach' type introductory material
* an *Analysis* box focusing students on the main language points
* a *Language summary* section at the back of the *Students' Book* providing more detailed information about what is covered in the *Analysis* boxes
* oral and/or written practice exercises.

These language areas are recycled through:
* the *Study ... Practise ... Remember!* sections at the end of each module.
* the *Consolidation* spreads after Modules 4, 8 and 12.

The *Workbook* includes additional practice material.

In the *Resource bank* of this *Teacher's Resource Book*, there are also a number of games and other activities designed to further consolidate the grammar areas covered.

❷ Be prepared to modify your approach

It is unlikely that you will discover that all students are using the target language perfectly and need no further work on it. However, you may realise they only need brief revision, that you can omit certain sections of the *Analysis* or go through some or all of it very quickly. Alternatively, you may decide to omit some of the practice activities, or set them for homework.

On the other hand, you may discover that many students know less than you would normally expect at this level. In this case, spend more time on the basic points, providing extra examples as necessary, and leave more complex issues for another day.

❸ Encourage students to share what they know and to make guesses

It is useful to do 'test-teach' exercises (for example, exercises 2b and c on page 106 of the *Students' Book*) in pairs or groups. In this way, stronger students can help weaker ones, and you do not have to provide all the input. If neither student knows, encourage them to guess – sometimes they have internalised rules without realising. This can be checked as you go over the answers together.

❹ Give students time to adjust

The idea of such exercises is that learners form their own hypotheses about new rules, which they then check and refine. Students not used to this approach may take time to adapt, but this does not mean that they will never get used to it. Some students get anxious if they do not have things explained immediately. In such cases, do not leave them to become more frustrated – either answer their questions briefly on an individual basis, or make it clear that you will be dealing with them later.

If there are language areas that you think your class will be unable to tackle without previous input, you can change the whole approach, presenting the rules at the beginning of the *Language focus* and setting the 'test-teach' exercises as controlled practice activities.

❺ Use Analysis *boxes in different ways*

Questions in the *Analysis* boxes can be tackled in different ways, depending on the ability/confidence of your students and the relative difficulty of the language point in question. Here are some possible approaches.

a **Answer the questions individually / in pairs, then check them together as a class:** this is a good way of encouraging a more independent attitude in the students. Make sure that students understand what they have to do for each question, and monitor carefully to see how they are coping – if they are obviously all stuck or confused, stop them and sort out the problem. As you check answers, write up examples to highlight any important problems of form, meaning, etc. The *Language summary* can be read at the end, either individually or as a class.

b **Answer the questions together as a class:** with weaker classes, or for areas that you know your students will find difficult, it may be best to read out questions to the whole class and work through them together, with examples on the board. Alternatively, set more straightforward questions for students to answer in pairs, and do more complicated ones together as a class. As students gain more confidence, you can set more and more questions for them to do on their own.

c **Students work through the questions individually / in pairs, then check the answers themselves in the *Language summary*:** stronger, self-sufficient students may be able to take most of the responsibility for themselves. Most classes should be able to do this with the simpler *Analysis* boxes. It is still important that you monitor carefully to make sure that there are no major problems, and check answers together at the end to clear up any remaining doubts.

Reading and speaking (PAGES 8–9)

1 Introduce students to the *Mini-dictionary*. Explain that for phrases like this, they need to think about which word to look up, e.g. for *working longer hours*, they may need to look up *work* or *hours*. Give students time to read the sentences and use their mini-dictionaries. Check the meaning of the words and phrases in bold. You may need to model, and get students to repeat, the pronunciation of *hours* /aʊəz/, *leisure* /leʒə/, *physically* /fɪzɪkəli/, *employee* /ɪmˈplɔɪ·ɪ/. Get students to think about the question individually before discussing the statements in small groups. Ask two or three groups to tell the class what they said about one of the statements.

2 Explain that the text is about how people spend their time in different countries. Students read the article, writing the name of the country (or countries) or *all over the world* next to each statement as appropriate. Check answers with the whole class.

ANSWERS AND LANGUAGE NOTE
a all over the world b all over the world
c the UK d Europe e Europe f the UK
g the UK h the US i the UK j the UK
k Sweden and Finland l the UK

Students may have written *Britain* rather than the *UK*. It is usual to describe the nationality as *British*, and the country as *Britain* or *the UK*. For the purposes of this exercise, either answer is correct.

3 Students read the text again and then work in pairs to discuss interesting points. Finish with a brief class discussion on points the whole class commented on.

4 Look at the example with the class. If necessary, write the two phrases on the board in number form, to clarify. Students work individually to decide on the meaning of the quantity expressions before comparing their answers with a partner. Check with the class as a whole.

ANSWERS AND LANGUAGE NOTES
a	two thirds / sixty-six percent	S
b	the main share of the work / most of the work	S
c	an average of six hours / exactly six hours	D
d	over eighteen hours / less than eighteen hours	D
e	the vast majority / ninety percent	S
f	almost half / fifty-two percent	D
g	more than half / forty-five percent	D
h	a fifth / twenty percent	S
i	at least twice a week / two times a week or more	S

Highlight the following.
* *An average of* is a generalisation; *exactly* is a precise number.
* *Over* means the same as *more than*.
* *Almost* means the same as *nearly but not quite*. Forty-seven percent would be *almost half*. However, *less than* is a more general description, so *less than half* could be any number between zero and forty-nine percent.

5 Look at the examples with the class. Ask them to discuss the numbers in pairs, then look at the text again if necessary. Check answers with the whole class.

ANSWERS
a **Eighty-five percent**: eighty-five percent of British people regularly read newspapers.
b **Six hours**: the average British husband does six hours of housework a week.
c **Eighteen hours**: the average British wife does over eighteen hours of housework a week.
d **Eleven minutes**: the average British family spends eleven minutes preparing the main evening meal.
e **Twenty-four**: the average Spanish or Italian person is twenty-four years old when they start full-time work.
f **Half an hour a day**: the average American fourteen-year-old spends half an hour a day on homework.
g **Seventy-five minutes**: on average British teenagers spend seventy-five minutes a day on physical activities.
h **Seventy-three**: seventy-three percent of Swedes and Finns do sport at least once or twice a week.
i **Fifty-five minutes**: the average British employee spends fifty-five minutes chatting every day at work.

6 Students discuss the questions in pairs or small groups. Finish off by asking each group to tell the class the most interesting/unusual thing they heard.

Vocabulary 2 (PAGE 10)

People around you

See *Teacher's tips: making the most of the* Mini-dictionary on pages 12–13.

1 **a** Students work in pairs and check any of the words they are unsure about. Practise the words with a repetition drill, marking the stressed syllables on the board. The pronunciation of the following words may need particular attention: *acquaintance* /əˈkweɪntəns/, *aunt* /ɑːnt/, *colleague* /ˈkɒliːg/, *mother-in-law* /ˈmʌðər ɪn ˌlɔː/, *niece* /niːs/, *neighbour* /neɪbə/, *parent* /peərənt/, *stranger* /streɪndʒə/, *cousin* /kʌzən/, *relative* /relətɪv/.

ANSWERS AND LANGUAGE NOTE
Family: aunt, cousin, husband, niece, mother-in-law, parent, relative, stepmother
Friends: best friend, (classmate), flatmate
Work: boss, colleague
School: classmate, headteacher
Other: stranger, acquaintance, ex-girlfriend, neighbour

There may be some variations in your students' ideas. For example, they may have put *ex-girlfriend* as a friend. Whilst this is an acceptable difference, it is not necessarily true for all people.

b When brainstorming other vocabulary to add to the columns, discourage words that are too simple (*mother*, *father*, etc.) and focus on vocabulary that students may not know, for example, *nephew*, *godmother*, *manager*, *partner*. Note that partner has different meanings. In the context of family and friends, it is similar to *husband*, *wife*, *boyfriend*, *girlfriend*. In the context of work, it means someone you run a business with. In the context of the classroom, it means the student you work with.

2 [1.4] Explain that each instruction will tell students to 'choose a shape' to write their answer in. Play the recording, pausing after each instruction to give students time to think and write.

3 Look at the examples with the class, then do one or two examples with them before they do the activity in pairs. Ask one or two pairs to tell the class something they found out.

ADDITIONAL ACTIVITY

RB Resource bank: *Vocabulary extension* (phrases for talking about people around you), page 115

Language focus 2 (PAGES 10–11)

Present simple and continuous

See *Teacher's tips: using a discovery approach in the teaching of grammar* on page 8.

1 [1.5] Focus students on the photos, and check that they understand the task. Play the recording and encourage students to compare answers in pairs before checking with the whole class.

ANSWERS
a brother   b friend/neighbour   c cousin
d grandmother   e brother

2 [1.5] Tell students to work individually before checking in pairs. Play the recording and check answers as a whole class.

ANSWERS

a	birthday party		
b	upstairs	girlfriend/partner	
c	with his parents	aunt and uncle	's doing
d	's enjoying	doesn't know	
e	like	cousin	
f	old	needs	weekend
g	grown up	tall	

Analysis

1 Write up the first examples of the Present simple and Present continuous as an example to illustrate the activity for the whole class.

ANSWERS
Present simple: lives (×2), is (×2), doesn't know, wants, looks (×2), needs, stays
Present continuous: is showing, 's staying, 's doing, 's enjoying, is getting (×2)

Full tables showing these verb forms are on page 144 of the *Language summary*. Although this should be revision, many students are unaware of their own lack of accuracy in this area, and may need to be reminded of the following problems:

Present simple
- the use of the third-person singular *s* in the affirmative form: *She lives in the flat upstairs from us.*
- the use of *do/does* in the question form: *Does he live with your parents, too?*
- the use of *don't/doesn't* in the negative form: *She doesn't go out much.*

Present continuous
- the use of the contracted form of the auxiliary verb *to be*: *He's enjoying the course (= he is enjoying).*

2 Check that students understand the key words in the explanations in B. Get students to do the matching activity in pairs or groups. Check the answers with the whole class.

ANSWERS

They're looking at photos.	an action happening at this moment
She stays with us every weekend.	a habit
She lives upstairs.	a permanent situation
He's staying with his aunt.	a temporary situation
Holly looks like Karina.	a state
He's getting really tall.	a changing situation

3 Students find more examples, discussing their ideas with a partner.

ANSWERS
She is also Karina's brother's girlfriend.
He doesn't know what he wants to do.
Nikita lives upstairs from Karina.
Richard looks so grown up.

The last two examples show verbs behaving as state verbs (*to live* and *to look*). They can also be dynamic verbs:
She's living with her brother for a month. (a temporary situation)
He's looking for a word in his dictionary. (a different meaning of *look*, an action rather than somebody's appearance)

PRACTICE

1 Students work individually before checking in pairs. Go through answers with the whole class, eliciting which explanation from *Analysis*, exercise 2, applies in each case.

> **ANSWERS AND LANGUAGE NOTES**
> a doesn't smoke   b is wearing   c I'm staying
> d plays   e I'm sitting   isn't moving
>
> a a habit – *isn't smoking* would be possible if you wanted to show that this is a temporary situation, e.g. *Ben isn't smoking – he's got a headache.*
> b a temporary situation – *wears* would be possible if you wanted to talk about a habit, e.g. *Every day he wears a tie.*
> c a temporary situation – *I stay with my uncle* would be possible to describe a regular event, e.g. *every weekend.*
> d a habit – *Eva is playing the piano; the guitar and the violin* would mean that she was actually doing it at that moment, an action in progress. This is not likely, though, with three instruments!
> e an action happening at this moment – these examples must be continuous as they describe events in progress right now.

2 **a** Do one or two examples with the class. Students work individually, then compare in pairs, before checking answers with the whole class.

> **ANSWERS AND LANGUAGE NOTE**
> 1 Do you like   2 Are you reading   3 Do you read
> 4 Are you studying   5 Do you listen
> 6 Do you prefer   7 Do you usually get up
> 8 Do you find / Are you finding*
> 9 Are you enjoying   10 Are you getting
>
> * The continuous form can be used here because students are actually studying English grammar now.

b Practise a few example questions by repetition drilling. Do this exercise as a mingle drill, possibly making it into a competition to see who can find a 'yes' answer to each question first.

3 Check the meaning of *to lose weight* and *to go grey*. This may be a useful opportunity to feed in *to put on weight*. Do an example about yourself with a student, eliciting a question, e.g. *Are you getting taller?*, and a negative, e.g. *I'm not getting taller*. Let students discuss the statements in pairs, then go through them with the class.

4 **a** Tell students to write the names of six people who are important in their lives.

b Give students time to think about what they want to say. Encourage them to ask you for any difficult or very specific vocabulary they need. Put students in groups to do the activity. If possible, put them in groups with people they do not normally work with. Encourage them to ask each other questions.

ADDITIONAL PRACTICE

 RB **Resource bank:** *Something in common* (Present simple and continuous), page 116

Workbook: Present simple or continuous, page 12

> *Language focus 2*: **alternative approach to the Present simple and continuous**
>
> A more task-based approach may be more challenging here (although it will require you to 'think on your feet' quite a lot during the lesson!).
>
> • Play the recording or give a short talk of your own about your family and friends. If possible, illustrate your talk with photos. Try to make it sound natural rather than scripted. Briefly check basic comprehension.
> • Move straight on to *Practice*, exercise 3, getting the students to talk about their family/friends in the same way that you/Karina did. Do not do any specific input on present tenses, but emphasise that you want them to talk about these people's lives as they are at the moment. Write up the following prompts to encourage this: *their jobs/studies, where they live, anything else important in their lives at the moment.*
> • Give students time to plan what they will say and feed in any necessary vocabulary. Put students in small groups and get each one to give a short talk. Circulate and note down any errors you hear with the use of the Present simple and continuous (these can be errors of form, meaning or pronunciation – it may help to divide your notes into these three sections).
> • Write up the errors and get students to correct them. Go over the problems on the board yourself, or direct them to the *Language summary*. Select exercises from the *Students' Book* (*Practice*, exercises 1 and 2) or the *Workbook* on the areas they need to practise.
> • If you do not feel confident about selecting material on the spot like this, spread this approach over two lessons, so you can analyse students' errors/needs more carefully.

Wordspot (PAGE 12)

Have (and *have got*)

See *Teacher's tips: working with lexis* on pages 9–10.

1 🔲 [1.6] Start off with a quick brainstorm of phrases with *have*. Check students understand *basket* and *run out of*. Students work individually or in pairs to fill the gaps. Play the recording before checking answers with the whole class.

> **ANSWERS**
> a lunch   b look   c headache   d humour
> e problem   f rest   g family

2 Tell students to copy the diagram into their notebooks. Make sure they have enough space for the answers.

ANSWERS
(section of diagram in brackets)
have lunch (b), have a look (a), have a headache (c),
have got a (great) sense of humour (d),
have got a (serious) problem (d), have a rest (a), have
got a (very large) family (d)

3 Get students to do this in pairs, then go through
answers with the class. If you feel that a lot of this
language is new for your students, do not overload them by
focusing on the additional phrases. This could be done as an
extension activity in a future lesson.

ANSWERS
(section of diagram in brackets)
have a bad back (c), have blue eyes (d),
have breakfast (b), have a walk (a), have flu (c), have a
holiday (a), have an ice cream (b),
have blond hair (d)

4 This activity helps students to activate the phrases by
requiring them to use them. Students discuss the
questions in small groups.

Task: Find things in common
(PAGES 12–13)

Preparation: listening

1 🖭 [1.7] Give students time to read through the topics
on page 13. Check that students understand the
instructions. Emphasise that they do not need to understand
everything at this stage. Play the recording, pausing after each
conversation to give students time to think, write and compare
in pairs. Play the recording again, if necessary, before checking
answers with the class.

ANSWERS

	Do they know each other?	Which topics did they talk about?
Conversation 1	No	Travelling, sport, work, childcare, housework, things they especially love/ hate, the area they live in
Conversation 2	Yes	Work, things they especially hate, ambitions, travelling

2 Check that students understand *in common*. Focus
them on the examples, then play the recording again.
Check answers in pairs and then as a whole class.

ANSWERS
Conversation 1: they both know Prague; they both like
football, and they went to the same match in Prague;
they both hate housework; they both live near the
university in Edinburgh.

Conversation 2: they are both looking for new jobs
because they don't like the jobs they have now; they
would both like to live abroad; neither of them speaks
Spanish.

3 Refer students to the tapescript on page 159. Do an
example as a whole class first. Let students check in pairs,
then go through answers with the class.

ANSWERS
Questions to find out more about each other
You were in Prague last year, weren't you, Phillip?
Were you there for a holiday?
Anyway, what are you doing here in Edinburgh?
So you look after the children and do the housework?
Oh, don't you like children?
Anyway, which part of Edinburgh are you staying in?
Do you know it?

Phrases to talk about similarities
I do, too.
I was at that match, too.
So am I!
Oh, it's the same with me.
I live very near there, too.

**Preparation: listening, exercise 3:
alternative suggestion**

Students work in pairs, A and B. A reads the tapescript
to find three questions that they ask to find out more
about each other, and B reads to find phrases that are
used to talk about similarities and differences. A and B
then share their answers.

Task: speaking

1 Tell students that they are going to interview somebody
to find out what they have in common and what
differences there are between them. Give students time on their
own to prepare the questions they will ask. Encourage them to
ask for you for any vocabulary they need. Some students may
feel more confident if they write down some of the questions,
but emphasise that they do not have to stick to these if others
seem more appropriate during the interview.

2 Explain that in the interview they should try to find out
as much as possible about each other. They should make
notes to help them when they report back to the class. Remind
them that they need to find things in common and differences
between them. As they interview each other, feed in any
language they need in an informal way. Do not correct at this
stage unless absolutely necessary, as this will interrupt
communication. Note down errors with language from the
module for analysis at the end of the task.

3 As each pair reports back to the class, ask the other
students to listen and decide which pair has the most in
common, and which pair the least. As students speak, note
down errors to focus on at the end of the task.

Writing (PAGE 14)

E-mail an old friend

Ask if students have heard of 'Friends Reunited' or similar
websites. If nobody has visited one, ask them to imagine why
people look at them, and what they want to find out. (People
want to find out what their old classmates and friends are
doing now. Often they want to make contact with them again,
and arrange a reunion.)

1 a Ask students to read the e-mail, ignoring the gaps.
Students read individually before checking answers as a
whole class.

ANSWERS

Laura: she went to university and wanted to work with
children; her boyfriend was called Simon; she knows
people called Joe and Katie – possibly in her family –
and knew Charlotte's family well in the past; she lives
in England.

Charlotte: she's a sales manager for a property
company, is living in Sydney (which she loves), is
getting married to an Australian man called Matt next
April, doesn't know where she will be living after she
gets married, has a brother called Anthony, a sister-in-
law called Rosie and two nephews or nieces; her
grandmother died a couple of years ago; her parents are
spending their retirement doing lots of travelling
(including a recent trip to Sydney).

b Give students time to read the phrases first, then work in
pairs to do the exercise. Remind them that there is one phrase
too many. Go through the answers with the class.

ANSWERS AND LANGUAGE NOTE

a   I decided to drop you a line.
b   How are things with you?
c   I really hope you're well.
d   How is all your family?
e   Send them my love, won't you?
f   My parents are really well.
g   Do write back – I'd love to hear your news.
h   Take care of yourself / Keep in touch*.
i   PS I've attached some photos of me now.

* *Keep in touch* and *Take care of yourself* are used in similar
ways, for closure. *Keep in touch* is more likely to be used
with someone you are in regular contact with. Both
phrases are also used in spoken English for the same
purpose, although it's more usual just to say *Take care*.

2 Remind students that there are other ways to finish a
letter or e-mail. In pairs, students discuss the four endings.
Then check answers with the class.

ANSWERS

All my love: this can be used as a romantic way of
signing off, or for family.
Regards: this is the most neutral way to sign off. It can
be used for people we do not know, acquaintances or
colleagues, and is sufficiently formal for a business
e-mail.
Lots of love: this is used for close friends or family.
All the best: this is used for people we know better:
friends, colleagues or regular business contacts.

3 You may want to decide which e-mail your students
write, or you may want to let them choose. Spend some
time explaining the two options. Students can do this writing
activity for homework.

Study ... (PAGE 14)

Using English in class

1 This should be revision for your students. If you are doing
this activity in class time, students work in pairs and write
the questions before trying to remember any others. Refer
them to their answers to *Practice*, exercise 4, page 7, to check.

2 Set this up as a class activity. Ask students to think of
other ways in which they can maximise their use of spoken
English. This is especially important if they are not studying in
an English-speaking environment, or if they get very few
chances to use English. For many of your students, English
lessons may be the only opportunity for spoken practice. For
this reason, although it may feel unnatural in a monolingual
class, it is a good idea if teacher–student and student–student
interaction take place in English as much as possible. Negotiate
with your students a realistic target to aim for, and then increase
it gradually once they are using more and more English in class.
In multilingual classes, encourage students to work with
students who do not share the same first language as they do,
so that they are constantly using English to communicate. You
could negotiate a set of 'rules' for the use of English in your
classroom and display them on the classroom wall.

ANSWERS

How do you spell 'acquaintance'?
How do you pronounce this word?
Can you write it/'stomachache' on the board, please?
Which page are we on?
Can you say that again, please?

The other classroom questions were:

What's the English word for this?

What's tonight's homework?

Practise ... (PAGE 15)

1 Auxiliary verbs

If this activity is done in class, students work individually before checking their answers in pairs. Monitor as students reread the *Language summary*, so that you are available to answer questions.

ANSWERS

a do   b has   c didn't   d haven't   e were
f doesn't   g is

2 Present simple and continuous

If this activity is done in class, students work in pairs. Emphasise that they should explain to each other why each tense is used. Monitor as students reread the *Language summary*, so that you are available to answer questions.

ANSWERS

a   *doesn't usually speak*
b   correct – an activity happening at the moment
c   correct – an activity happening at the moment
d   correct – describes a change
e   *I don't know – know* is a state verb, and so cannot be used in the continuous form.
f   *has* or *has got* – a state
g   correct – describes a change
h   *I understand – understand* is a state verb which does not usually appear in the continuous form.

3 The correct form of the verb

Students work in pairs before checking answers on page 8 or with the whole class.

ANSWERS

a jogging   b getting   c swimming

4 People around you

Students can work in pairs to do this. Each student takes turns to give a definition; their partner tries to remember the word.

ANSWERS

a cousin   b brother-in-law   c neighbour
d colleague   e acquaintance   f stranger
g stepfather   h niece

5 Words that go together

Emphasise that all the phrases have been studied in Module 1. Students work individually to make phrases before comparing answers in pairs. They test each other by covering up part A and trying to remember the phrases.

ANSWERS

a 6   b 4   c 10   d 9   e 1   f 2   g 8   h 5
i 7   j 3

6 Quantities

ANSWERS

a 5   b 2   c 1   d 4   e 3

Pronunciation spot

Stress and the /ə/ sound

Focus students' attention on the dictionary extract, and show them how they can find the stressed syllable.

a   Students work in pairs, saying the words to each other to help them hear where the stressed syllable is. Encourage them to check answers in their mini-dictionaries as this is good dictionary skills practice.

ANSWERS

(stressed syllables underlined)

<u>a</u>verage	<u>coll</u>eague	<u>cou</u>sin
emplo<u>yee</u>	<u>fa</u>ther-in-law	<u>lei</u>sure
<u>neigh</u>bour	<u>par</u>ents	<u>pen</u>sioner
per<u>cent</u>	<u>rel</u>ative	<u>stom</u>achache

b   🔊 [1.8] Use the word *acquaintance* to demonstrate the schwa sound for students. Play the recording or model the words for students to listen for the schwa. Because it is unstressed, they may find this difficult at first.

ANSWERS

(schwa sounds underlined)

av<u>e</u>rage	colleague	cousi<u>n</u>
employee	fath<u>e</u>r-in-law	leisu<u>re</u>
neighb<u>ou</u>r	par<u>e</u>nts	pension<u>e</u>r
perc<u>e</u>nt	rel<u>a</u>tive	stom<u>a</u>chache

Colleague and *employee* do not contain a schwa sound.

c   Highlight the schwa sound on its own for students, before putting it into a word (for example, /faːðə/ > father. Drill each of the words as a class before students work in pairs to practise.

Remember! (PAGE 15)

After looking back at the areas they have practised, students do the *Mini-check* on page 156. Check answers as a whole class, and ask students to tell you their scores out of 20.

ANSWERS

1 sense	11 (no change needed)
2 Were	12 Excuse me, what <u>does</u> this word mean?
3 full-time	
4 keeping	13 I must go to the hairdresser's – my <u>hair's getting</u> very long.
5 How	
6 Take	
7 have	
8 Her husband is a taxi driver, so <u>he gets</u> home very late.	14 (no change needed)
	15 Sorry, but <u>I think</u> you're wrong.
9 <u>Do</u> you like my new shoes?	16 cousins
	17 relatives
10 She wants to find a job where she looks <u>after</u> children.	18 an acquaintance
	19 mother-in-law
	20 is having

module 2

Memory

Listening and speaking (PAGE 16)

First meetings

1 Before students discuss the questions in small groups, check any unknown vocabulary. Circulate during the discussion and nominate groups to report back on any interesting information you have heard.

2 [2.1] Ask students to look at the photos and read the names. Play the recording, pausing after each speaker to give students time to check in pairs. Check answers with the whole class.

> **ANSWERS**
> a 2   b 3   c 1

3 First get students to discuss in pairs how much they can remember from the recording. Play the recording again, pausing after each speaker to allow students time to write, and encourage them to compare ideas in pairs. Check answers with the whole class at the end.

> **ANSWERS**
> **Sung and Nixon:** Datong (China), 1972; 'Hello', 'Welcome'
> **Andy and Karen:** disco, nearly two years ago; 'Oh, I'm so sorry. I'm really, really sorry.'
> **Raul and Vieri:** outside a hotel in Raul's home country, a few years ago; 'Oh, sorry, sorry', 'Do you mind if we take a photo?', 'Yes, OK.'

Language focus 1 (PAGES 16–17)

Past simple and continuous

Students work individually or in pairs with the tapescript. As you elicit answers from the students, write up the full form of the Past simple and Past continuous using an example verb (see the tables in the *Language summary* on page 145).

They should have studied these forms before and so be able to recognise the different forms. If they clearly have no idea, give the answers and move on to highlighting how the Past simple and Past continuous are formed.

Highlight the following:

- that in the Past simple, regular verbs are followed by -ed
- that irregular verbs have to be learnt individually (point out that there is a list on page 155)
- that questions and negatives are formed with *did* and *didn't* in all persons
- that the question and negative forms in both cases are with the 'bare' infinitive (*Did they start …. ?* not *Did they started … ?*, *We didn't start* not *We didn't started*.)

- that the form of the Past continuous is the same as the Present continuous, except that *was/were* is used.

> **ANSWERS**
> **Regular Past simple:** wanted, dropped, started
> **Irregular Past simple:** met, was, couldn't, said, found, gave
> **Past continuous:** was working, was carrying, was sitting

Analysis

Students work individually to choose the correct alternative in the rules. As you check the answers to a, b and c, encourage the students to find other examples of these rules in the tapescripts.

> **ANSWERS**
> a Past simple   b Past continuous
> c Past continuous   d when; Past simple

PRACTICE

1 [2.2] Focus students' attention on the picture. Introduce the characters, asking students to guess what their first impressions of each other were, etc. Check the meaning of *date, barbecue, chaos, to be direct, to seem, Hawaiian shirt*. Students work individually, then check in pairs. Play the recording, pausing the recording after each verb to check students' answers.

> **ANSWERS**
> a met   b went   c was staying   d was visiting
> e invited   f was helping   g arrived
> h were still tidying   i offered   j started
> k were preparing   l was   m asked   n seemed
> o liked   p was wearing

Pronunciation

1 Students work in pairs, saying the verbs to decide on the number of syllables.

2 [2.3] Play the recording and check answers with the class. Students discuss the question in pairs, then play the recording again to check answers, pausing after each one. Encourage students to practise saying each verb.

> **ANSWERS**
> **1 syllable:** asked, helped, liked, seemed, stayed
> **2 syllables:** arrived, offered, prepared, started, tidied
> **3 syllables:** invited, visited
>
> /ɪd/ invited, started, visited
> /t/ asked, helped, liked
> /d/ arrived, offered, prepared, seemed, stayed, tidied

ANSWERS
decided – (3 syllables) /dɪˈsɪeˈdɪd/
played – (1 syllable) /pleɪd/
tried – (1 syllable) /traɪd/
expected – (3 syllables) /ɪkˈspektˈɪd/
remembered – (3 syllables) /rɪˈmemˈbəd/
wanted – (2 syllables) /wɒnˈtɪd/
hoped – (1 syllable) /həupt/
studied – (2 syllables) /stʌˈdɪd/
watched – (1 syllable) /wɒtʃd/
noticed – (2 syllables) /nəutɪsd/
talked – (1 syllable) /tɔːkd/
worked – (1 syllable) /wɜːkd/

Pronunciation: **helping students with stress**

Regular past forms: if students have difficulty in hearing the number of syllables, break them down slowly like this: *tra – velled*. Count the number of syllables on your fingers at the same time.

2 **a** Check the meaning of *to give somebody a lift, curtains, to pay attention to something*. Go through the example with the class, then tell students to work in pairs to match the beginnings and endings. Go through the answers with the class.

ANSWERS
2 a while   3 g because   4 f when   5 h because
6 d when   7 b while   8 c when

b Ask students to look at the example, then write the sentences individually and check in pairs. Circulate as students work, noting down any common problem areas to focus on. Check answers with the class.

ANSWERS
2 My relatives arrived while we were having dinner. +a
3 The police stopped him because he was driving too +g fast.
4 It was snowing when I opened my bedroom curtains this morning. + f
5 You fell off your bike because you weren't paying attention to the road. +h
6 I was waiting for the bus this morning when Marco drove past me. + d
7 Anna broke her leg while she was skiing in Austria. +b
8 I was doing a summer job in a hotel when I met my husband. + c

3 Give students a few minutes to think about the language they will need before they work in groups. While they are working, make a note of students' problems with the use and form of the Past simple and Past continuous. If there are a lot of problems, write some examples on the board and ask the students to look at the *Analysis* again, and then try to correct their mistakes as a class.

ADDITIONAL PRACTICE

RB **Resource bank:** *Past tense pelmanism / What about you?* (irregular Past simple forms), page 117; *Alibi* (Past simple and continuous), pages 118–119

Language focus 2 (PAGES 18–19)
used to

1 **a** Focus students on the photo and the title of the song, check the meaning of *schoolyard* and get students to predict the content in pairs. Check ideas quickly as a class.

b [2.5] Ask students to complete the gaps individually before comparing in pairs. Play the recording, then check answers as a class.

ANSWERS
1 had   2 had   3 laughed   4 needed
5 remember   6 cry   7 had   8 had   9 laughed
10 needed   11 remember

2 Students discuss their ideas in groups. Check ideas as a class.

ANSWERS
The writer of the song remembers good times and sad times. The line 'We used to cry a lot' shows that everything was not completely happy.

Analysis

See *Teacher's tips: using a discovery approach in the teaching of grammar* on page 8.

1 Give students time to work individually before answering the questions as a whole class. Highlight:
- the forms of *used to*:
  - *used to* + verb for all persons
  - the question form *Did you use to ...?*, etc.
  - the negative form *I didn't use to*, etc.
- the pronunciation of *used to* /juːstə/
- that there is no equivalent present form (this is particularly important where there is an equivalent present form in students' own language, for example Spanish).

ANSWERS
Single action in the past: d
Repeated actions / states in the past: a, b
Repeated actions / states in the present: c

2 Point out that:
- *not ... any more / not ... any longer* have the same meaning
- *any more* and *any longer* always come after the verb
- we can also say *no longer*, but this is more formal
- *still* comes before most verbs but after *be*:
  They still live in the same house.
  He is still at school.

PRACTICE

1 **a** Check that students understand *frightened*, *neat*, *tidy*, *get into trouble*. Students work individually to decide for them which statements are true.

b Focus on the examples, and do a couple of examples about you. Monitor the groups, helping and correcting any errors with *used to*. Finish the activity by asking each group to report any surprises.

Practice, exercise 1: alternative suggestion

Ask students to work in pairs with somebody they know or have worked with before. Individually, they should guess which of the statements is true for their partner. They then compare answers to see if their guesses were correct.

2 Give students a few minutes to think about what they are going to write. Explain that they don't have to include any topics they don't want to. Focus on the examples, and tell students to write similar sentences about themselves. Encourage them to ask for any language they need. Go round checking and correcting if necessary as students write their sentences.

Practice, exercise 2: alternative suggestion

Ask the students not to write their name anywhere on the sentences they write about themselves. Collect the written work in and display it on the classroom walls. The students circulate and decide who they think wrote each piece.

ADDITIONAL PRACTICE

RB **Resource bank:** *School reunion (used to, still, not ... any longer/more)* pages 120–121

Workbook: *used to*, pages 19; *still, not any more / longer*, page 19

Listening and speaking (PAGE 19)

A childhood memory

1 **a** Explain that students are going to hear two different stories, and that each picture illustrates one of them. Focus students' attention on the pictures and ask them to predict what the stories will be about.

b Once students have checked in their mini-dictionaries, deal with any words they are still not sure about. As a class, students predict which story they come from.

2 📻 [2.6] Tell students that they will hear Justin's story first. Play the recording, pausing after the first story for students to check. After the second story, let students compare in pairs, then check answers with the class. Discuss the questions as a class.

3 **a & b** Give students time to read the questions. Play the stories again, pausing after each one for students to compare their ideas in pairs. Check answers as a class.

4 **a** Explain that students are going to tell a childhood memory of their own. Emphasise that it does not need to be something serious or sad – a story of something silly or amusing might be more appropriate.

b Emphasise that students do not need to write the story, but they can make notes and think about how they will tell it. Go round the class supplying any special vocabulary that students need. As students tell their stories, encourage the others in the group to ask questions or respond to what they hear. Remind students that they may need to explain unknown words in their stories, but encourage them to do so in English.

Listening and speaking, exercise 4: alternative suggestions

a *If you want to make the activity more personalised*: tell a story yourself about a childhood memory.

b *If personal memories of childhood are not suitable*: students may not wish to talk about incidents which are personal to them. If so, suggest alternatives such as:
 • a funny/interesting/unusual story about someone else's childhood/children

- a family anecdote that is often retold
- something funny/adventurous/frightening, etc. that has happened to them as adults.

Reading (PAGES 20–21)

1 Have a quick class discussion of the first question. To start this off, you could give examples of your own. Give students time to look at the pictures and read the captions. Put them into groups to discuss the questions. Circulate, making sure students understand what is shown in each picture. Check answers with the class.

ANSWERS
Top left: forming a mental picture
Top right: inventing a story
Bottom left: repeating things
Bottom right: forming a word from the first letter of each item

2 Ask students to read the list. Check that they understand *puzzles, crosswords, oxygen, brain, chewing gum.* Students discuss the questions in pairs. Do not check their answers, as they are going to read and check.

3 **a** Before reading, check the meaning of: *responsibility, an expert, consciously, to pat, to invent, logical, brainy.* Students should read the text to check their predictions. As you check the answers, get students to read out the part of the text where the answer is found.

ANSWERS
Things which help: listening to classical music, doing puzzles and crosswords, keeping fit, increasing your heart rate, getting oxygen to your brain, eating fish, eating fruit and vegetables, chewing gum
Things which don't help: listening to rock music, stress

b Put students into pairs to discuss the question. Let them read the text again if necessary. Check answers with the class, asking students to say where in the text the technique is mentioned.

ANSWERS
forming a mental picture, inventing a story, repeating things

4 Get students to read the statements and answer any which they can remember. Then they should read the text again to complete the task. Put them in pairs to compare their answers before checking as a class. Again, ask students to locate the part of the text in which each answer is found.

ANSWERS
a T b F c F d F e DK f F g F

5 Ask students to work together and decide what the missing prepositions are. It can be helpful to put each verb into a sentence to feel which preposition 'sounds right'. If students are struggling, or when they have finished guessing, ask them to

read the text to find the answers. Emphasise that they should write any verbs they couldn't remember in their notebooks, and that they should always write the preposition as well.

ANSWERS
a in b with c on d about e with f to
g to h down

Reading, exercise 5: additional suggestions

a Give students small texts and get them to read to find other verb phrases with dependent prepositions.
b Encourage them to record further examples they come across when reading outside class.

6 Students discuss their ideas in small groups before sharing them with the whole class.

Vocabulary (PAGE 22)

Remembering and forgetting

See *Teachers' tips: working with lexis* on pages 9–10.

1 Check that students understand the instructions, and go through the example with the class. Students work individually, using their mini-dictionaries, before comparing in pairs. As you check answers with the class, elicit / write up examples of full sentences with the correct forms, highlighting possible constructions, using the examples.

ANSWERS
b learn someone how to use a computer
c remind to phone someone
d forget of something
e recognise to do something
f lose a bus

2 **a** Emphasise that students should only add a word if they think it is necessary. You could demonstrate this by doing the first two as examples with the class. Encourage the use of mini-dictionaries, as this is an important dictionary skill for students to practise.

ANSWERS
1 to 2 not necessary 3 not necessary 4 to
5 by 6 when 7 to 8 of 9 not necessary
10 to 11 not necessary 12 not necessary

b Allow time for students to select and prepare the questions they will ask. Circulate as they ask and answer, so that you are aware of any problem areas. Focus on these with the class at the end of the activity, if necessary. Get faster students to ask and answer all the questions.

Task: Test your memory (PAGES 22–23)

See *Teacher's tips: making tasks work* on pages 13–14 and *Responding to learners' individual language needs* on pages 11–12.

Preparation: reading

1 Students work individually to check the words in bold in their mini-dictionaries. Note that *appointments* are more formal arrangements, either for work or with a professional person such as a doctor or lawyer. *Arrangements* are more general future plans. Put students into groups for the discussion.

2 Emphasise that the memory quiz is not a serious memory test. Give students ten minutes to look at the memory tasks individually. Remind them to try and use some of the techniques mentioned earlier in the module.

Task: speaking

1 Refer students to the *Useful language* box, sections a and b. Put students into pairs and check they know where to find their instructions. Remind them to take turns to ask questions. Monitor and help with any difficulties. Students record how well their partner does in the memory quiz.

2 In the same pairs, students discuss what their partner was good / not very good at remembering. Give students a few minutes to prepare how they will report back to the class. Refer students to the *Useful language* box, section c. Emphasise that students do not need to write their report, but just make notes and think about how they will say it. Give students about 15 minutes to compare their results and prepare their report. Go round the class providing any support that students need. Each pair reports back to the class.

Task: speaking: alternative suggestions

a *If you have a large class*: put students into groups to report back.

b *If you have a small or teenage class*: get students to make a poster using a graph or bar chart to show, as a class, which things they found it easy and difficult to remember. They write a report on the survey findings.

ADDITIONAL ACTIVITY

RB **Resource bank**: *Learner-training worksheet 5* (recording and remembering vocabulary), pages 110–111

Real life (PAGE 24)

Showing interest

1 [2.7] Focus students on the picture to establish who the characters are. Ask them to read the instructions and statements, and check that they understand them. Play the recording, more than once if necessary, and let students compare in pairs. Check answers with the whole class.

ANSWERS

1 She decided to go for a walk.
2 She left the bar.
3 She walked around for a bit.
4 She decided to return to the bar.
5 She couldn't find the bar.
6 She spoke to a woman.
7 She saw someone in a 'Steam Patrol' T-shirt.
8 She followed the man.
9 She saw the rest of the group.

---

2 Refer students to the tapescript on page 160. Do an example as a whole class before students work individually. As you elicit the answers, highlight the following points about short questions (like *Don't you?*).

- Short questions are formed using just the auxiliary verb.

- The auxiliary verb matches the first sentence in tense, person, negative form, etc.

ANSWERS

Really? Yeah, yeah. Uh-huh. No! You're joking!
Don't you? Oh, right. Wow! That was lucky!

Pronunciation

1 [2.8] Look at the examples, then play the recording. As students listen, highlight the rising intonation to show interest, either by drawing an arrow pointing upwards, or by gesturing as the phrases play.

2 Pause the recording after each phrase so that students can repeat chorally.

Pronunciation: helping students with intonation

Remind students that rising intonation can be used to show interest in English. Ask students whether or not this is the same in their language. Emphasise that, in English, if your intonation is very flat, you may sound bored and rude. Focus on the intonation curves in the example, modelling the pattern yourself (possibly exaggerating), or replaying the first couple of examples on the recording. Humming or exaggerating the intonation pattern may well help students to hear this more clearly. If students produce flat intonation, pulling an exaggeratedly bored face may help to reinforce the importance of intonation.

---

3 Give students a few minutes to think about what they are going to say. Students should try to use as many different ways of expressing interest as possible.

Study ... (PAGE 24)

Using the mini-dictionary

1 Students have used the *Mini-dictionary* in Modules 1 and 2 to find the meaning of words and learn where the stress is. This activity focuses on other information students can find out when they look something up.

2 If this activity is done in class time, set it up as a competition. The first student to answer all the questions correctly wins.

ANSWERS
a a noun and a verb
b on the second syllable /əˈrɪθmətɪk/
c uncountable   d on   e unfit   f /t/
g a phrasal verb   h ate

Practise ... (PAGE 25)

1 Past simple

If this activity is done in class time, students work in pairs to match sentences and definitions. For further practice, students write another sentence to match each definition. Circulate and check that they are correct before students pass them to another pair to match.

ANSWERS
a 2   b 5   c 1   d 3   e 4

2 Past continuous

Students work in pairs to correct the sentences. For a further check of understanding, get students to draw a timeline for each corrected/checked sentence. Check answers with the whole class.

ANSWERS
b when we arrived   c the doorbell rang
d didn't want   e I heard   f I liked

3 Contrasting past and present

Students work individually or in pairs before checking answers with the whole class.

ANSWERS
a used   b use   c any   d more   e still

4 Short questions to show interest

You could do this as a spoken activity first. Write the possible short questions on the board and drill them. Students close their books. Say each sentence prompt; students respond with a short question. They then write the answers.

ANSWERS
a Are you?   b Did you?   c Was he?
d Were they?   e Didn't they?

5 Remembering and forgetting

Use this for dictionary skills practice. Students work in pairs to choose the correct alternative before checking the answers in their mini-dictionaries.

ANSWERS
a remember   b reminds   c learn   d lost
e recognise

6 Words that go together

Write the words on separate pieces of card. Students work in pairs to match the verbs and prepositions before checking answers with the whole class.

ANSWERS
a 4   b 5   c 2   d 3   e 6   f 1

Pronunciation spot

a [2.9] If this activity is done in class time, encourage students to try listening without reading the text. It is very good listening practice. Pause the recording after each sentence, and repeat several times.

ANSWERS
1 three   2 three   3 two   4 four   5 three

b Put students into pairs and ask them to take turns saying the sentences. Monitor and help if necessary.

Remember! (PAGE 25)

After looking back at the areas they have practised, students do the *Mini-check* on page 156. Check answers as a whole class, and ask students to tell you their scores out of 20.

ANSWERS
1 saw   11 at
2 were playing 12 how
3 were arguing 13 any
4 walked   14 in
5 stopped   15 of
6 lasted   16 about
7 me   17 Were
8 was   18 recognise
9 am   19 used
10 are   20 when

module 3

Around the world

Language focus 1 (PAGES 26–27)

Comparatives and superlatives

See *Teachers' tips: using a discovery approach in the teaching of grammar* on page 8.

a Start by naming some of the countries in the quiz and asking students what they can tell you about them. Check the meaning of *area, populated, coastline, further/furthest, theme park*. Put students into pairs to do the quiz. Emphasise that they must use English (you could deduct 'penalty points' if the students use their mother tongue!).

b 🖭 [3.1] Emphasise that students will hear a lot of extra information in addition to the answers. Play the recording. If your students need support with listening, pause the recording after each question to give them time to check in pairs. Finish the activity by checking which team got the highest score.

ANSWERS
1 a Russia   b China
2 River Nile
3 Seoul, Mumbai, São Paulo, Jakarta, Moscow
4 Canada
5 a Chicago   b Los Angeles
6 a China   b Ireland   c India   d the UK
   e France   f Japan

Analysis

1 Revision of basic forms

Check that students understand the questions, including grammatical terminology such as *comparative*, *superlative* and *syllable*. Students compare answers in pairs before checking as a class.

ANSWERS AND LANGUAGE NOTES
a *long – longer/longest*
   big – bigger/biggest
   busy – busier/busiest
   popular – more popular/the most popular
   *far – further/furthest**

*It is also possible to say *farther/farthest*. The meaning is the same.

b one-syllable adjectives: adjective + -er/-est
   two-syllable adjectives   adjective + -er/-est
      ending in -y:
   other two- or three-   *more / the most* + adjective
      syllable adjectives:
   other irregular forms: *good/better/best*
                                         bad/worse/worst

Highlight the following spelling rules.
• In one-syllable adjectives with short vowel sounds,

the final consonant doubles:
(*big > big**g**er > big**g**est*)
• Adjectives ending in *-e*, add *-r / -est*:
(*nice > nic**er** > nic**est***)
• Adjectives ending in *-y, -y* changes to *-i-*:
(*pretty > prett**ier** > prett**iest***)

2 Big and small differences

Do the first example together. Students work in pairs. In feedback, highlight the following points:
• *much higher / a lot higher* have the same meaning
• the pronunciation of *slightly* /ˈslaɪtli/
• the opposite of *a lot* is *a little bit*. (*Note*: it is also possible to say *a little*, but it is not possible to say *a lot bit*.)

ANSWERS
Picture a – *X is slightly higher than Y; X is a little bit higher than Y.*
Picture b – *X is much higher than Y; X is a lot higher than Y.*

3 Superlative phrases

Emphasise that students should complete the sentences by inserting one word in each space. In feedback, highlight.
• *By far* + superlative shows a big difference between this and the rest
• Before superlative adjectives (*biggest, best,* etc.), **the** is needed. We also say **the** *second*, **the** *third*, **the** *fourth*, etc. *biggest.*
• *One of the biggest cities* means there are several big ones, but we are not saying it is the biggest of all.

ANSWERS
by far the biggest city **in** *the world*
second/third/fourth biggest city **in** *the USA*
one **of** *the biggest cities*

Analysis: alternative suggestions

a *If you are short of time:* set the revision of basic forms as homework in advance of the lesson.

b *If you have a weak group:* provide additional practice of the basic forms before, or instead of, moving on to the more complex forms in 'Big and small differences'. Use students in the class to talk about height, age, etc. or choose other countries in the world to compare size, population, etc.

PRACTICE

1 Students work in pairs to complete each sentence. Emphasise that they should use two words. Encourage them to attempt each question before looking at the tapescript.

ANSWERS
a slightly longer   b most populated
c bit bigger   d fifth biggest   e much longer
f lot further / lot farther   g much bigger
h more popular   i the busiest   j most popular

2 a [cassette] [3.2] Emphasise that students can write their answers in any order they choose. Pause the recording after each instruction to give students time to think and write.

b Do an example or two, using students' own answers.

3 a [cassette] [3.3] Give students time to read the table on page 138. Check that they understand *population density*, and explain how to say *km²*. Demonstrate the activity by playing the first statement, and asking the class to decide if it is true or false. Pause after each statement to allow students time to decide, and to correct the false statements. Check answers in pairs and then as a class.

ANSWERS
1	False	France is by far the largest of the three countries.
2	False	France is a lot less crowded than the UK.
3	False	The UK is much more popular than Ireland with tourists.
4	True	
5	True	
6	False	Heathrow is the busiest of the three airports.

b Circulate as students work in pairs to create six more statements. Check that they are using comparative and superlative forms accurately. Help students to self-correct before giving them the right answer.

4 a Encourage students to work in pairs or small groups to find differences.

b Students compare their ideas in groups. Finish off by eliciting a few ideas from different groups.

> **Practice, exercise 4: alternative suggestion**
>
> *If your students are from the same country*: use this activity as a competition to write as many differences as possible in five minutes. Points are awarded for correct sentences and for the ability to correct another pair's mistakes.

ADDITIONAL PRACTICE

[RB] **Resource bank:** *The best place in the world* (superlatives and Present Perfect), pages 122–123

Workbook: Comparatives and superlatives, pages 22–23

Reading (PAGES 28–29)

1 Before students discuss the question, check the meaning of *natural wonder, archaeological site, monument*.

2 a Explain that the text shows the results of a vote by viewers of a TV travel programme. Students scan the text quickly to find the five categories and winners.

ANSWERS
Natural wonder: the Grand Canyon, USA
Ancient wonder: Petra, Jordan
Romantic city: Venice, Italy
Modern city: Las Vegas, USA
Beach: Koh Samui, Thailand

b Students work in small groups to brainstorm information they know or think they know about each place. Set a time limit to ensure that they work quickly.

c Give students time to use their mini-dictionaries. Check answers with the whole class.

ANSWERS
The Grand Canyon: layers of rock, stretches for 443 kilometres
Petra: cliffs and temples
Venice: canals and bridges, paintings and sculptures
Las Vegas: extravagant hotels, neon lights, gambling
Koh Samui: white sand, coconut trees, turquoise sea

3 Students work in pairs or groups before checking with the whole class. As you check the answers, get students to read out the part of the text in which each answer is found.

ANSWERS
a Elvis Presley and Richard Gere
b more than 2,000 years old
c Phuket (Koh Samui is the second largest)
d Egyptian Pyramids and Roman Palaces
e Iguazu Falls
f famous paintings and sculptures
g on average, five
h Swiss
i Sunbathe, swim, go shopping, eat in restaurants, experience the nightlife
j 400

4 Students read alone before discussing their ideas in small groups. After students have compared ideas, do some brief feedback with the whole class to find out which places your students have been talking about.

Language focus 2 (PAGES 30–31)

Phrases for comparing

See *Teachers' tips: using a discovery approach in the teaching of grammar* on page 8.

1 Get students to look at the photos to help them with ideas, then work in small groups to brainstorm.

26 + 27

2 [cassette] [3.4] Ensure that students read the phrases in the box before listening. Play the recording, let students check in pairs, then go through answers with the whole class.

ANSWERS

a	economic problems	M
	tourists	I
	how clean/dirty the city is	I
	new shops and buildings	I
	standard of living, prices, etc.	M & I
	street names	M
	language(s) spoken	M & I
	pace of life	M
	traffic and driving	M & I

b They both mention changes in the standard of living, prices, etc. and in the languages spoken. Michael is generally happy. Irina is generally unhappy.

They also both mention traffic and driving, but in Hong Kong there is no change, although in Moscow there is more traffic than before.

3 [3.4] Emphasise that these are not the exact words Michael and Irina use. Students work in pairs to choose the best alternative before listening again to check their answers.

ANSWERS

a more or less the same as   b more
c very similar   d slightly   e completely   f less
g much worse than   h very different from

Analysis

1 Students match the adjectives and prepositions in pairs. (If you have a weak group, refer them to the sentences from the previous exercise where each adjective–preposition combination can be found.)

ANSWERS

the same as   worse than   similar to

2 Check that students understand that the line is a scale from one extreme to the other. Students work individually before going through the answers with the whole class.

ANSWERS

a exactly the same as   b the same as
c about the same as   d very similar to
e similar to   f slightly different from
g different from   h very different from
i completely different from

Highlight the fact that comparisons can also be made using the following forms:
• *not as* + adjective + *as*: this does not mean *is not the same as*. It means *less than*. This may be different in the students' own language and difficult for students to understand.
• *fewer … than / less … than*: they mean the same, but *less* is used with uncountable nouns, whereas *fewer* is used with countable nouns.
Refer students to *Language summary D* on page 146.

PRACTICE 28

1 **a** [3.5] Refer students to page 135. After looking at the pictures for a few minutes, they listen and answer true or false.

ANSWERS

1 T   2 F   3 F   4 T   5 T   6 F   7 F   8 T

> **Practice, exercise 1a: alternative suggestion**
>
> *If you have time*: allow students a few minutes to study the pictures on page 135. Then ask them to close their books. In small groups they try to answer true or false from memory as they listen. In feedback, find out which group had the most correct answers.

b Emphasise that students should use the phrases from the *Analysis*, and also those from *Language Focus 1*, to express six more similarities and differences as precisely as possible. The focus here is on accuracy, so go round checking and correcting sentences. In feedback, check that the meaning is also correct by referring to the pictures.

POSSIBLE ANSWERS
(*The same ideas can obviously be expressed in a number of different ways.*)
The post box in picture A is completely different from the one in B.
The church steps in picture A are exactly the same as the ones in B.
The people at the kiosk are more or less the same in picture A as they are in B.
The couple walking across the square in picture A are slightly different form the couple in B.
The people sitting outside the café in picture A are very different from the people in B.
The cashpoint in picture A is exactly the same as the one in B.
The tourist information office in picture A is exactly the same as the one in B.
The souvenir shop in picture A is exactly the same as the one in B.

2 Give students a few minutes to think about similarities and differences between their town now and at a time in the past. Look at the example with the class before they start their sentences. Go round the class supplying any special vocabulary that students need, for example, with adjectives. Then put students into small groups to compare with each other.

Pronunciation   29

1 [3.6] Play the recording as many times as necessary, pausing after each sentence for students to write. Alternatively, read out the sentences yourself. (Keep to a natural speed, with natural use of weak forms and linking – maintain this speed no matter how many times students ask you to repeat the words.)

2 🔊 [3.7] Make sure that students are familiar with the schwa sound. Read out the phrases, exaggerating the /ə/ sounds slightly and getting students to copy. Alternatively, play the recording, pausing to allow the students to repeat. Replay the recording several times.

3 Refer students back to the sentences they wrote in *Practice*, exercise 1b. Ask them to decide where the schwa sounds are, before they practise saying each sentence with their partner. Go round the class to check that students are using the schwa sound correctly.

ADDITIONAL PRACTICE

Workbook: Different phrases for comparing, page 24

Vocabulary and writing (PAGE 31)

Describe towns and cities

1 Students work individually or in pairs to check the meaning of the words. (Note that *docks* always has an *s* on the end, but can be a singular noun – *a docks*.) Give students five to ten minutes to answer the questions individually.

2 *For students who all come from the same town/city*: the emphasis here is on comparing opinions. Students can run quickly through the first two bullet points, and spend more time discussing the last two.

For students who come from different towns/cities: this is an opportunity for students to tell each other about their towns and cities. First, give students a few minutes to plan a short talk, using the vocabulary in the questions. Encourage them to ask each other questions.

3 Students write a description of the town or city they chose. This could be done for homework or as a class activity.

Task: Design a tour (PAGES 32–33)

See *Teacher's tips: making tasks work* on pages 13–14 and *Responding to learners' individual language needs* on pages 11–12.

Preparation: listening

1 Focus students' attention on the pictures and ask if anyone has visited Australia before going through the questions. If students do not know very much about Australia, encourage them to tell you anything at all they know. Before students discuss the questions in small groups, encourage them to check unknown vocabulary in their *Mini-dictionaries*.

2 🔊 [3.8] Focus students' attention on the map and check that they can see all the places mentioned in the recording (see tapescript on page 162). Check the pronunciation of *Melbourne* /ˈmelbɔːn/, *Ayers Rock* /eə(r)s rɒk/, *Cairns* /keə(r)ns/.

3 🔊 [3.8] Check students' understanding of the words and phrases in the box (especially *Aboriginal culture*, *jellyfish*, *snorkelling*, *the Outback*, *the rainforest*) before they work in pairs to decide in which place(s) Elaine mentions them. Play the recording before checking answers as a whole class.

4 🔊 [3.9] Give students time to read through the sentences. Explain that they will just hear the answers, not the whole sentences. Play the recording. Check answers in pairs and then as a whole class.

5 Students discuss the questions in small groups. Circulate during the discussion and nominate one or two groups to report back on their ideas.

Task: speaking

1 **a** *If you have a multinationality class*: it is probably most motivating if students prepare the tour for each other, either in nationality groups or individually. It is particularly important that they draw a map of their countries, as other students may be unfamiliar with the basic geography. Each student will need to draw their own map.

If you have a mononationality class: designing the tour for one of the other specified groups, or choosing one of the other tour options, will probably work better. This can be done in pairs or groups of four, to facilitate the pairwork stage later.

b Talk students through the decisions they have to make, then give them time to think. If this is done in class, they will need about half an hour for planning, map-drawing and note-making (with reference to the tour itself and the language needed). Students do not need to write out the tour in full at this stage.

2 Circulate, answering vocabulary questions, and helping students to plan the tour. If necessary, ask prompt questions, for example, *How long do you think they should stay in ... ?* Remind students to look back at the phrases in the tour of Australia, and in the *Useful language* box, to use in their own tours, if appropriate.

3 If students have prepared carefully, this stage could take between twenty and forty minutes, so make sure that you allow enough time. Students may need to be regrouped to ensure that they work with someone who has planned a different tour. Encourage students to ask each other questions. Circulate as students work, noting down any errors or useful language for analysis at the end of the task. Students report back briefly to the whole class about what appeals / doesn't appeal about their partner's tour.

Follow up: writing

The focus here is on accuracy, so go over any corrections that you have from the spoken tours. Remember only to select the most useful errors, and to limit the number of points to a maximum of ten.

Task: alternative suggestions

a   *If you want to provide a model yourself*: it may be more motivating for students if you present a tour of an English-speaking country/region that you have visited. If you are a native speaker of English, students may be interested in your own region and town.
  Plan briefly what you will say, incorporating useful phrases (*It's really worth visiting*, etc.). If possible, take a map of the country to refer to, marking the place you talk about with stickers. Encourage students to ask any questions they have as you present your tour.

b   *If you are short of time, or have short lessons*: do the model for the task (either the Australia model or your own) on one day, then set the planning stage (*Task: speaking*, exercise 1) as homework. Students can talk through the task in the next lesson, after asking you about any vocabulary they need.

c   *If your students choose to design a tour for a group of people other than the students in their class*: help them to select the target group.
  • You could bring in photos of your own foreign friends or relatives. Explain that they are coming to the students' country for a week and want to see as much as they can. Give brief details of their ages, interests, budget, etc. and ask students to design a tour for them.
  • Alternatively, bring in some photos of famous foreigners likely to interest the students, or get them to think of someone themselves (actors, rock stars, etc.). Tell students that this person is coming on holiday to their country, that they are going to be his/her personal guide for a week and that they must plan a tour for them.
Once the tour is organised, tell students to imagine they are having lunch with the person/people they organised the tour for. Students talk through the tour in a similar way to Marco and Elaine. At this role-play stage, some students will have to take the part of

the visitor. Mix the pairs so that students do not see the same tour that they themselves planned.

Real life (PAGE 34)

Booking a flight

1 Students work in pairs to brainstorm questions. Go through them with the class.

POSSIBLE ANSWERS
How much does/will it cost?
Is it a direct flight?
What time does it leave/arrive?
What time is the return flight?
Can I reserve a seat/ticket?
Can I book a ticket/the flight?

2 [3.10] Give students a few minutes to look at Rachael's notes. Remind them that they will not hear the information in the same order as her notes. This is good practice for them in focusing on specific information. Before playing the recording, check the meaning of *stopover*. Students compare answers in pairs before checking as a whole class.

ANSWERS
a 979 Euros   b 3rd   c 06:50   d 4th   e Madrid
f 13:35   g 08:20   h two   i 7 887 9345

3 [3.10] Before playing the tape, check that students understand the difference between *Mrs*, *Miss* and *Ms* (in terms of meaning and pronunciation). Play the tape as many times as necessary for students to check the spelling and numbers.

ANSWERS
Mr   Mrs   Miss ✔   Ms
Surname   *Stewart*
First name   *Rachael*
Contact number   *07711 737385*

4 Students work in pairs to match sentence halves. Check answers as a whole class, and drill each sentence chorally and individually.

ANSWERS
a   When do you want to travel?
b   And coming back when?
c   How many seats do you want?
d   I'll just check availability.
e   It's completely full, I'm afraid.
f   Can you try the 3rd of April instead?
g   I can do it for €979 return including taxes.
h   It's a twelve-hour flight from Madrid.
i   There's an hour stopover in Madrid.
j   I can hold it for two days.

5 a Put students in pairs to act out the conversation.
   b Check that students know where to find their information.

As students act out their conversations, circulate to check that they are using the sentences from exercise 4 accurately. If there is time, pairs can perform their dialogues in front of the class.

Study ... (PAGE 34)

Keeping notes

1 Students have used the *Mini-dictionary* in Modules 1 and 2 to find the meaning of words and learn where the stress is. This activity focuses on what students do with the information they find when they look something up in a dictionary. If this activity is done in class time, ask students to read through the example, and to add a translation and another example sentence for *crowded*.

2 This activity could be done for homework or in class. If it is done in class, it could be done as a competition. Encourage students to compare their notes in small groups, and to decide who has made the clearest/best notes.

Study ... additional suggestion

Students keep a vocabulary box as a whole class. At the end of each lesson, spend a few minutes deciding with the students which vocabulary from the lesson is the most important. Choose at least eight new words. Nominate one or two students to make cards on cut-up pieces of paper, one for each vocabulary item, in the same way as shown in exercise 1. The cards are handed in at the start of the next lesson and kept in a box. Use the vocabulary cards for revision games or 'warmers' at the start of lessons.

Practise ... (PAGE 35)

1 Comparative and superlative adjectives

If this activity is done in class time, do it as a spoken drill. First, say the phrase as given (for example, *the smallest*). Then give the prompt. Students have to say the opposite form. Students can write the answers for further consolidation if necessary.

ANSWERS
a the biggest   b the busiest
c further than / farther than   d the cleanest
e worse than   f the most difficult
g more boring than

2 Large and small differences

If this activity is done in class time, get students to cover the box and guess what the missing words are before uncovering them and completing the sentences. Check answers with the whole class.

ANSWERS
a by   b one   c slightly   d much   e bit   f lot

3 Making comparisons

Students work individually or in pairs before checking answers with the whole class.

ANSWERS
a as   b quite   c less   d less   e to   f completely
g from   h exactly

4 Prepositions

ANSWERS
a in   b from   c with   d on   e for   f on

5 Word building

Use this activity for dictionary skills practice. Students work in pairs to write the adjectives before checking the answers in their mini-dictionaries.

ANSWERS
a industrial   b historical/historic   c crowded
d romantic   e polluted

Pronunciation spot

The sounds /ɪ/ and /iː/

a 📼 [3.11] Play the recording, pause after each pair of words, and repeat several times. Alternatively, model the pairs of words, exaggerating the /ɪ/ and /iː/ sounds slightly.

b 📼 [3.12] Pause the recording after each word, and repeat several times.

ANSWERS
/ɪ/   big, built, busy, city, which
/iː/   beach, clean, easy, street, tea, three

c Drill the words from exercise b chorally and individually, then get students to practise saying them in pairs.

Remember! (PAGE 35)

After looking back at the areas they have practised, students do the *Mini-check* on page 156. Check answers as a whole class, and ask students to tell you their scores out of 20.

ANSWERS

1 further/farther	11 the
2 worst	12 to
3 tall	13 more
4 better than	14 in
5 least expensive	15 for
6 less	16 on
7 recommend	17 border
8 as	18 seeing
9 the second best	19 flight
10 exactly	20 view

module 4

Life stories

Reading (PAGES 36–37)

1 Check the meaning of *take after*, *facial expressions*, *tastes*. Look at the examples with students, and perhaps demonstrate the activity by telling students about the similarities and differences between you and somebody in your family. Students work in pairs.

2 Check the meaning of *twins*, *identical*, *non-identical*. Students discuss the questions in pairs or groups.

3 Check the meaning of *telepathic* if it didn't come up in the previous discussion about twins. Emphasise that students only need to scan the text for the relevant information; they don't need to understand everything.

> **ANSWERS**
> a   Greta and Freda Chapman
> b   Margaret Richardson and Terry Connelly
> c   Jim Springer and Jim Lewis (the 'Jim Twins')
> d   Grace and Virginia Kennedy

4 Before students read the text in detail, give them time to use their *Mini-dictionaries*. Check the meaning of the words and phrases in the box, and of *IQ* – intelligence quotient, a figure arrived at by doing a special test. Give students time to read the statements.

> **ANSWERS**
> a T   b T   c F   d F   e F   f T

5 Give students time to think about the questions individually first. This discussion can be brief or lengthy, depending on time and interest level.

Language focus 1 (PAGES 38–39)

Present perfect simple

See *Teacher's tips: using a discovery approach in the teaching of grammar* on page 8.

a Before students read, check the meaning of *fan*. Emphasise that students should not try to choose the verb forms yet. They should simply answer the question about the twins' life.

> **POSSIBLE ANSWERS**
> (*The same ideas can obviously be expressed in a number of different ways.*)
> The twins have been TV stars since they were nine months old.
> They were the youngest Hollywood producers ever at the age of six.
> They were in a TV show for eight years.
> They are famous all over the world.

They have published a book and sold more than thirty million copies, making more than $130 million.
They have also produced their own brands of clothing, jewellery, make-up and perfume.
They are extremely rich, with more than $150 million each.
In 2003 they were the highest paid TV stars in the world.

b 🔊 [4.1] Check briefly that students understand the basic difference between the Present perfect and Past simple (*have/has* + past participle, verb + *-ed*). Students work individually or in pairs to choose the correct verb form. If they are not sure, encourage them to guess. When checking answers from the recording, students may have difficulty catching the answers as the weak forms of *have* are used. Encourage students to listen again rather than giving the answer yourself, as this is useful practice in listening closely to the language used. With each answer, ask students to explain why that form is used – the *Analysis* should act as a summary of what has been discussed, with the *Language summary* providing further detail. You can draw timelines on the board as follows:

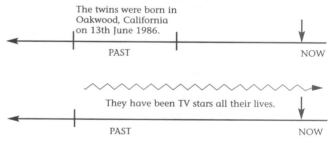

	ANSWERS AND LANGUAGE NOTES	
1	*were*	(This is clearly finished / in the past – a definite time is given.)
2	*have been*	(This refers to their whole lives, which have not finished.)
3	*appeared*	(This is clearly in the past – a definite time is given.)
4	*started*	(This is clearly in the past – they are not six years old now.)
5	*appeared*	(This is in the past. The next sentence tells us that the TV show is finished.)
6	*finally ended*	(This is clearly in the past – a definite time is given.)
7	*have become*	(This is still continuing – point out that sentences with *since* are in the Present perfect.)
8	*published*	(This is clearly in the past – a definite time is given.)
9	*have sold*	(This is still continuing – their book is still for sale – and so related to the present.)
10	*have made**	(This refers to their whole lives, which have not finished.)
11	*have also produced*	(This refers to their whole lives, which have not finished.)

| 12 | *have built up* | (This refers to their whole lives, which have not finished.) |
| 13 | *were* | (This is clearly in the past – a definite time is given.) |

*It is possible here to say *made*, because it is not necessary to repeat the auxiliary *have*. The form is still the Present perfect simple, though, because if there were a new sentence, it would read *They have made ...*.

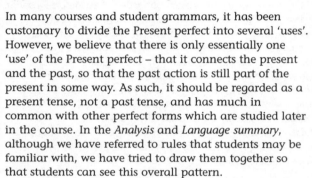

Language focus 1: notes on the approach to the Present perfect

In many courses and student grammars, it has been customary to divide the Present perfect into several 'uses'. However, we believe that there is only essentially one 'use' of the Present perfect – that it connects the present and the past, so that the past action is still part of the present in some way. As such, it should be regarded as a present tense, not a past tense, and has much in common with other perfect forms which are studied later in the course. In the *Analysis* and *Language summary*, although we have referred to rules that students may be familiar with, we have tried to draw them together so that students can see this overall pattern.

Analysis

Students work individually or in pairs before discussing answers with the whole class. As well as checking meaning, it may be necessary to check form. In particular, highlight:
- The Present perfect simple is formed with *have/has* + past participle.
- *Have* and *has* are often shortened to *'ve* and *'s*.
- Regular past participles are verb + *-ed*; irregular ones have to be learnt individually (see page 155 of the *Students' Book*).
- In questions, *have/has* and the pronoun are inverted.
- Negatives are formed with *haven't/hasn't*.

> **ANSWERS**
> 1 *have/has* + past participle
> **Regular:** *have appeared, have started, has ended, have published, have produced*
> **Irregular:** *have been, have become, have sold, have made, have built up*
> 2 a Present perfect b Present perfect
> c Past simple
> 3 **Past simple:** *ten minutes ago, yesterday, when?*
> **Present perfect:** *all my life, since, ever?*

PRACTICE

1 Get students to look at the photos. Ask them what they know about the famous people in the photos. Check meaning of *cover versions, hit singles, number ones, release*. Put students into pairs to match the texts to the photos, and check answers with the class. Then students do the verb exercise in pairs before going through answers as a class.

ANSWERS AND LANGUAGE NOTES
a Lennon and McCartney

| | 1 *wrote* | (In the past – time is given.) |
| | 2 *have been* | (Present perfect with *since*) |

b Elvis Presley

	3 *died*	(In the past – time is given.)
	4 *has had*	(Present perfect with *since* – although his life is in the past, he can still have hit singles.)
	5 *had*	(His life is in the past – he is no longer alive.)

c Jack Nicholson

	6 *has received*	(This refers to his whole career, which has not finished – he may be nominated again.)
	7 *has won*	(This refers to his whole career, which has not finished – he may win again.)
	8 *won*	(Time is given.)
	9 *received*	(Time is given.)

d Kate Winslet and Leonardo DiCaprio

	10 *starred*	(The filming is completed in the past.)
	11 *has made*	(Present perfect with *since*)
	12 *cost*	(The filming is completed in the past.)

2 **a** 📼 [4.2] Focus students' attention on the dialogue descriptions before playing the recording. Students compare answers in pairs before checking answers as a class.

> **ANSWERS**
> | A teacher talking to some students | 4 |
> | A woman meeting her friend in the street | 2 |
> | A couple at home | 1 |
> | Some business people meeting at a party | 5 |
> | Some colleagues in an office | 3 |

b Explain that the sentences come from the five dialogues students have just heard. Students complete the gaps individually or in pairs.

> **ANSWERS**
> 1 Have ... seen 2 've lost 3 've changed
> 4 've lost 5 's ... gone 6 's gone 7 've finished
> 8 haven't finished 9 have ... met

c Students check their answers with the tapescript on page 163. Make sure that students have focused on the contracted form of the Present perfect.

Pronunciation

1 📼 [4.3] Play the first dialogue, asking students to count the number of times they hear *have* and *'ve*. Play the tape more than once if necessary.

> **ANSWERS**
> | *have* | three times |
> | *'ve* | twice |

Play the recording again, stopping after each *have/'ve*,

writing up the verb and getting the students to tell you whether or not *have* is weak or strong. It may be useful to write up the phonemic spellings /hæv/ and /həv/, and to model the two several times for your students.

> **ANSWERS**
> | | | |
> |---|---|---|
> | a | the strong form: | I don't know if I have. |
> | b | the weak form: | Have you seen my glasses anywhere? Have you looked under the … |
> | c | the contracted form: | I can't believe you've lost them again! Okay, so I've lost my glasses. |

Highlight the following about *have*:
- It is strong if it stands alone without a main verb.
- It is weak in the question form.
- It is often contracted in the affirmative if it is followed by a main verb.

2 Get students to repeat the pronunciation chorally and individually. Start with the stressed word in each phrase, so students get the weak forms and contractions right. The other phrases can be 'back-chained' in a similar way.

3 In pairs, practise strong, weak and contracted forms of *have* using the tapescript on page 163.

3 Check the question form for asking about a life experience by referring students to the example in the *Students' Book*. Set this up as a competition. Students work in pairs to find six experiences they have had which their partner hasn't. Go through the example with the class. Emphasise that they can use the ideas on page 138 or their own ideas. The winner is the first person to find six differences.

ADDITIONAL PRACTICE

RB **Resource bank:** *Find someone who … lied!* (Present perfect simple for experience), page 128

Workbook: Present perfect simple and Past simple, page 30; Time words with the Present perfect, pages 30–31

Vocabulary 1 (PAGE 40)

Describing life events

See *Teacher's tips: working with lexis* on pages 9–10.

1 a Focus students' attention on the pictures and elicit what they represent. Students will be familiar with most of the words in the box, but may not be able to use the full phrases correctly. The pronunciation of the following may need drilling: *retire*, *get engaged*, *get married*. Students check the meaning of any unknown words in their mini-dictionaries before working in pairs. Check answers with the whole class.

> **ANSWERS**
> | | |
> |---|---|
> | **Love and relationships:** | fall in love, get engaged, get married |
> | **Home and family:** | bring up your children, |

have children, rent or buy a house, leave home, move house
Education:	get a degree, go to university, pass your exams, start school, leave school
Career:	retire, change job, get promoted, get a job, start work

b Elicit ideas on the order in which these things usually happen. Emphasise that there are different possibilities. Students discuss the questions in pairs.

2 Check the meaning of *split up* and use this as an example. Students discuss their ideas in pairs before checking answers as a whole class.

> **ANSWERS AND LANGUAGE NOTE**
> | | |
> |---|---|
> | **Love and relationships:** | get married again (positive), get divorced (negative), split up (negative) |
> | **Education:** | fail your exams (negative) |
> | **Career:** | become very successful (positive), make a lot of money (positive), lose your job (negative) |
>
> *Split up* and *get divorced* can both mean the same thing. However, if a couple are not yet married, they can only *split up*, they cannot *get divorced*. *Lose your job* means that the person did not choose to leave.

3 Emphasise that students should study the phrases before doing the quiz in pairs. If they have started to make vocabulary notes (*Study …* , exercise 1, on page 34 of the *Students' Book*), this may help them to memorise the phrases. Set the quiz up as a competition. Check the answers as a whole class and see which pair has the most points.

> **ANSWERS**
> 1 buy a house, get a degree, get a job
> 2 children (the verb should be *have*)
> 3 a become very successful   b bring up children
>   c fail an exam   d lose your job
>   e make money   f pass an exam
>   g rent a house
> 4 a to   b with   c to   d from

ADDITIONAL ACTIVITY

Workbook: Describing life events, page 31

Language focus 2 (PAGES 40–41)

for, *since* and *ago* and Present perfect continuous

See *Teacher's tips: using a discovery approach in the teaching of grammar* on page 8.

39

1 [cassette] [4.4] Focus students' attention on the photo of Sara and ask one or two questions to check that they understand the concept of the 'lifeline'. For example, did she start learning English before or after she began studying medicine? (before).

ANSWERS
a 1979   b 16   f 1999   h 2001   i first house

2 Students work individually or in pairs before checking answers with the whole class. All the verb forms can be completed on the basis of what the students have already studied in *Language Focus 1* except j. Students' choice of verb form here will help you to establish if they have noticed the use of the Present perfect continuous in the tapescript. If they find this difficult, they should be able to go back and answer it after the *Analysis*.

ANSWERS
a   It depends what the year is when students are answering the question.
b   moved   1999
c   It depends what the year is when students are answering the question.
d a year   e 1999   f met   g 2003   h 's known
i since   j 's been studying   k 's had

Language focus 2: notes on the approach to the Present perfect continuous

It is not our intention to introduce the students to all 'uses' of the Present perfect continuous. For example, we do not focus on the 'activity/result' contrast between the Present perfect simple and continuous, which is more suitable for Upper Intermediate students. Instead, we focus on a very common use for the Present perfect continuous with *for* and *since*, which:
• is, at least, likely to be familiar to students
• can be drawn into their existing knowledge of continuous/simple aspect
• will form a confidence-building basis for understanding other contexts in which the Present perfect continuous is used.

Analysis

Students work in pairs, looking back at the examples from *Language focus 2*, exercise 2, to help them.

ANSWERS
Past simple: a, b, d, f
Present perfect simple: e, g, h, k
Present perfect continuous: c, i, j

Focus mainly on the difference in form here, as the difference in meaning is dealt with later. Write the form *have / has been* + verb + *ing* on the board, and highlight.
• that in the question form, only *have* is inverted, *been* doesn't change position
• the negative form
• the use of *has/hasn't* in the third-person singular

• the fact that *been* never changes form
• the contracted forms of *have/has*
• the weak form of *been* /biːn/.

2 *for*, *since* and *ago*

ANSWERS
a   The Past simple is used with *ago*.
    The way students change the time phrases will depend on when they do the exercise. For example, if it is 3:00 p.m. on a Friday in June 2005, the answers would be as follows:
    three days ago, nine hours ago, ten months ago, four years ago, twenty years ago.
b   *For* is used with periods of time: twenty years, a long time, five minutes.
    Since is used with points in time: I was born, 1999, six o'clock.
c   Sentence d

Point out that *ago* can only be used with the Past simple; *for* can be used with both Past simple and Present perfect. Check that students can see the difference between the use of *for* in sentences d and h. The following timelines may be useful:

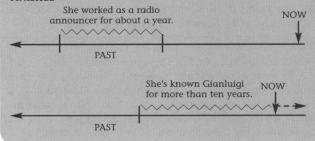
FINISHED

3 Present perfect continuous with *for* and *since*

ANSWERS
a   sentences c, i, j
b   Because *know* is a state verb (this is the same as with other tenses).

Point out that the idea of long/repeated actions is one of the most important distinctions between the Present perfect simple and continuous.

PRACTICE

1 Students work in pairs before checking answers with the whole class. Emphasise that they should choose between the Past simple, the Present perfect simple and the Present perfect continuous.

ANSWERS
a   1 's been driving   2 for   3 took   4 didn't pass
b   5 studied   6 for   7 started
c   8 's been   9 for   10 was   11 since
    12 's been working
d   13 worked   14 retired   15 's been   16 since
    17 bought   18 for   19 's been painting

Pronunciation

1 📼 [4.5] Play the recording, pausing after each phrase to allow the students to repeat. Students may find it useful to see/hear where the linking occurs. To show this, write the phrases on the board like this:

for about six months

If students still find it difficult, 'back-chain' the sentences breaking the words up where the linking occurs. For example:

about > r about > for about

2 📼 [4.6] Pause the recording after each sentence to allow students time to write. Play each sentence several times. Students check their answers in pairs before checking with the class as a whole.

> **ANSWERS**
> 1 He passed his driving test about a year ago.
> 2 We haven't had a holiday since October.
> 3 They got married a few weeks ago.
> 4 They've been married for ages and ages.
> 5 She hasn't been well for a long time.
> 6 He's been working here since about 1990.

2 **a** 📼 [4.7] Stress that students only need to write a phrase with *for*, *since* or *ago*, not a complete sentence. Stop the recording after each sentence, replaying if necessary.

b Use the recording to check answers and work on pronunciation as you go along. Insist on the correct use of the verb forms in the reconstructed questions – if students are having problems, remind them of the appropriate rules. Use the recording to correct their answers, focusing on the weak forms and linking at the same time.

3 **a** Remind students of the kind of information on Sara's lifeline and give them ten minutes to prepare their own.

b Circulate giving help, suggestions and vocabulary. To make the practice more controlled/accuracy-oriented, get them to write sentences about themselves similar to the ones in *Language focus 2*, exercise 2, on page 40. Check and correct them as you go round.

c Look at the examples and demonstrate the activity with a student. Circulate and note down both good and bad examples of the use of verb forms and time words. Write up about ten sentences and ask students to identify the correct ones, and correct those that are wrong.

d Students could do this for homework if time is short.

ADDITIONAL PRACTICE

RB **Resource bank:** *How long have you had it?* (Present perfect simple and continuous for unfinished past), page 129

Workbook: *for*, *since* and *ago* and Present perfect continuous, page 32

Vocabulary 2 (PAGE 42)
Positive characteristics

1 **a** Students check the meaning of any unknown words in their mini-dictionaries. Check the pronunciation of *ambitious* /æmˈbɪʃəs/, *courageous* /kəˈreɪdʒəs/, *imaginative* /ɪˈmædʒɪnətɪv/, *tolerant* /ˈtɒlərənt/, *determined* /dɪˈtɜːmɪnd/, paying particular attention to word stress.

b Students work in pairs to discuss their ideas.

c Encourage students to tell their partner why they believe the person they describe has these characteristics.

2 Do an example with the class before students work in pairs. Check the meaning of *principles*, *crisis*, *attitude*.

3 Check the meaning of *admire* before students work together in small groups.

Task: Talk about someone you admire (PAGES 42–43)

See *Teacher's tips: making tasks work* on pages 13–14 and *Responding to learners' individual language needs* on pages 11–12.

Preparation: listening

a Focus students' attention on the photos. Students work in groups of three or four. Emphasise that not all the photos are of famous people; some represent vocations or roles in life. Use them to help students think about the kind of person they might admire (for example, someone who has dedicated their life to helping other people). *Note:* the pictures represent the following (clockwise, from top left):
- Pablo Picasso (1881–1973), Spanish cubist artist
- Serena Williams (1981–), American tennis player. She is one of the first black female players to become really successful. Her sister, Venus, is also a famous tennis player.
- Nelson Mandela (1918–), first black president of South Africa. He spent more than 25 years in prison in his fight for equal rights for black people in South Africa.
- a teacher
- a grandmother
- J.K. Rowling (1966–), author of the Harry Potter series of children's books (also popular with adults).
- a doctor
- a wheelchair athlete
- David Beckham (1975–), English footballer, He is famous for being England captain and for being married to 'Posh Spice' (formerly a member of the pop group The Spice Girls).

b 📼 [4.8] Emphasise that students only need to make notes about the person's life the first time they listen. Encourage students to share their information.

> **ANSWERS**
> | Nelson Mandela: | president of South Africa in 1990s; before that, imprisoned for more than 25 years due to political beliefs; made famous speeches at his trial |
> |---|---|
> | Father: | civil engineer for 33 years, |

suddenly made redundant;
returned to university and retrained
as a maths teacher; lots of people
say he is 'one of the best teachers'
they have ever had

c 🔊 [4.8] Students listen again. After comparing notes in pairs, they check their ideas as a whole class.

ANSWERS

Nelson Mandela:	never changed his views; not bitter or angry; forgiving
Father:	strong in a difficult situation; didn't give in to depression; showed flexibility and creativity

Task: speaking

a Make sure that students understand what the task is, and encourage them to quickly choose a person to talk about.

b It is important for students to have time to plan their talks. Tell them to think about the language they need to explain their choices – they can use the phrases from *Vocabulary 2*, the tapescript from *Preparation: listening* on page 164 or the phrases from the *Useful language* box, or they can ask you for phrases they need. Emphasise that students should not write down everything they want to say, but just make notes.

> **Task: speaking: notes on describing people**
>
> Traditional adjectives for describing people form only a small part of what native speakers say when they describe someone. Far more common are sentences with verbs which describe the person's typical behaviour. Phrases like *He's the sort/kind of person who …* and *She's someone who …* are far more generative and easier to use.

c Students work in pairs. Practice time helps students to try out their talks and to ascertain if there is any other vocabulary or language they need to ask for. Encourage them to spend a few minutes after the practice reviewing their notes.

d Students give their talks to the class. Encourage the other students to ask questions.

> **Follow up: writing**
>
> This can be done either in class or as homework. Display the students' finished work on the classroom wall.

Wordspot (PAGE 44)

take

1 **a** Students work in small groups to discuss the phrases before checking the meaning in their *Mini-dictionaries*.
b Students work individually or in pairs.

ANSWERS
Different meanings are as follows:

3 If you *take an exam*, you do an exam and wait for the results. If you *pass an exam*, you are successful.
5 You *take a picture* with a camera; you *paint a picture* with a brush and paints.
9 If you *take off* (*clothes*), you remove (them). If you *put on* (*clothes*) you add (them).

2 Students work in pairs or groups before checking with the whole class.

ANSWERS
(*section of diagram in brackets*)
take after (c), take a holiday (d), take a test / an exam (a), take up a sport/hobby (c), take a picture (a), take someone out for a meal (e), take a train (f), take care of (e), take off (clothes) (c), take part in (e), take over (c), take notes (b)

3 Put students into pairs and refer them to the appropriate page at the back of the book. Allow a few minutes for them to check that they remember the meaning of the phrases with *take*. When students finish interviewing each other, put them into small groups to report their findings, or ask a few pairs to report back to the whole class.

Writing (PAGES 44–45)

A curriculum vitae

1 Introduce the topic and check that students understand what a *curriculum vitae* is. Also, check the meaning of *store*, *salary*, *candidate*. Students read the job advertisement before checking their answers in pairs.

ANSWERS
It's a part-time job, which would be suitable for Birgitte. She would have to work Saturdays and Sundays.

2 Students work in small groups to brainstorm topics. There is no need to correct students, as they will read a model CV in the next stage.

3 Students read individually before checking answers as a whole class.

ANSWERS
her contact details (address, telephone number, etc.)
her work experience
the name of her secondary school
her education and qualifications
whether or not she can drive
a profile of her skills and achievements
what languages she speaks
what makes her suitable for the job

4 **a** Students work in pairs and read the CV again. Do at least one example to ensure that they understand.

ANSWERS
1   proven ability
2   excellent personal skills

3 work placement
4 graduate
5 to be completed
6 mother tongue
7 fair
8 non-smoker

b Focus on the examples and the words which are not included. Give further examples if students are unsure.

Note: the following are usually not included: personal pronouns, articles, auxiliary verbs, *to be*, *to have* and *to do* as main verbs.

5 Choose whether it is more relevant for students to write their own CV or to use the fictional person on page 139. Ensure that they use the headings given in Birgitte's CV and remind them not to include unnecessary words. Students work individually. Circulate as they work, providing any vocabulary and noting down common errors to focus on as a class at the end. Encourage students to read each other's work.

Consolidation modules 1–4 (PAGES 46–47)

A Questions and auxiliaries

1 Check that students understand the context before they work in pairs to predict questions.

4-5

2 [C1] Pause the recording after each question to allow students time to write down each question. This is good intensive listening practice and provides them with concrete examples to compare their own questions with. After the listening, check answers as a whole class. Students might have suggested other questions which were equally possible.

ANSWERS
a Do you speak any other languages?
b How long have you been here?
c What are you doing at the moment?
d Did you have a good holiday?
e So where were you born?
f How often do you go swimming?
g Where are you staying while you're here?
h Have you got any brothers or sisters?

B Present and past verb forms

Students work in pairs before checking answers with the whole class. Use the relevant *Language summary* to clarify any problem areas.

If necessary, check the meaning of *supply, symbol, footprint, ceremony, common, factory* and *soul* before students read.

ANSWERS
1 voted   2 was having   3 later   4 has grown
5 came   6 stands   7 has only been   8 since
9 leave   10 was   11 wait   12 once missed
13 was playing   14 is becoming   15 still come
16 have been   17 died

C Listening and speaking: Comparing the past with the present

1 [C2] Students listen for the topics before comparing their answers in pairs.

ANSWERS
Topics mentioned: her friends, her hairstyle, her clothes, her home, her personality, a typical Friday night

2 After students have checked answers in pairs, check with the whole class.

ANSWERS
Her hairstyle and clothes: she used to spend a lot of time on these, but now she would rather sleep and spend less time.
Her personality: she used to be quite serious and worry about things, but now she's less serious and she doesn't worry so much.
A typical Friday night and her home: she used to go to clubs and go out dancing. Also she drank and smoked. Now she stays at home and watches TV or reads a book.

3 As a class, brainstorm other topics which students might use to talk about how their lives have changed in the last ten years. Circulate as students discuss in pairs, and note down any language problems to focus on as a class. Ask a few pairs to report back to the class.

D Speaking: Getting to know you

1 Put students in pairs and refer them to the appropriate role card. Allow a few minutes for them to check that they understand their role. Emphasise that students do not need to write the conversation, but just make notes and think about what they will say. Circulate so that students can ask you for any vocabulary they need.

2 Encourage students to speak for the full ten minutes by using a clock or stopwatch. A time limit provides them with a motivating challenge. As students speak, note down errors or useful language to look at together.

E Vocabulary: Alphabet quiz

Set this up as a competition. The first pair to complete the alphabet quiz correctly are the winners.

ANSWERS
A acquaintance   B border   C colleague
D determined   E engaged   F fail   G gambling
H hardworking   I industrial   J jellyfish   K keep
L local   M mother-in-law   N niece
O old-fashioned   P prize   R   recognise
S stepmother   T twins   W waves

Students can now do *Test one: modules 1–4* on pages 161–163.

module 5

Success

Reading and vocabulary (PAGES 48–49)

1 Give students between five and ten minutes to discuss their view of success in small groups.

2 **a** Emphasise that students should not answer the 'psychometric test' questions yet. Students work individually before checking answers with the whole class.

b Students work individually or in pairs checking the meaning of the words and phrases. The pronunciation of *jealous* and *workaholic* may need drilling.

c Students work in pairs, asking each other the questions and recording their partner's answers. Emphasise that students should give a reason for each answer they give.

3 Get students to add up their scores, then direct them to the assessment on page 140. Ask them if they agree with the assessment, and to explain why.

4 Look at the example with the whole class. Students work in pairs to complete the table.

ANSWERS

Noun	Adjective
success	successful
jealousy	a jealous
b intelligence	intelligent
importance	c important
d happiness	happy
e ambition	ambitious
f determination	determined
g imagination	imaginative
confidence	h confident
i possibility	possible

Pronunciation

1 Students mark the stress, saying the words aloud to their partner to help them decide where the stress falls.

ANSWERS

success	successful
jealousy	jealous
intelligence	intelligent
importance	important
happiness	happy
ambition	ambitious

determination	determined
imagination	imaginative
confidence	confident
possibility	possible

2 [5.1] Play the recording as many times as necessary, pausing after each word for students to decide where the stress is.

ANSWERS
The following words change their pattern:

determination	determined
imagination	imaginative
possibility	possible.

3 Drill the phrases before students practise saying them aloud with a partner.

ADDITIONAL ACTIVITY

RB **Resource bank:** *Have you got what it takes?* vocabulary extension (dependent prepositions), page 131

Language focus 1 (PAGES 50–51)

Future forms

See *Teacher's tips: using a discovery approach in the teaching of grammar* on page 8.

1 Students discuss the questions in small groups.

CD2 Tracks 3 – 8

2 **a** Before listening to the recording, students check the vocabulary in their mini-dictionaries.

b [5.2] Focus students' attention on the photos of the six students before they listen. Students check answers in pairs before checking as a whole class.

ANSWERS

Student	Has been studying	Plans/ideas about future career
Nora	Drama and Education	She will probably teach Drama at secondary school. Nora plans to travel to the West Indies first, and possibly to do some work there.
Oliver	Ancient History	He starts in the army in September if he passes his medical. Oliver has signed for five years.

Dino	Fashion	He is going to do a master's degree in Fashion Design if he gets good enough grades in his exams.
Caroline	Modern Languages – Spanish and Russian	She has got a job as a trainee manager with an international clothing company, starting in September.
Zak	Business Studies	He hasn't decided what to do yet, but is considering applying for a course in Journalism.
Alice	Law	She doesn't want to be a lawyer and doesn't know what she wants to do. Alice expects to get a temporary job, possibly working in a shop or in telephone sales.

Track ~~4~~ 9

3 **a** 🔊 [5.3] Students listen before checking answers in pairs and then as a whole class. Pause the recording after each sentence to allow students to write the missing words.

ANSWERS
1 I'll probably
2 I'm not going to apply *~~I'll probably~~*
3 ~~I'm hoping to go~~
4 I'm about to join
5 ~~I'm starting~~ *I'll start*
6 I'm having
7 I'm leaving
8 I'm planning to do
9 I'm due to start
10 I'm having
11 I'm going to find
12 I'm thinking of applying
13 I'm definitely not going to be
14 I'll do some kind

b Students work in small groups to discuss the six students they heard about. Check answers as a whole class.

ANSWERS
Have made arrangements to start a job/course:
Oliver, Caroline – *Dino*
Know what they want to do: Nora, Dino
Don't really know what they want to do: Zak, Alice

Language focus 1: notes on the approach to future forms

• *Will* versus *going to*: we have chosen not to contrast *will* for 'spontaneous decisions' with *going* to for 'plans' for several reasons. Research suggests that *will* is the most common way of talking about the future, and that the most common use of *will* is the one described here. *Will* for 'spontaneous decisions' is less frequent. When it does occur, it is often in the communicative context of 'offers' or 'on the spot' responses. This is dealt with separately in Module 7 within the context of polite social behaviour.

• The Present continuous versus *going to*: students may find the difference between these two forms difficult to

see. This is partly because there is a genuine overlap: *going to* can almost always be used instead of the Present continuous. However, the Present continuous cannot be used where there is just a vague intention; there must be some kind of arrangement.

Analysis

1 Get students to underline the verb forms in sentences 1, 7 and 11. Explain or translate the following: *to predict, an intention.* Students work in pairs to try to complete the rules. All three forms should be familiar, but it may be useful to remind the students briefly of the following points:

• the contraction of *will* (*'ll*) and *will not* (*won't*)

• the difference in form between the Present continuous and *going to* (with *going to*, the main verb is in the infinitive).

ANSWERS
a *will* + verb — sentence 14
b *going to* + verb — sentences 2 and 13
c the Present continuous — sentences 5, 6 and 10

2 Discuss this with the whole class. Check the meaning of the verbs and phrases, especially *about to* and *due to.* Point out, by using examples, which constructions are followed by a gerund and which are followed by an infinitive. Highlight the following:

• the use of prepositions with these verbs/phrases

• that *due to* can be used either with an infinitive (as in the example given) or without (*You're due at a meeting*).

ANSWERS
I'm hoping to go there for a few months.
I'm due to start work at the beginning of September.
I'm thinking of applying for a course in journalism.

PRACTICE

1 Students work in pairs before checking answers with the whole class. Emphasise that form is important.

ANSWERS AND LANGUAGE NOTE
a I'm planning to study engineering.
b My sister is thinking of joining the army.
c I'm due to take my driving test next week.
d Alex says he's not going to / he isn't going to apply for university.*

*There are two possibilities for expressing this form. The first one emphasises the negative more.

e I know I won't get the job.
f My boss is about to retire.
g My son's starting a new job on Monday.
h I probably won't see you before you go.

43

2 Look at the examples with students. Emphasise that students should make sentences with a future meaning and that they don't need to use all the prompts. Circulate as students work individually, checking the accuracy of their work. Check answers as a whole class.

3 Put students into pairs. Refer them to page 141. Do an example with the class by choosing three numbers yourself and asking a student to read out the three instructions to you. As students write complete sentences, circulate and help with any extra vocabulary they need. Note down any errors with the use of future forms for correction later on.

Vocabulary (PAGE 51)

Work

1 Check the meaning of *wouldn't mind doing*. Emphasise that students should keep their notes secret until later.

2 **a** Students work individually or in pairs, using their mini-dictionaries. At the feedback stage, check the meaning and pronunciation of *physically* /ˈfɪzɪkəli/, *qualifications* /ˌkwɒlɪfɪˈkeɪʃənz/, *secure* /sɪˈkʊə/, *competitive* /kəmˈpetɪtɪv/, *challenging* /ˈtʃælɪndʒɪŋ/, *responsibility* /rɪˈspɒnsɪbɪlɪti/, *opportunities* /ˌɒpəˈtjuːnɪtiz/.

> ### *Vocabulary*: additional language notes
>
> Students may have difficulty distinguishing between *training*, *qualifications* and *skills*.
> - *Training* is education aimed at teaching you to do a job (*training to be a doctor, teacher-training,* etc.).
> - *Qualifications* are exams/certificates you get, especially those which enable you to do a particular job.
> - *Skills* mean the abilities you have in a particular area; you get them from training courses or experience, or you have them naturally. This word is often used in the plural – *people skills, management skills,* etc.

b Put students into pairs to discuss their opinions.

3 Students decide which jobs they think would interest their partner, before working in pairs. Do some class feedback to find out if anybody's suggested jobs matched what their partner had written.

ADDITIONAL ACTIVITY

RB **Resource bank:** *Vocabulary extension* (talking about work and training), page 134

Listening and speaking (PAGE 52)

Doing something different

1 Focus students' attention on the photos and explain that all the people have made a career change. Check the meaning of *to resign, to retrain, supervisor, solicitor*. Students read about the people in the photos, then discuss the questions in pairs.

> **ANSWERS**
> | Clare: | a | geography teacher |
> | | b | plumber |
> | Kevin: | a | supervisor |
> | | b | house-husband |
> | Lorna and Ian: | a | solicitor and accountant |
> | | b | run a hotel |

2 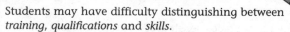 [5.4] Check the meaning of *disadvantages, stressful, exhausted, depressed, unemployed, change places, desperate*. Emphasise that students should just write notes. Play the recording, pausing after each person to give students time to write and compare ideas in pairs. Check answers with the whole class.

> **ANSWERS**
> **Clare**
> a really fed up; children were badly behaved and hard to control; had to mark homework and plan lessons in the evenings; felt stressed and depressed
> b practical problems to solve every day; no work in the evenings
> c start work early; older people think she can't do the job because she's a woman
> **Kevin**
> a lost his job when the company closed down
> b gets to see his children growing up
> c very hard work; lonely at times; misses colleagues
> **Lorna**
> a didn't want to bring up children in London
> b meeting new people; lovely view; near the sea
> c people in the village weren't friendly at first; money problems

3 Students work in pairs to answer true (T) or false (F) before listening again. Check answers as a whole class.

> **ANSWERS**
> a T
> b F They sometimes tease her, but she doesn't mind.
> c T
> d F He became a house-husband because he couldn't find work, but his wife could.
> e T
> f F He misses his friends from work.
> g F They had successful careers.
> h F They still work very hard. She says it's a twenty-four-hour job.
> i T

4 Check that students understand the questions/statements. Students discuss the questions in groups whilst you circulate and supply any vocabulary needed.

Language focus 2 (PAGE 53)

Future clauses with *if, when,* etc.

See *Teacher's tips: using a discovery approach in the teaching of grammar* on page 8.

Check the meaning of *staff, to be fully qualified, to fail an exam, full-time*, *part-time*, *to redecorate*. Students discuss the answers briefly in pairs before checking with the whole class.

ANSWERS
a Clare b Ian c Clare d Kevin and Sally
e Sally f Lorna

Analysis

1 Do the first example with the class and then get students to do the other examples before checking answers together.

ANSWERS
a If I <u>don't enjoy</u> it, I'll try something else.
b <u>When</u> she <u>has</u> the baby, we'll have to get more staff to help us.
c I'll be fully qualified in about three years, <u>unless</u> I <u>fail</u> my exams, of course!
d We can't both work full-time <u>until</u> our youngest child <u>starts</u> school in about three years' time.
e <u>As soon as</u> he <u>finds</u> a job again, I'm going to change to working part-time.
f I'm hoping to redecorate a lot of the hotel <u>before</u> I <u>have</u> the baby.

2 Discuss the question with the whole class.

ANSWER AND LANGUAGE NOTE
The sentences refer to the future, but the verb after these words is in the Present simple.

This is probably different in the students' own language – with a monolingual group, it may be worth contrasting this with examples from their own language.

3 Students discuss this in pairs before checking with the whole class.

ANSWER
A future form is used in the 'main' clause (*will* is most common here, but *going to* and modal forms are also common).

PRACTICE

1 Students work individually or in pairs before checking answers with the whole class.

ANSWERS
a When; qualifies, will earn
b will make; unless; gets
c will go; if; doesn't find
d will have; before; have
e will go; as soon as; is
f won't get; until; are
g will be; if; waits
h will get; when; has

2 This exercise can be either spoken or written. Give some examples of your own first.

3 Look at the examples with the class. Students work in small groups. Allow a few minutes for each student to think of somebody to talk about. As students work, circulate

and note down any errors in the use of future clauses with *if*, *when*, etc. to focus on in feedback.

ADDITIONAL PRACTICE

RB **Resource bank:** *The great diamond robbery* (future clauses with *if*, *when*, etc.), pages 132–133

Workbook: Future clauses with *if*, *when*, etc., pages 41–42

Task: Choose the best candidate
(PAGES 54–55)

See *Teacher's tips: making tasks work* on pages 13–14 and *Responding to learners' individual language needs* on pages 11–12.

Preparation: reading

1 Check the meaning of: *employment agency, to recruit, staff, nanny, an applicant, an application form, an interview, suitable*. Focus students' attention on the advertisement and get them to scan it to answer the question. Ask if students would be interested in applying to this agency. Discuss answers with the whole class.

ANSWER
They recruit for management and office staff, catering staff (hotel and restaurant staff), domestic staff (nannies, private teachers and nurses).

2 a Students read about Jean-Luc and Marion. Ask them the following questions to check that they have understood the context.
• Which one works for Horizons Unlimited?
• Which of them has recruited staff from Horizons Unlimited?
b Check the meaning of *childminder* and *remote*. Students read the first two paragraphs and answer the questions in pairs before checking with the whole class.

ANSWERS
1 His wife has died and he has been neglecting the hotel because he has been so busy looking after his children.
2 He wants one person to do two very different jobs; nanny and assistant hotel manager.

3 Get students to predict the duties and qualifications before reading. Check the meaning of a *barman*, a *chef*, *to be absent on business*, *computer skills*, *skier*, *skiing*, *salary*, a *ski pass*, a *driving licence*. Students read the rest of the e-mail to complete the information. Encourage them to make notes rather than copying whole sentences from the text. It is reading practice, so the emphasis is on finding the information.

ANSWERS

Size/Location of the hotel	• 25-bedroom family hotel in remote ski resort in France.
Hotel duties	• running reception/office in the mornings and evenings • organising part-time staff

	when Jean-Luc is absent • helping in the restaurant and bar when they are busy.
Childcare duties	When Jean-Luc is away on business trips: • take Karine to and from school • cook the children's dinner • put them to bed • look after them at the weekend.
Information about the children	• David is 13, Karine is 8. • Both are well-behaved, but they have had a difficult time for the last two years.
Essential qualifications	• fluent French and English • good computer skills • previous experience of hotel work • kind and sympathetic.
Other useful qualifications	• ability to speak German • knowledge of skiing • driving licence.

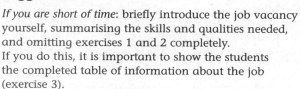

Preparation: reading: alternative suggestions

If you are short of time: briefly introduce the job vacancy yourself, summarising the skills and qualities needed, and omitting exercises 1 and 2 completely.
If you do this, it is important to show the students the completed table of information about the job (exercise 3).

Task: speaking

1 Divide students into groups of five and allocate each student a candidate. (If you don't have the correct number of students, put weaker students together in pairs.) Give students time to read the notes at the back of the book, and help with any comprehension problems. Explain that the task is to find the best candidate for the job. Ask students to make notes about the strengths and weaknesses of their candidate.

2 Give students five to ten minutes to think about what they will say about their candidate. Get them to close their books and remember, rather than reading the notes. Circulate amongst the students as they work so that you are available to provide any difficult vocabulary or phrases. Remind them to refer to the *Useful language* box for ideas, too.

3 Students work in their groups again. It is useful to appoint a chairperson for each group, to ensure that everyone gets a chance to speak. Emphasise that they need to listen and make notes about each candidate, asking questions about anything that is not clear. As they discuss the candidates, circulate and make notes of errors or useful language, for analysis and correction later on.

4 Give students time to think about how they will express their decision before each group tells the class which candidate they chose. If there is disagreement, encourage further discussion to see if the class can agree on the one most suitable candidate.

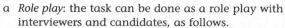

Task: speaking: alternative suggestions

a *Role play*: the task can be done as a role play with interviewers and candidates, as follows.
  • Divide the class into two groups, the interviewers and the five candidates. The interviewers should make a list of questions they want to ask the candidates, while the five candidates read and memorise the information at the back of the book. They should think about how they can express these personal details in English.
  • The candidates are then interviewed one by one (you may need to set a time limit of five minutes per candidate).
  • The interviewers then discuss who they think is most suitable for the job. Whilst this is going on, the five candidates can either 'drop' their roles and join in the discussion, or remain in their roles and be available to answer any further questions that interviewers might have.
If you have a larger class, the groups of interviewers and candidates can be duplicated and final decisions on the best candidate compared.

b *Using the feedback/correction stage of the task for revision purposes*: this task brings together much of the language that students have studied in the first five modules of this book. Whilst performing the task, students will almost certainly need to use: present tenses, past tenses, the Present perfect simple and continuous, comparatives, superlatives, future time clauses. Collect errors in these five categories, as a lead-in to a revision session. Copy these onto the board and give them to students to correct in pairs. Refer students to the appropriate rules and *Language summary* for revision where necessary.

Writing (PAGE 56)

A covering letter

1 Focus students on the pictures of Louisa, and make sure that everyone understands *CV* (curriculum vitae) and *covering letter* (a letter you write enclosing something else).

ANSWERS
a Louisa's address   b date
c the address of Horizons Unlimited

2 Ask students to guess what they think she might write in her covering letter. Check the meaning of *to be available, to be qualified, to be bilingual*. Students order the letter individually or in pairs before checking answers with the whole class.

ANSWERS
a 4 b 6 c 8 d 9 e 7 f 3 g 2 h 1 i 5 j 10

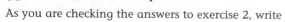

Writing, exercise 2: alternative suggestion for focus on phrases

• As you are checking the answers to exercise 2, write

the letter in order onto the board (or slowly reveal it on an overhead projector if you have one). Students close their books and read through the whole letter on the board, aloud or silently, trying to remember the important phrases.

- Rub one of the important phrases out of the letter, replacing it with dots. Get a student to read out the letter, supplying the missing phrase at the appropriate point.
- Rub out another phrase, and get another student to read it out as before, supplying the missing phrase. Repeat this until the letter disappears and is replaced by dotted lines.
- When the letter has been reduced to no more than a few prompts, get students to write it out from memory, either in pairs or individually.

3 Point out/elicit any similarities or differences between a formal letter in English and in the students' own language. Discuss the useful phrases the students have underlined.

> **POSSIBLE ANSWERS**
> Students may have underlined the following sentences / sentence stems, which could be used in any formal letter:
> Dear Sir or Madam,
> I am writing in reply to …
> I am interested in …
> I enclose …
> I look forward to hearing from you soon.
> Yours faithfully,

4 Refer students back to the job advertisement on page 54 and ask them to guess what other jobs the agency might have. Students can invent experience if necessary.

Real life (PAGE 57)

A formal telephone call

1 a [5.5] Explain that Louisa has had a job interview, but has not heard whether or not she has got the job. She is phoning to find out what is happening. Ask students to predict what she might say. Play the recording and go through the answers with the class.

> **ANSWERS**
> She is phoning because she has not heard from Marion O'Neill since her interview.
> She is going to pass on the message and ask Marion O'Neill to call back.

b Get students to guess what the missing phrases might be before playing the recording. Stop the recording after each phrase for students to tell you the exact words used.

> **ANSWERS**
> 1 I'd like to speak
> 2 put you through
> 3 could I speak
> 4 who's calling
> 5 a message
> 6 her to call you
> 7 just phoning because
> 8 I'll pass on
> 9 she can contact you on
> 10 is there a mobile number
> 11 leave a message
> 12 for calling

Pronunciation

1 [5.6] Play the recording, stopping after each phrase and pointing out the intonation marked on the page. Alternatively, use your hand to indicate where the intonation rises or falls. Point out that this is how people make themselves sound polite and that it is important to practise this.

2 [5.7] Get students to practise saying the phrases, either providing a model yourself, or playing the recording, pausing after each phrase. Do not spend too long on this if students are having difficulty reproducing intonation patterns – passive awareness is a good start.

> ***Real life*: alternative suggestion for focus on phrases**
>
> - Copy the dialogue onto slips of card – each line should be on a different card, and ideally each speaker should be a different colour. Either make large words to stick on the board big enough for the whole class to read, or small cards, a separate set for each pair of students.
> - After exercise 1a, get students to close their books and give/show them the set of cards with the dialogue mixed up. Students put the dialogue in order, using the recording to check if necessary.
> - Get students to read aloud the dialogues from the cards – you could focus on the intonation as you are going along.
> - Leaving the dialogue in the correct order, turn over one or more of the cards, preferably some of the ones which include useful phrases for making a formal telephone call. Get a pair of students to read it aloud, supplying the missing phrases. Repeat the process until students gradually memorise the dialogue. Correct pronunciation, focusing especially on the polite intonation highlighted in the pronunciation section.

2 Introduce the situation and get students to guess the sort of thing that each speaker might say. Divide the class into As and Bs. Focus students' attention on the flow chart, and read through the instructions, checking that they understand them. *If you have a less confident group*: elicit a possible dialogue first as a class, then get them to practise it in pairs. *If you have a stronger group*: get students to try it in pairs straight away. Circulate, supplying/correcting phrases as necessary, or noting down errors for work later.

Song (PAGE 58)

Manic Monday

1 Students discuss their ideas for a few minutes before comparing with the class as a whole.

2 [5.8] Students work in small groups to complete the gaps. Emphasise that the final words at the end of each gapped line should rhyme, so it is important that they say the words aloud to each other. Play the recording for students to check their ideas. Pause the recording and replay sections if students find it difficult to hear.

ANSWERS
a dream b stream c paid d made e Monday
f Sunday g fun day h run day i Monday j train
k nine l aeroplane m time n wear o there

3 Students discuss the questions in pairs or small groups.

ANSWERS
She's going to tell the boss that the train was delayed or late.
If she's late, she won't get paid.
It's manic because she's in a rush and she feels disorganised.

Study ... (PAGE 58)

Improving your spoken fluency

1 This activity could be done for homework or in class.
If it is done in class, it could be done as a discussion. Students work in small groups and compare which of the tips they already use and any additional ideas they have.

2 *If you have one-to-one tutorials with your students:* this would be a good thing to follow up with them.

Practise ... (PAGE 59)

1 Future plans and intentions

If this activity is done in class, get students to cover up the descriptions a–e and underline the future forms. Students work in pairs to discuss why each form has been used before uncovering the descriptions and matching them.

ANSWERS
a 5 I'm going to phone and tell him exactly what i think.
b 3 We're going to look for a new flat in a few years.
c 4 I'm having lunch with Simon on Friday.
d 2 My birthday will be on a Friday next year.
e 1 Shall I carry that suitcase for you?

2 Talking about the future

Students work individually before checking answers as a class.

ANSWERS
a planning b he'll get back c due d thinking of
e you will leave

3 Future clauses

Get students to cover the words in the box and try to predict what the missing words will be before uncovering the box and completing the sentences. Check answers with the whole class.

ANSWERS
a until b if c before d as soon as e unless

4 Work

If this activity is done in class, each half of a phrase written on a piece of card. Students work in pairs to match them.

ANSWERS
a 8 b 5 c 2 d 1 e 6 f 7 g 3 h 4

5 Adjectives

Use this activity for dictionary skills practice. Students work individually or in pairs to identify the odd one out and change it to form an adjective. Get them to check their answers in their mini-dictionaries.

ANSWERS
a success   successful
b happiness   happy
c imagination   imaginative
d determination determined
e jealousy   jealous

6 Prepositions

ANSWERS
a for b in c through d to e on f in

Pronunciation

a [5.9] Play the recording, pausing after each group of words.

b [5.10] Students work in pairs, saying the words aloud to each other to help them decide which one is different. Play the recording, pausing after each word to give students time to decide.

ANSWERS
1 old 2 qualification 3 bored 4 gone
5 told 6 confidence

c Students work in pairs, saying the words aloud.

Remember! (PAGE 59)

After looking back at the areas they have practised, students do the *Mini-check* on page 157. Check answers as a whole class, and ask students to tell you their scores out of 20.

ANSWERS
1 'm going   11 skills
2 to go   12 run
3 going   13 call you back
4 go   14 due
5 to go   15 to travel
6 'll go   16 for
7 imaginative   17 on
8 jealousy   18 for
9 successful   19 in
10 ambition   20 for

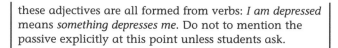

In the media

Listening and vocabulary (PAGE 60)

TV and radio

1 Check the meaning of *terrestrial TV* and *satellite TV*. Students discuss the questions in groups or with the whole class.

2 a Check the meaning and pronunciation of *documentary* /ˌdɒkjʊˈmentari/, *coverage* /ˈkʌvərɪdʒ/, *mystery* /ˈmɪstəri/, *sitcom* /ˈsɪtkɒm/ (= situation comedy). Students work individually before comparing answers in groups. Emphasise that they can use their *Mini-dictionaries* to check meaning.

b Students work in pairs or small groups. If they come from different countries, ensure that there is a mix of nationalities in each group. If they come from the same country, ask them to think of one or two examples for each type of programme.

3 Students work individually before comparing answers in pairs.

4 [6.1] Emphasise that students only need to identify the type of programme. Pause the recording after each extract for students to compare answers in pairs. Check answers with the whole class at the end.

ANSWERS
1 game show / quiz – TV   2 sports coverage – TV/radio
3 phone-in – radio   4 travel news – radio/TV
5 soap opera – TV

5 After listening again, students compare their answers in pairs.

ANSWERS
a Geography and Art
b Berlin
c a runner
d an open-air rock concert
e She thinks it's really unfair to criticise young people.
f A broken-down lorry is blocking the central lane.
g better
h He loves her.
i no

Language focus 1 (PAGE 61)

-ed/-ing adjectives

Language focus 1: notes on the approach to -ed/-ing forms

These adjectives have been put before the passive in this module in the hope that this will help students understand the passive better, since the *-ed* adjectives are, in origin, passive forms. You could point out that

these adjectives are all formed from verbs: *I am depressed* means *something depresses me*. Do not to mention the passive explicitly at this point unless students ask.

1 Check the meaning of *invent* and *violence*. Students discuss their opinions in small groups.

2 [6.2] Students match the opinions to the statements. They do not need to write down the opinions.

ANSWERS
1 statement b – agrees
2 statement d – partly agrees
3 statement c – completely disagrees
4 statement a – agrees

3 Ask students if they understand the basic meaning of the adjectives, but do not explain the difference between the *-ed* and *-ing* forms. If necessary, replay the recording.

ANSWERS
Speaker 1: exciting, bored
Speaker 2: upsetting, confusing, worried
Speaker 3: depressing
Speaker 4: annoying, interested

Analysis

1 Students work in pairs, matching the adjectives to the man and the programme.

ANSWERS
The man is *excited*. The programme is *exciting*.

2 Ask if anyone can explain the difference between the *-ed* and *-ing* forms of the adjectives.

ANSWERS AND LANGUAGE NOTE
-ed adjectives describe a feeling; *-ing* adjectives describe something/someone that makes us feel like this.

Point out that *-ed* adjectives are, in fact, past participles – adjectives like *upset* are not exceptions, but are simply formed from irregular verbs.

PRACTICE

1 Check the meaning of the adjectives by describing typical situations in which you might feel *disappointed*, *embarrassed*, *frustrated*, etc. Students work individually or in pairs before checking answers with the whole class.

ANSWERS
a interesting, shocked   e confusing,
b pleased, worrying   frustrating
c exciting, surprised   f annoyed,
d fascinated,   disappointing
   embarrassing   g frightened

49

2 Focus on the example and the suggested responses, highlighting the following.

- *I'd* (*I would*) is used because you are imagining this situation / it is hypothetical.
- The *-ing* adjectives are very often used in the construction *I find ... boring/annoying*, etc.

Check the meaning of *empty, civil war, developing country*. Students discuss their responses in groups, then do brief feedback as a class.

ADDITIONAL PRACTICE

Workbook: *-ed/-ing* adjectives, page 44

Reading and vocabulary (PAGES 62–63)

News stories

1 **a** Students work in pairs to discuss their reading habits.

b In pairs, students think of possible topics for news stories. Circulate and supply any vocabulary they need.

2 **a** Tell students they are going to read some news items from English newspapers. Check the meaning of: *an immigrant, to be horrified, to threaten someone, familiar, to be persuaded, a pair of trainers, to blame something or someone (for something), a trilby hat, a firefighter*.

In groups, students predict what the articles are about. As they are doing this, copy the headlines onto the board. Write their suggestions under each headline on the board, without saying whether or not they are correct.

b As a whole class, discuss which headlines the vocabulary relates to.

3 Students read the articles and match them to the headlines.

ANSWERS
a 5 b 7 c 6 d 2 e 8 f 4 g 1 h 3

4 Students work in pairs to remember the answers. Emphasise that they may need to use their *Mini-dictionaries*. Allow a few minutes for them to remember, before they read to find the answers. Check with the whole class.

ANSWERS
a a teenager, Emilio Sanchez, and his two friends
b a youth called Billy Camlia
c Pete Twigger, a passenger
d Bono, the U2 star
e Raul Hortena
f Shaun Kenna, a Brisbane firefighter
g Phin Suy, a gardener and Cambodian immigrant
h Bono   i air traffic controllers
j carpets   k envelopes

5 Students discuss the questions in groups or with the whole class.

Language focus 2 (PAGES 63–65)

The passive

See *Teacher's tips: using a discovery approach in the teaching of grammar* on page 8.

1 Look at the example with the class. Students work individually or in pairs before checking answers with the whole class. Some students may ask about the passive at this point. This is fully dealt with in the *Analysis*.

ANSWERS
a rescued   b was rescued   c tried   d was put
e are caused   f will be raised   g has been fined

2 Emphasise that some sentences do not tell us who or what did each action.

ANSWERS
a Shaun Kenna   b her ex-husband
c a Chilean teenager   d We don't know.
e ordinary items   f We don't know.   g We don't know.

Analysis

Note: we have used the term 'doer' in preference to 'agent' because it seems more transparent, but if your students know 'agent' already, make it clear that this is what is meant.

1 Active and passive

a This is a good way to find out if students are familiar with the passive.

ANSWERS
The verb *rescued* is active. The verb *was rescued* is passive.

b Check (by translation if necessary) that students understand what the subject of a verb is. Write out the first two sentences, underlining the subject and verb in each. The 'doer' (agent) of the verb can be shown with arrows, like this:

Shaun Kenna rescued his ex-wife from a burning house.
   (subject)   (verb)   (object)

A Melbourne woman (subject) was rescued (verb) from a burning house by her ex-husband.

In the second sentence, the subject is not the 'doer'. If students have problems with this concept, go through more of the sentences, identifying the subject and 'doer'.

2 Forming the passive

Remind students of the basic form of the passive verb, then ask them to identify the tenses one by one, contrasting them with a similar active sentence, for example:

Thousands of accidents <u>are caused</u> by ordinary items. / Ordinary items <u>cause</u> thousands of accidents.
Shaun Kenna <u>rescued</u> his ex-wife. / a woman <u>was rescued</u>.

ANSWERS
Present simple passive: *are caused* (sentence e)
Past simple passive: *was rescued* (sentence b), *was put* (sentence d)

Present perfect passive: *has been fined* (sentence g)
Future passive: *will be raised* (sentence f)

Point out also:

- the formation of the negative and question form in each case, particularly in the Present perfect, where students have two auxiliary verbs to manipulate
- that contractions can be used with the passive as with other verb forms
- that the *be* + past participle rule for forming the passive is completely regular.

3 The 'doer' (agent) in passive sentences

Students discuss their ideas in pairs, and find an example of each, before checking with the whole class.

ANSWERS
a obvious: sentence g; unimportant/unknown: sentences d and f
b *by* + doer: sentences b (*by her ex-husband*) and e (*by ordinary items*)

PRACTICE

1 Check the meaning of *to be attacked by someone, a burglar, an attack, a bill, to pay in instalments, to estimate*. Students read the stories quickly to see what happened in each one. Feed back briefly with the whole class before getting students to select the correct form.

ANSWERS
a was attacked b heard c phoned
d were contacted e was sent f was rescued
g happened h has apologised i sent
j was told k owed l said m admitted
n was sent o has been estimated p is stolen

2 [6.3] Introduce the idea of a quiz and check the meaning of *to be produced, to be widely watched, to be manufactured*. This quiz can be done in pairs, individually or as a team game. If you do it as a team game, you may prefer to play the relevant section of the recording after each question/answer rather than waiting until the end to check the answers all together. After checking the answers, get students to underline the passive forms in each question.

ANSWERS
a 1 b 2 b 3 c 4 a 5 c 6 a 7 c 8 b
b were ... produced, is ... watched, is ... watched, was ... used, was ... created, have been made, has been made, are manufactured

3 Students work individually or in pairs before checking answers with the whole class. Remind them to think about the tense of the verb as well as whether it is passive or active.

ANSWERS
a were written b has been translated
c is watched d was first used e was awarded
f was created g named h have been based
i have made j are manufactured

4 **a** Tell students that each question in the quiz must contain a passive phrase. Remind them of the passive phrases in the quiz they have just done, and check the meaning and pronunciation of the words/phrases in the box. Put students into groups of four or five and set them a number of questions to write. Put up categories or questions for them to include (*sport, films*, etc.). Suggest that students follow the same format as the questions in the book. Set a time limit of ten to fifteen minutes.

b Put students into groups of two teams each, or do the quizzes as a whole class, with each team taking turns to read out a question and answer. Allocate points for correct answers.

ADDITIONAL PRACTICE

RB Resource bank: *Passive dominoes* (passive forms), page 135; *Vocabulary extension* (passive verbs often in the news), page 136

Workbook: The passive, page 46; Active or passive, page 47

Vocabulary (PAGE 65)

Extreme adjectives

1 Check that they understand what a review is by asking questions such as *Where can you read film reviews?* Focus students on the film reviews, and check the meaning of *a blockbuster, special effects, a joke, to admit, a commanding officer*. Students read and discuss the questions in pairs.

ANSWERS
a	good review	blockbuster/action movie
b	bad review	comedy
c	good review	comedy
d	mixed review	romance

2 Students work individually or in pairs before checking answers with the whole class.

ANSWERS
a terrific, superb b terrible, dreadful
c hilarious d ridiculous

3 **a** Look at the example together and check that the students understand 'extreme'. Students do the rest of the exercise individually or in pairs. Check the pronunciation and stress of the 'extreme' adjectives.

ANSWERS
1 astonished – very surprised
2 boiling – very hot
3 brilliant – very good
4 delighted – very happy
5 freezing – very cold
6 furious – very angry
7 terrified – very frightened
8 tragic – very sad

b Discuss the question with the class. Use examples on the board to explain that:

- *absolutely* can only be used with extreme adjectives, for example, *absolutely boiling, absolutely delighted*

- *really* can be used with both extreme adjectives, for example *really brilliant, really furious*, and non-extreme adjectives, for example, *really good, really angry*
- *very* can only be used with non-extreme adjectives, for example, *very happy, very cold*.

ANSWER
Very cannot be used with the extreme adjectives in A.

4 Ask students about the type of language used in headlines in their own country. Point out that 'extreme' adjectives are often used in headlines in English newspapers. Check the meaning of *a performance, the opposition, a nomination*. Students work in pairs before checking answers with the whole class.

ANSWERS
a   United manager <u>delighted</u> with <u>brilliant</u> performance
b   <u>Tragic</u> death of teenager
c   Prime Minister <u>furious</u> at opposition's criticism
d   We made some <u>terrible</u> mistakes, admits United captain
e   <u>Freezing</u> temperatures in north of country
f   <u>Boiling</u> weather to continue
g   Film star <u>astonished</u> at Oscar nomination

Pronunciation

1 [6.4] Look at the example together. Play the recording and pause after each word to allow students to compare their answers in pairs.

ANSWERS

●●	●●●	●●●●	●●●●
boiling dreadful freezing tragic	brilliant furious terrible terrified	hilarious ridiculous	astonished delighted terrific

2 Drill chorally and individually, using your hand to indicate when a syllable is stressed, like a conductor. If students are confident, put them into pairs to practise further.

ADDITIONAL ACTIVITY

RB **Resource bank:** *Adjective snap* ('extreme' adjectives), page 137
Workbook: Vocabulary: Extreme adjectives, page 47

Task: Review a book/CD/concert
(PAGES 66–67)

See *Teacher's tips: making tasks work* on pages 13–14 and *Responding to learners' individual language needs* on pages 11–12.

Preparation: listening

1 Explain that students are going to do a survey in groups to find out about what forms of entertainment are the most and least popular in the class. Check the meaning of *a musical, a novel, ballet*. Students work individually to rank the activities before working in groups. Each group reports back to the class.

2 Students work individually or in pairs before checking with the whole class. Check the meaning of *set* carefully. Note that *set* (noun) is the place in a studio or theatre which is made to look like, for example, a room in a house or another planet in a science fiction film; *to be set in* + place/time describes where/when the story takes place, for example, *The film is set on the moon in the year 2075*.

ANSWERS
acting – musical, cinema, video/DVD, TV, ballet, play
characters – musical, cinema, video/DVD, computer games, TV, novels, ballet,
play costumes – musical, cinema, video/DVD, TV, ballet, play
graphics – computer games, TV
language – cinema, video/DVD, TV, novels, play
lyrics – musical, classical concert, music at home, rock concert
music – musical, cinema, video/DVD, classical concert, music at home, computer games, TV, ballet, rock concert
photography – cinema, video/DVD, TV
set – musical, cinema, video/DVD, TV, ballet, rock concert, play
singing – musical, classical concert, music at home, rock concert
special effects – cinema, video/DVD, computer games, TV, ballet, rock concert, play
story – musical, cinema, video/DVD, TV, novels, ballet, play

3 **a** [6.5] Explain that students will hear three people talking. Emphasise that they should make notes as they listen. Pause the recording after each person, to allow students to compare answers in pairs. If necessary, play the recording more than once.

ANSWERS
Person 1
1   a book
2   They liked it.
3   It's very easy to read and really witty.
4   The story is a bit predictable.

Person 2
1   a film
2   They liked it.
3   It's like theatre in the cinema, with fantastic songs, marvellous staging and inspiring dance routines.
4   The beginning of the film is extremely fast-moving, and it gives you a headache.

Person 3
1 a pop concert
2 They liked it.
3 Justin Timberlake is an amazing singer, especially
   live; his dancing and the dancers were fantastic; the
   concert had amazing lighting, incredible musicians
   and a brilliant atmosphere.
4 They were sitting too far back to see Justin
   Timberlake's face properly.

b Students discuss the questions in groups or as a whole class.

Task: speaking

1 **a** Give students two minutes to make their decision,
and then check that everyone has made a choice.

b Focus students' attention on the *Useful language* section and
get them to read it, asking you about any phrases they do not
know, pronunciation problems, etc. Give students at least fifteen
minutes to prepare their reviews. Make it clear that they do not
need to write out a script, but should make notes based on the
questions. Circulate, supplying vocabulary and making a note of
any errors or useful phrases to analyse later.

2 Put students into pairs to rehearse their reviews. At
this point you can feed in some of your corrections /
alternative suggestions if appropriate.

3 Tell students that they are going to present their reviews
to the class, and listen to the other students. Ask students to
make a note of what they would like to see most and any
questions they would like to ask. As they give their talks, make a
note of further errors for analysis and correction.

Task: alternative suggestion

*If you want to make your own student radio/TV programme,
follow this procedure.*
• Make it clear that you will be recording/filming
  students later to make a class radio/TV programme,
  so they understand what they are preparing for.
• Appoint a presenter to introduce and link together
  the items. This could be yourself or a strong student,
  with plenty of initiative. The following tips are useful.
  – Get the 'presenter' to circulate amongst the rest of
    the class and make a list of what items to include
    and in what order.
  – Give him/her the following useful phrases:
    Hello and welcome to …
    Later in the programme we have …
    First of all on today's programme we have …
    And next we have …
    And now for something different …
    And finally …
  – Make sure that he/she has an opportunity to
    rehearse, as with the other students.
  – If you want to video the programme, nominate one
    student to plan any visual aids or props which might
    be used, for example, a desk for the 'presenter'.
• Include items other than reviews too, according to the
  interests of your students. Feed in useful language
  yourself, as necessary.

• Before recording the programme, give students ample
  opportunity to rehearse what they are going to say.
  They are bound to be more nervous when recording
  'formally'.
• Either record the whole programme in front of the class,
  or send students (including the 'presenter') to a different
  room to record their sections in private. If you are using
  video, either you or a competent student will need to be
  in charge of the camera.
• Use the finished programme for correction and
  further language input. The first time students listen
  or watch, they may be preoccupied – it may be more
  appropriate to listen/watch a second time for
  correction work.

Writing (PAGE 68)

A consumer review

1 Focus students' attention on the reviews, and make
sure that they understand the context: that they are from a
website, and that they are written by members of the public.
Students read individually and compare their answers in pairs.

ANSWERS
Love and hate – film; ***
Desert island – computer game; 0
Attack! – computer game; *****
The real me – book; *****
Manic Days – CD; ***

2 Students work in pairs to find words and phrases. Check
answers by drawing the table on the board.

ANSWERS

Positive words and phrases	Negative words and phrases
… the best thing on the market	… not a movie I'd recommend
great storyline/game play	(really) hard to follow
really cool	… by the end I'd lost interest.
What more could you ask?	I'm afraid I was bored.
Highly recommended!	annoying
terrific	repetitive
funny	… a waste of money
well written	Don't buy it.
… had me laughing out loud	…. to be honest … isn't up to much
Buy it now – you won't regret it!	… sounds the same after a while
	… isn't really any different from hundreds of other …

3 Give students time to look at the example phrases.
Circulate as students write, supplying useful vocabulary
and noting any corrections for later analysis.

Writing: additional suggestions

a *If students find writing accurately very difficult*: ask them to write just one review, with a word target of exactly 35 words. This ensures that students review and edit their own writing.

b *If students produce reviews of current interest*: compile them into a magazine format and make this available to other groups of students to read. Having written work 'published' is highly motivating.

Study ... (PAGE 68)

English outside the classroom (1): Using the media

1 This activity could be done for homework or in class.

2 Students work in groups and compare which of the tips they already use and any additional ideas they have.

Practise ... (PAGE 69)

1 *-ed/-ing* adjectives

If this activity is done in class time, first brainstorm the difference between *-ed* and *-ing* adjectives. Students work individually before checking answers as a whole class.

ANSWERS
a interesting b surprising c embarrassed
d annoying e boring f upsetting
g worrying h confused

2 The passive

If this activity is done in class, divide the class into A and B. Give all A students the active sentences to put into the passive. Give all B students the same sentences in passive form to convert into active sentences. Put students into pairs A and B to compare their answers. Discuss problems with the class.

ANSWERS
a Over thirty demonstrators were arrested.
b A number of buildings have been damaged.
c Thousands of trees are destroyed every year.
d The man will be sentenced tomorrow.
e My computer had been stolen.
f Are you being looked after?
g Sarah was presented with a gold watch.
h The museum was built in 1874.

3 Extreme adjectives

Students work in pairs before checking their answers in the *Vocabulary* section on page 65. Get them to take it in turns to test each other – one student closes their book, and the other student gives a definition of an extreme adjective.

ANSWERS
a brilliant/fantastic b terrible/dreadful c tragic
d furious e ridiculous f hilarious

4 Words that go together

If this activity is done in class, put the verbs and nouns on pieces of card. Students work in pairs to match them.

ANSWERS
a 5 commit suicide
b 3 raise money (for charity)
c 1 cause an accident
d 4 hear a voice
e 6 to give up your job
f 2 take a day off

5 Prepositions

ANSWERS
a on b to c in d about e into f by

Pronunciation spot

a ▣ [6.6] Play the recording, pausing after each pair of words. If students find it difficult to hear the difference, model the individual sounds /æ/ and /ʌ/, and get students to repeat them, putting one hand under their chin. When they say /ʌ/, their jaw should drop down lower.

b ▣ [6.7] Play the recording, pausing after each phrase to give students time to decide which they heard.

c Students work in pairs, saying the phrases aloud.

ANSWERS
1 has begun   2 rang   3 ran   4 've drunk
5 swam   6 've sung

Remember! (PAGE 69)

After looking back at the areas they have practised, students do the *Mini-check* on page 157. Check answers as a whole class, and ask students to tell you their scores out of 20.

ANSWERS	
1 surprising	11 will complete/are
2 disappointed	going to complete
3 confused	12 in
4 exciting	13 about
5 depressed	14 to
6 are injured	15 by
7 have been found	16 about
8 is being built	17 happy
9 cost	18 angry
10 was stolen	19 hot
	20 surprised

module 7

Socialising

Reading and vocabulary (PAGES 70–71)

1 Check that everyone understands what is meant by *go out*, and ask one or two students to tell the class what they did when they went out recently. Check the meaning of *live music* and *karaoke*. Students work in small groups to discuss the questions before reporting back to the whole class.

2 a Introduce the article by writing the title on the board and ask students to predict which activities from exercise 1 it will be about. Students quickly scan the text – just the introduction in the top-left corner – to see if they are right.

> **ANSWERS**
> go for a pizza, go dancing, go to a karaoke bar

b Students work individually before comparing answers in small groups. Emphasise that they should use their mini-dictionaries to check the meaning of words and phrases in the box if necessary.

> **ANSWERS**
> **Go for a pizza**: to bake, a chain of restaurants, an oven, an ingredient, an international dish
> **Go dancing**: to applaud a live band, a dance craze, a DJ (disc jockey – the person who plays the records), laser lights
> **Go to a karaoke bar**: to applaud, a DJ, laser lights

3 Students work in pairs to read again and complete the sentences.

> **ANSWERS**
> a   jazz bands
> b   the sixteenth century
> c   Kobe, Japan
> d   Rafaele Esposito, a baker from Naples
> e   Havana, Cuba
> f   1961
> g   soldiers
> h   twenty

4 Using the first word (*flat*, line 2), go through an example with the whole class, following this procedure.
- Students find the word in the text and underline it.
- They decide what type of word it is (verb, noun, adjective, etc.).
- They try to guess its meaning. If they are unsure, they try to guess something about the word, for example, if it is positive or negative.
- They check the meaning in their mini-dictionaries.
Note: guessing the meaning of unknown vocabulary from context is a very important reading skill. It helps students to increase their vocabulary, and also makes them more independent learners.

5 Students discuss the questions in groups or with the whole class. Circulate, supplying any vocabulary they need.

Language focus 1 (PAGES 72–73)

Polite requests

See *Teacher's tips: using a discovery approach in the teaching of grammar* on page 8.

1 Give students time to read the list, then get them to discuss the questions. *If your students are all from the same country*: discuss the questions with the whole class. *If your students are from different countries*: put them into small groups to share information about their different cultures. Give further examples of the different ways of being polite, if necessary.

2 Focus students' attention on the pictures. In pairs, they decide who is making requests in each picture, and guess what they are saying. Compare ideas with the whole class.

3-2

3 a 🔊 [7.1] Pause the recording after each request for students to look at the pictures and decide who is talking, and then compare their ideas in pairs. If they do not hear the first time, replay the request rather than repeating it yourself.

> **ANSWERS**
> 1   the man with his hand raised on the left of picture a
> 2   the woman in the grey T-shirt on the centre right of picture b
> 3   the woman in a blue dress in the middle of picture b
> 4   the woman with blonde hair and glass raised in picture a
> 5   the woman with a red top reaching across the table towards the mobile phone in picture a
> 6   the man in a blue sweater talking to the barman, holding a banknote, in picture b
> 7   the woman standing up behind the two children in picture a
> 8   the man in a green sweater on the centre left of picture b
> 9   the man standing on the far left in picture b

b Pause the recording after each sentence, and allow plenty of time for students to write their answers and to check what they have written in pairs.

> **ANSWERS**
> 1   Could I have the bill, please?
> 2   Is it okay if I take this chair?
> 3   Excuse me, can I get past, please?
> 4   Could you pass me the water, please?
> 5   Do you mind if I borrow your mobile, really quickly?
> 6   Could you possible change this five-pound note for me?
> 7   Would you mind watching the children, just for a second?
> 8   Is it all right if we sit here?
> 9   Can you tell me the time, please?

4 [7.2] Students listen to the full dialogues and answer the questions before comparing their answers in pairs.

ANSWERS AND LANGUAGE NOTE
1 yes
2 no – someone's sitting there.
3 yes
4 yes
5 no – the battery is flat.
6 no – they have no change.
7 yes
8 yes
9 yes

Students may be confused by 7, as the answer is in the negative. Further explanation can be found in the *Analysis*.

Analysis

Check that students understand the difference between asking if you can do something (*a request for permission*) and asking someone else to do something (*a request*). Students work in pairs, underlining the different types of phrases in the tapescript before checking answers with the whole class.

ANSWERS
Ask if you can do something: Could I ... ?; Is it okay if I ... ?; Do you mind if I ... ?; Is it all right if we ... ? Excuse me, can I ... ?
Ask another person to do something: Could you ... ?; Could you possibly ... ?; Would you mind ... ?; Can you ... ?
Say yes: Certainly; Sure; Here you are; Of course not; Go ahead.
Say no: Sorry, but ... ; I'm afraid ...

Point out the following.
• *Will/would* are only used to ask other people to do things; *can/could* can be used with both types of request.
• The modal verbs here are followed by an infinitive without *to*, but *Do you mind ... ?* / *Would you mind ... ?* are followed by either a gerund or an *if* clause.
• Strictly speaking, with *Do you mind ... ?* / *Would you mind ... ?*, if you want to grant a request (say yes), the answer is *No* or *Of course not.*
Other common phrases are: *Will you ... ?; Would you ... ?; Could/Can I possibly ... ?*

More polite phrases are: *Do you think you could possibly ...? Would you be so kind as to ... ?* These are not used very often, however, and students may sound sarcastic or ridiculous to native speakers if they use them inappropriately.

Pronunciation 34

1 [7.3] Point out that how you say these polite requests is just as important as the words you choose. Play the recording and point out the intonation patterns. Get students to copy them. Exaggerate or hum the pattern to help them hear it better, if necessary.

2 Students practise the requests, saying them first to themselves and then, when they are more confident, to a partner.

PRACTICE

1 Write the example up, without the handwritten additions, and ask students what is wrong with it. Ask for their suggestions about how to make it more polite, and compare what they say with the corrections in the book. Check the meaning of *to pass someone something*, *to lend someone something*, *to bring something*, *to charge something* (for example, *a phone* or *a battery*), *to give someone a lift*, *to tell someone the way*, *to pick something up from somewhere*.
   Students work in pairs before checking answers with the whole class. Focus on appropriate levels of formality and remind students that an overly polite phrase for a simple request can sound sarcastic. Get students to practise the dialogues in pairs, paying attention to intonation.

ANSWERS AND LANGUAGE NOTE
a A: Could I use your pen?
   B: Yes, of course.
b A: Could you pass me my coat, please?
   B: Sure, here you are.
c A: Could you possibly* lend me €10 till tomorrow?
   B: I'm afraid I haven't got any money.
d A: Could you bring me another coffee?
   B: Certainly.
e A: Can you lend me your phone?
   B: Sorry, it needs charging.
f A: If you're going into town, would you mind giving me a lift?
   B: Of course not.
g A: Could you tell me the way to the bus station?
   B: I'm sorry, but I don't know this area.
h A: Can you pick up my suit from the dry cleaner's?
   B: I'm afraid I won't be able to. I'll have too much to carry.

* Asking for money is potentially quite embarrassing even between friends, so this very polite language is appropriate.

2 a Give one or two examples of the kinds of requests students could make. Give them a few minutes to think of the requests, circulating to supply any vocabulary they need.

b Look at the examples with the class, then put students into pairs to do the activity. Insist that if students say no, they give a reason why. Alternatively, students could circulate making the requests, or ask each other across the class.

ADDITIONAL PRACTICE

RB **Resource bank:** *Vocabulary extension* (informal words and phrases), page 138

Workbook: Polite requests, pages 52–53

Language focus 2 (PAGE 73)

will for offers and instant decisions

See *Teacher's tips: using a discovery approach in the teaching of grammar* on page 8.

> **Language focus 2: language notes**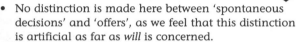
>
> - No distinction is made here between 'spontaneous decisions' and 'offers', as we feel that this distinction is artificial as far as *will* is concerned.
> - Students are not asked to discriminate between *will* and *going to* as we feel it is more useful to practise common phrases used for 'responding on the spot'. The distinction between *will* and *going to* is mentioned in the *Language summary*.

1 **a** Focus students' attention on the pictures, and get them to guess as a class what the relationship and small problem are in each case. Keep this stage very brief.

b [7.4] Pause the recording after the first conversation to give students time to check in pairs. After both conversations, go through answers in pairs before checking with the whole class.

ANSWERS
1 The speakers are colleagues. Speaker A is about to go home. Speaker B tells him that Tony, another colleague, needs to speak to him urgently, but is in a meeting. Speaker A has a date in an hour. He will come in early tomorrow to see Tony.
2 The speakers are friends. Speaker A has missed the last bus. She'll get a taxi.

2 Students work in pairs to complete the sentences, before listening to check. Play the recording more than once as students may have problems hearing the contracted form of *will*. Check answers with the whole class.

ANSWERS
a I'll go   b I'll come   c I'll give   d I'll phone

Analysis

1 Students answer the questions individually or in pairs before checking answers in the *Language summary*.

ANSWERS
They decide at the moment of speaking in response to what the other person has just said.
Will (usually contracted to *'ll*) is used.

2 As you read the notes in the *Language summary*, emphasise that if the speaker has decided beforehand, *going to* should be used.

PRACTICE

a Look at the example with the whole class. Explain that the quiz is hypothetical, and that students should imagine that they are in each situation now.

b Check the meaning of *to babysit*. Students work in pairs to do part a) of the quiz. Monitor and help any students who are not sure. For part b), pairs choose the best answers from the ones they have been given. Go through answers with the whole class, comparing different answers and what different students chose. Correct the pronunciation of *I'll* where necessary.

> ## Pronunciation
>
> **1** [7.5] Elicit from students the correct pronunciation for *I'll*. Pause the recording after each sentence to give students time to compare their ideas in pairs. If necessary, play the sentences again.
>
> **ANSWERS**
> sentences 2, 4 and 5
>
> **2** Students work in pairs and practise saying each sentence, using the contracted form *I'll*. Circulate as students practise, correcting their pronunciation of *I'll* if necessary.
>
> **3** Students work in pairs. Tell them to choose three situations from page 142. Refer them to the tapescript on page 167 to remind them of the sort of dialogue they should write, including at least one offer or response with *I'll*. Circulate as students work, supplying any vocabulary or phrases students need. Get some pairs to act out their dialogues for the class. Note down any useful errors for correction later.

> **Language focus 1 and 2, additional activity: make a wall poster**
>
> Amongst the language studied in this module are many 'fixed' or 'semi-fixed' polite phrases which will be useful in a wide range of social situations. It might be useful to make a wall poster or a series of posters to remind students of these phrases. Possible sections are:
>
> **in a restaurant:** *Could you bring me the bill? / Could I have a light? / Could you bring me the menu?*
>
> **at someone's house:** *Could you pass me the salt? / Is it all right if I smoke? / Would you like me to open the wine? / Could I use your phone? / I'll do the washing-up.*
>
> **in the street / on the train, etc.:** *Can you tell me the time? / Could you tell me the way to … ? / Could I get past, please? / Is it all right if I open the window?*
>
> **helping people:** *I'll do that for you if you like. / I'll lend you … if you like. / I'll help you with that. / I'll give you a lift.*

ADDITIONAL PRACTICE

Workbook: *will* for offers and instant decisions, page 53; *will* or *going to*, page 54

Vocabulary and speaking (PAGE 74)

Social behaviour

1 Check that students understand *social behaviour*. Check the pronunciation of *refuse* /rɪˈfjuːz/, *shake* /ʃeɪk/ and *bow* /baʊ/. Students work in pairs, using their mini-dictionaries as necessary, before discussing ideas with the whole class.

2 Look at the examples with the class before students discuss the question in groups or with the whole class. Encourage them to give reasons.

Listening (PAGE 74)

Social customs in Thailand

1 Focus students' attention on the map and pictures of Thailand and ask what they know about it. If necessary, ask questions to prompt students.

Which part of the world is it in? What's the capital city? What sort of climate does it have? What is the religion? What kind of buildings/scenery would you expect to see there? What kind of food would you expect to find? Is it a popular tourist destination?

If students have no idea about social customs, move straight on to the extract from the travel guide.

2 Focus students' attention on the extract, explaining that it's about social behaviour and customs in Thailand. Check the meaning of: *hospitality, to address someone, to say a prayer, to be respectful, chopsticks*. Get students to read the text carefully to guess the best alternatives before comparing their ideas in pairs. Emphasise that it is not important if their guesses are right or wrong. If students cannot guess, move on quickly to the listening.

3 **a** 📼 [7.6] Focus students' attention on the photo of Nikam Nipotam. Check that students understand who he is and who he is talking to before playing the recording.

> **ANSWERS**
> a first name   b both men and women
> c older people   d not acceptable   e not respectful
> f take your shoes off   g a spoon and fork

b Students discuss the questions in small groups. *If you have a multicultural class*, ensure that there is a good mix of cultures in each group.

Language focus 3 (PAGE 75)

Making generalisations

Analysis

1 Point out the generalisations which have been taken from the travel guide to Thailand. Students work individually or in pairs to find three more in the text. As you check answers, highlight:
- the impersonal construction *It is ... for ... someone ... to ... do something*
- some other adjectives often used in this construction, for example, *normal, common, okay, rude, sensible*
- the use of adjective + infinitive to talk about general situations, and adjective + for to talk about people.

> **ANSWERS**
> It is polite to use ....
> It is not respectful to ...
> It is very important to show ...

2 Draw students' attention to the use of the verb *tend* for making generalisations, in paragraph g of the travel guide. Point out that the negative can be expressed in two ways, *don't tend to* or *tend not to*.

PRACTICE

1–3 Do one or two examples with the class to start them off. Students do exercises 1 and 2 individually or in pairs, before comparing answers in groups for exercise 3. There will obviously be differences in multinationality groups, but even in mononationality groups there will probably be differences of opinion for students to discuss/explain.

ADDITIONAL PRACTICE

RB **Resource bank:** *Doonbogs* (making generalisations), page 139

Task: Give tips on how to behave
(PAGES 76–77)

See *Teacher's tips: making tasks work* on pages 13–14 and *Responding to learners' individual language needs* on pages 11–12.

Preparation: listening

1 **a** 📼 [7.7] Explain that students will hear the eight people in the order in which they are listed on the page. Give students time to read the topics in the box. Students listen and match. Warn students that the extracts are quite short, and that they should listen for gist by finding clues as to the topic(s) being talked about by each person. Emphasise that they only need to listen for the topic, and they will listen again to find further information. You could pause the recording after each speaker to give students time to think and compare answers. Go through answers with the class.

ANSWERS
Amy: behaviour between the sexes
Pawel: how you greet and address people
Rosa: being late
Ian: smoking
Dong-Min: typical times for going out / eating
Lee Kuan: the way people dress
Ramon: typical times for going out / eating
Khalid: behaviour between the sexes and what people
do when they go out

b Pause the recording after each extract to give students time to make a few notes and to compare their ideas in pairs. Check answers with the whole class.

ANSWERS
Behaviour between the sexes: Amy says that a woman on a date should always offer to pay/split the bill. Khalid says that it's normal to go on dates with a girlfriend; a couple must be engaged first.
Being late: Rosa says that it's okay to arrive an hour late when visiting friends, unless they ask you to be punctual by saying 'hora inglesa'.
How you greet and address people: Pawel says that men usually shake hands to greet each other every time they meet.
Smoking: Ian says that it's not acceptable to smoke in people's houses, unless the hosts smoke.
The way people dress: Lee Kuan says that it's important to be fashionable, especially for women, and to dress smartly.
Typical times for going out / eating: Ramon says that it's normal to meet friends at 10:00 or 11:00 p.m. to go out for a meal, and to stay out until 5:00, 6:00 or 7:00 a.m. if you go dancing or go to bars. Dong-Min says that friends normally meet at about 7:00 p.m., eat at about 7:30 p.m. and go home at about 11:00 p.m.
What people do when they go out: Khalid says that he normally goes for a drive with friends, and sometimes goes to a shopping mall.

2 [7.8] Tell students that the extracts are not in the same order as the phrases. Pause the recording after each extract to allow students time to write the missing words. Play the recording again if necessary rather than giving the answers yourself.

ANSWERS
a	Generally you	f	Generally nowadays; not really acceptable
b	always offer		
c	usually shake	g	People expect you
d	quite common	h	It's important
e	It's perfectly okay to	i	It's normal to

Task: speaking

1 Decide if it is better to choose an option for your students or to let them choose. If you let them choose, explain both sets of instructions and then give them two or three minutes to decide on an option in their groups.

For the first option, ask students to imagine that someone from a very different culture is coming to their country. They are going to advise this person about social behaviour in their country in the same way as Nikam Nipotam.

For the second option, ask students to imagine that they are going to go on a radio programme for people over fifty. They are going to talk about the way young people behave when they go out.

For both options, check the list of topics from *Preparation*, exercise 1, and put students into groups to brainstorm ideas. Focus their attention on the phrases in the *Useful language* box, briefly explaining any language problems. Highlight the following if necessary: the meaning of *should*, *expect*, *polite*; the use of the plural after *people* and the singular after *nobody*; the use of the impersonal pronoun *it* + infinitive. Circulate, supplying useful language they need and noting down useful language points to look at later. Encourage students not to write everything they want to say, only to make notes. Allow ten to fifteen minutes for this stage. *If you have a multinationality class*: group students so that they are in groups of the same nationality, if possible.

2 This stage will need to be conducted differently depending on which option(s) you chose, and what type of class you have.

If students have worked on the first option, put them into groups to compare ideas.

If students have worked on the second option, put them into pairs to give their talk. Encourage them to ask questions or make suggestions as they listen.

If you have a multinationality class: pair students so that each pair has students with different nationalities. The tips students give will be of genuine cross-cultural interest. There may be some big differences. Ask each pair to note similarities and differences to report back to the whole class.

Task: **alternative suggestions**

a *If you do not have enough time to cover the whole task in one lesson*: do *Preparation: listening* and get students to make a list of tips/points in one class (*Task: speaking*, exercise 1) and present them in the next class (*Task: speaking*, exercise 2).

b *If you have a young mononationality class who have difficulty in seeing their own culture from an outside perspective*: we have included the radio option as an alternative. However, if you do not wish to use this, it might be useful to try the following.
 • Get students to think of a specific culture or person to focus their advice on. It could be a Thai person, such as Nikam Nipotam, or a famous British/American person they identify with (a film star, footballer, etc.).
 • Get students to think about British/American films and any differences in social behaviour they have noticed, before imagining what British/American people would find strange in their culture.

59

• Tell students about some of the things you found different when you first arrived in their country.

c *If you have well-travelled students in your class:* get students to work separately on tips about a country they have visited, to present to the whole class.

Real life (PAGE 77)

Making a social arrangement

1 🔲 [7.9] Focus students on the photo and give them time to read the questions. Students listen to the recording before comparing their answers in pairs. Check answers with the whole class.

> **ANSWERS**
> a They're friends.
> b Relatives (Millie's sisters) are round for lunch.
> c to his house, next Saturday
> d They're going to a friend's wedding in Scotland.
> e He invites them for the following Saturday instead.
> f in a week or so

2 Refer students to the tapescript on page 168. Using three different colours, or different types of line, students work in pairs to find useful phrases. Check answers with the whole class. An overhead transparency of the tapescript is a useful way of ensuring that everyone can check the answers.

> **ANSWERS**
> Students might choose to underline some of the following useful phrases.
> **Telephone**
> *Hello?*
> *Hello + name, it's + your name.*
> *I haven't heard from you for ages! How are you?*
> *I was just phoning to …*
> *Thanks for calling.*
> *See you!*
>
> **Inviting:**
> *I was just phoning to ask if you are doing anything + day.*
> *Would you like to come over for a meal?*
>
> **Arranging**
> *How about + day + instead?*
> *I'll check and call you back if there's any problem.*
> *Give me a ring in a week or so to arrange a time.*

3 a Students work in pairs before checking answers with the whole class.

> **ANSWERS**
> 1 A 2 R 3 A 4 R 5 R

b Students listen before checking answers with the whole class. Play the recording again or model the phrases yourself, for students to drill. Encourage them to copy the intonation pattern.

> **ANSWERS**
> Roger uses phrases 1, 4 and 5.

4 Put students into pairs and go through the role play. Explain that they can act out several conversations, but that in some they should accept and in some refuse the invitation. Remind them that if they refuse, they need to give a reason. Circulate, making a note of errors and language for correction and analysis later on.

ADDITIONAL ACTIVITY

[RB] **Resource bank:** *What time shall we meet?* (making a social arrangement), pages 140–141

Wordspot (PAGE 78)

go

See *Teacher's tips: working with lexis* on pages 9–10.

1 a Students spend a few minutes individually looking at the diagram.

b Students work in pairs before checking answers with the whole class.

> **ANSWERS**
> 1 go on   2 go off   3 go bald

c Students work in pairs or small groups to brainstorm possible situations. Check answers with the whole class.

> **ANSWERS**
> 1 *Go away!* – if someone is annoying you
> 2 *Go to sleep!* – to a child who won't sleep, or to someone who wakes up in the night
> 3 *Oh, no! I'm going grey!* – the first time someone finds some grey hairs
> 4 *He went mad at me!* – when telling someone about a person who lost their temper or got very annoyed with you
> 5 *Let's go for a drink!* – a way of suggesting a visit to a pub or bar

2 Remind students to form the questions correctly, and emphasise that they only need to find one person for each sentence. Do this as a mingling activity.

Study … (PAGE 78)

Using revision techniques

1 This activity could be done for homework or in class. If it is done in class time, it could be done as a discussion. Students work in small groups and compare which of the tips they already try to use and any additional ideas they have.

2 *If you have one-to-one tutorials with your students:* this would be a good thing to follow up with them.

Practise ... (PAGE 79)

1 Offers and requests

If this activity is done in class time, first get students to cover the explanations in B, and work in pairs to try to guess what they are.

ANSWERS
a 2 b 4 c 1 d 5 e 3

2 *will* for instant decisions and responses

If this activity is done in class time, have each sentence half written on a separate piece of card. Students work in pairs to match before deciding on the function/meaning of each sentence.

ANSWERS
a 3 (offer)
b 5 (decision made at the moment of speaking)
c 1 (decision made before the moment of speaking)
d 6 (offer)
e 2 (decision made at the moment of speaking)
f 4 (decision made before the moment of speaking)

3 Words that go together

If this activity is done in class time, do it as a race. Students work in pairs to decide on the correct word or phrase to complete the sentences.

ANSWERS
a order some food   b book in advance
c split the bill   d give someone a lift home
e send someone a card

4 Word building

If this activity is done in class time, use it for dictionary skills practice. Students work individually or in pairs, and use their dictionaries to check/find the answers.

ANSWERS
a acceptable   b respectful   c important

5 Making generalisations

If this activity is done in class time, students work individually or in pairs before checking answers with the whole class.

ANSWERS
a to go b for c of d - e not to

6 Phrases with *go*

If this activity is done in class time, set it up as a competition. The first part is a race to see who can think of the correct phrases with *go*, and the second part a competition to see who can remember the most phrases in three minutes.

ANSWERS
a go bald   b go on   c go away / go out
d go home

Pronunciation spot

a [7.10] Play the recording, pausing after each set of words. If students find it difficult to hear the difference between the two sounds, model the individual sounds /θ/ and /ð/, and get students to repeat them, putting a finger gently on their throat. When they say /θ/, there should be no vibration as the voice is not used (it is an unvoiced sound), but when they say /ð/, they should feel vibration as the voice is used (it is a voiced sound).

b [7.11] Play the recording, pausing after each phrase to give students time to decide which sound they heard.

ANSWERS
1 /θ/ (unvoiced)
2 /ð/ (voiced)
3 /ð/ (voiced), /ð/ (voiced)
4 /θ/ (unvoiced)
5 /ð/ (voiced)
6 /θ/ (unvoiced)

c Students work in pairs, saying the phrases aloud.

d Students work in pairs to brainstorm words before checking in their mini-dictionaries. Make this into a competition by setting a time limit. The winning pair is the one with the most correct answers within the time limit.

Remember! (PAGE 69)

After looking back at the areas they have practised, students do the *Mini-check* on page 157. Check answers as a whole class, and ask students to tell you their scores out of 20.

ANSWERS
1 of
2 mind
3 not
4 to
5 if
6 Could
7 I'll lend
8 Will you
9 Would
10 I'll have
11 closing
12 to close
13 to close
14 close
15 closing
16 the
17 become
18 to (*between go and home*)
19 having
20 for

module 8

Things you can't live without

Reading (PAGES 80–81)

1 Ask students to work in pairs to guess what the objects are. Go through answers with the class.

ANSWERS
a CDs b Game Boy c computer keyboard
d laptop e mobile phone

2 Check students' understanding of the phrases in the box. Put students into groups to discuss the questions.

3 Students match words and phrases with the things from the previous exercise. Check answers with the class.

ANSWERS
A better quality picture: digital TV
Hardware: laptops / palm tops, computer help desks
Being out of date: mobile phones, laptops / palm tops
A spare part: laptops / palm tops, digital TV
Using your thumbs: texting
The customer care department: call centres, computer help desks
Instruction manuals: laptops / palm tops, mobile phones, digital TV
saving time: e-mail, the Internet
Software: laptops / palm tops, computer help desks, mobile phones

4 **a** Refer students to the title of the text. Ask if they think the writer feels positively or negatively about technology. Get students to read the headings. Emphasise that they do not need to read in detail, only to match headings and paragraphs.

b Students work individually before comparing their answers.

ANSWERS

1 It does things you don't need	paragraph B
2 It doesn't save you time	paragraph A
3 It was out of date before you bought it	paragraph D
4 It's anti-social	paragraph G
5 It's destroying the English language	paragraph F
6 More choice does not mean better	paragraph C
7 No one takes responsibility when things go wrong	paragraph E

5 Students work in pairs to answer the questions. Check answers with the whole class.

ANSWERS
a Learning how to use it takes up all the time the computer saves.
b Because spare parts are no longer manufactured.
c Because very few people understand how their machines work, so aren't in a position to question when they are passed to different departments.
d There are a lot of channels but the programme quality is worse – there isn't one single programme worth watching.
e They are developing larger thumbs, not learning how to spell properly, and would prefer to text than talk.

6 Using *anti-social* (heading 4 in exercise 4a), go through an example with the whole class, following this procedure.

• Students find the phrase in the text and underline it.

• They try to guess its meaning by underlining other words or phrases which relate to it. If they are unsure, they should try to guess something about the word, for example, if it is positive or negative.

• They check the meaning in their mini-dictionaries.

7 **a** Students discuss the questions in groups or with the whole class.

b In groups, students decide which option they would choose.

Language focus 1 (PAGES 82–83)

Defining relative clauses

Start by asking students how much they know about computers. Tell them they are going to do a quiz to find out what they know. Check the meaning of *virus* and *dominated*. Students do the quiz in pairs or groups. Check answers with the class.

ANSWERS
a a technophobe b the Internet
c broadband d an anti-virus
e a mouse f cyberspace g a techie

Analysis

1 Focus students' attention on the example, showing the relative pronoun underlined. Students underline the relative pronouns in the quiz. Check answers with the whole class.

ANSWERS
a who b which c that d no relative pronoun used
e which f where g whose

2 Students work individually or in pairs before checking answers with the whole class. Emphasise that they should look at the examples to help them work out the rules.

ANSWERS AND LANGUAGE NOTES
a *who* (*that* is less usual for people – it's quite informal)

b *which*; *that* (students may want to use *what* here – emphasise that this is not correct)
c *whose* (this might be difficult for students to understand – the best way to explain is by changing the relative clause back into a normal sentence (*his life is dominated by computers*), and pointing out that *whose* replaces *his/her/its/their*, etc.)
d *where* (point out that no preposition is used with the relative pronoun *where*; if you use a preposition, *where* is replaced by *which*: *an imaginary place in which electronic messages exist*)

3 Students work in pairs. Encourage them to guess the answers if they don't know.

ANSWERS AND LANGUAGE NOTES
The relative pronoun can be omitted in sentence d because *A piece of software* is the object rather than the subject of the relative clause. In sentence e, *which* can be left out for the same reason.

If students have difficulty understanding this, write sentences a and d on the board, and ask students to break them into two simpler sentences. Write these underneath the original sentence d.

An anti-virus is a piece of software <u>which</u> you install on your computer to protect it from viruses.
An anti-virus is a piece of software. You install <u>it</u> on your computer to protect it from viruses.
(which = it = OBJECT)

Ask the students which word in the second sentence *which* refers to. (Answer: *it.*) Point out that *which* is the object of the verb (*install*) and that we can leave it out. Then write these under the original sentence a.

A technophobe is a person <u>who</u> doesn't like machines, especially computers.
A technophobe is a person. <u>He</u> doesn't like machines, especially computers.
(who = he = SUBJECT)

Ask the students which word in the second sentence *who* refers to. (Answer: *He.*) Point out that *who* is the subject of the verb (*like*) and that we cannot leave it out.

Emphasise that we cannot omit relative pronouns when they are the subject of the sentence. Point out that *whose* and *where* cannot be omitted.

PRACTICE

1 a Students work in pairs before checking answers with the class. Do not pre-teach the words, but offer help if necessary. When discussing the answers, check if the pronoun can be omitted.

ANSWERS
1	photocopier; which/that	(cannot be omitted)
2	bodyguard; who	(cannot be omitted)
3	launderette; where	(cannot be omitted)
4	plumber; whose	(cannot be omitted)
5	vacuum cleaner; which/that	(can be omitted)

b To focus students' attention on the example, write the

prompts on the board, elicit first the item, and then the definition. Students work in pairs before checking with the class.

ANSWERS
1 A cooker is a machine which/that cooks food.
2 A cook is a person you pay to cook for you.
3 A cleaner is a person you pay to clean your house or office.
4 A typewriter is an old-fashioned machine you use for typing.
5 A boiler is a machine which/that heats water for baths, etc.
6 A dry cleaner's is a shop where they clean jackets, suits, etc. for you.
7 A decorator is a person whose job is to paint houses.
8 A stationer's is a shop where you buy office supplies.

2 Put students into pairs, A and B. Demonstrate the activity with a strong student. Circulate and note down any errors.

3 Put students into teams, A and B. Direct students to the appropriate page, and do one example together. Emphasise that they should not use the relative pronoun if it is not needed.

ADDITIONAL PRACTICE

RB Resource bank: *Relative clauses crossword* (defining clauses), page 143
Workbook: Defining relative clauses, pages 59–61

Vocabulary 1 (PAGE 83)

How machines work

1 a [8.1] Before listening, emphasise that students only have to identify which machine is being discussed, and any words or phrases which helped them to decide.

ANSWERS
1 a cassette player   2 a laptop computer
3 a photocopier   4 a mobile phone

b Students listen and read, underlining verbs before comparing answers in pairs. Check answers as a whole class.

ANSWERS
1 play, set, rewind (×2), use, switch off, press, plugged in.
2 keeps crashing, freezes, switch off, restart, re-installing
3 gets stuck, breaks down, fix, switch off (×2), unplug, open, holding down
4 recorded, play, recharge

2 [8.2] Do an example before the students work in pairs. Play the recording to check answers.

ANSWERS
a	switch off	your mobile phone
b	plug in	the vacuum cleaner
c	press	the button

d	rewind / fast forward	the tape
e	restart	your computer
f	turn up	the volume
g	replay	your messages
h	shut down	your computer
i	hold down	the button
j	pause	the tape
k	My computer	's crashed
l	My mobile phone	needs recharging
m	The batteries	need replacing

3 Put students into pairs and focus their attention on the examples. Circulate, supplying vocabulary.

Pronunciation

1 Explain what a compound noun is (a noun consisting of two parts, noun + noun / gerund or adjective + noun), and give an example. Go through the two rules, writing the examples on the board and marking the stress. Repeat the examples yourself several times to make sure that students can hear the difference.

2 Give students time to work out where the stress should be, without giving the answers at this stage.

3 [8.3] Play the recording, stopping after each compound noun to allow students time to check/correct their answers. Drill the compound nouns.

ANSWERS

call centre, spare part, swimming pool, mobile phone, dining room, washing machine, fan heater, instruction manual, dark glasses, video recorder, personal computer, car radio

Language focus 2 (PAGES 84–85)

Quantifiers

1 Focus students' attention on the picture, and check the meaning and pronunciation of *desert*. Discuss the questions as a class and write students' suggestions on the board. Feed in the following items: *fuel, map, compass, first-aid kit, knife, matches, sun screen*.

2 [8.4] Check that students understand who the speaker is. Play the recording and check the answers.

ANSWERS
Items mentioned by Jeff: plenty of water, plenty of fuel, one or preferably two maps, a compass, a small first-aid kit (including a pair of scissors, some bandages and a sharp knife), some matches, sun screen, warm clothes

3 [8.5] Ask students to tell you to stop the recording when they hear one of the sentences. Give students time to write. Play the recording again rather than giving the answers yourself.

ANSWERS
a several b a bit of c a few d one or two
e much f plenty of g too much h no
i enough j some k some l lots of m any

Analysis

1 Check that students know the difference between countable and uncountable nouns. Elicit further examples from the classroom and its surroundings (for example, *chair*, *noise*).

ANSWERS AND LANGUAGE NOTE
*chance** (uncountable), *fuel* (uncountable), *rule* (countable), *water* (uncountable)

**Chance* has several meanings in English. Here it is used to mean '*likelihood*', and as such it is an uncountable noun. When used to mean '*opportunity*', it is countable. If you have a strong class, it would be useful dictionary training to show them this in their *Mini-dictionaries*.

2 Do examples together, using the sentences from exercise 3. Students do the rest in pairs. Check answers with the class, and feed in any other quantifiers students know (for example, *many*, *loads of*).

ANSWERS AND LANGUAGE NOTES
a **Quantifiers which are used with countable nouns** several, a few, one or two
b **Quantifiers which are used with uncountable nouns:** a bit of, much, too much
c **Quantifiers which are used with both:** plenty of, no, enough, some, lots of, any

Too much / a lot of
Too much often carries negative meaning. For example, *I've eaten too much*. However, *a lot of* does not have any negative implication.

Enough / plenty
Enough means that you have as much as you need. For example, *I've got enough money to buy a new car*. *Plenty* means 'more than enough'. For example, *I've got plenty of money if I buy this car. I can afford to go on holiday as well.*

Any
Remind students that *any* is only negative when accompanied by a negative verb. For example, *I haven't got any money*. A common mistake is: *I've got any money* instead of *I've got no money*; on the other hand, *I didn't have no money* is wrong because it is a double negative.

Loads of
Loads of is informal, and is usually spoken, not written.

PRACTICE

1 Do the first example together, eliciting possibilities, and making clear that students should make the sentences true in their opinion. This is best done by asking them to explain their answers. Do this as a spoken exercise initially, but get students to write their sentences afterwards for consolidation.

2 Do this as a spoken exercise in pairs. If you teach a mononationality class: group students from different areas together so they have more to talk about. Multinationality classes can either discuss where they are staying, or tell each other about the place they are from.

ADDITIONAL PRACTICE

RB **Resource bank:** *Camping holiday* (quantifiers – *a few, a lot of*, etc.), pages 144–145

Workbook: Quantifiers, pages 62–64

Vocabulary 2 (PAGE 85)
Describing everyday objects

1 Check that students know the words (and pronunciation) for the objects in the photo. Check the pronunciation of *calculator* /ˈkælkjʊleɪtə/, *torch* /tɔːtʃ/, *Sellotape* /ˈseləteɪp/, *tissues* /ˈtɪʃuːs, – sjuːs/, *comb* /kəʊm/, *scissors* /ˈsɪzəz/, *purse* /pɜːs/, *saucepan* /ˈsɔːspən/.

> **ANSWERS**
> a calculator, a plastic bag, a torch, a ring, some drawing pins, a mirror, a roll of sellotape, some cotton wool, an alarm clock, a packet of tissues, a comb, a pair of scissors, a purse, a saucepan, some make-up

2 **a** Explain that students are going to play a memory game. Set a time limit for them to study the words.

b Students write as many words as they can remember.

3 **a** Students work in pairs to match a phrase to each object.

> **POSSIBLE ANSWERS**
>
> | | |
> |---|---|
> | calculator | It's got batteries. |
> | plastic bag | It's made of plastic. |
> | torch | It's long and thin. |
> | ring | It's valuable. |
> | drawing pins | They're sharp. |
> | mirror | It's easy to break. |
> | sellotape | It's used for sticking things together. |
> | cotton wool | It's soft. |
> | alarm clock | It's used for waking up on time. |
> | tissues | They're made of paper. |
> | comb | It's made of plastic. |
> | scissors* | They're sharp. |
> | purse | It's made of leather. |
> | saucepan | It's got a lid. |
> | make-up | It's used for making us look good. |
>
> *Scissors* are always plural.

b Students work in pairs to brainstorm more words.

> **POSSIBLE ANSWERS**
> 1 metal, wood, cotton, wool, cardboard
> 2 hot, cold, shiny, huge, rough, smooth, bendy, heavy, light
> 3 flat, square, thick

4 Give students time to write their clues individually. Then students work in pairs, guessing each other's objects.

5 Emphasise that students can choose any object and ask any questions they want, as long as the answer is *yes* or *no*. Look at the example questions with them. Circulate, supplying vocabulary.

Task: Make a list of things you'd hate to be without (PAGES 86–87)

See *Teacher's tips*: *making tasks work* on pages 13–14.

Preparation: listening

📼 [8.6] Check that students know the words for the items in the pictures. Pre-teach: *to be out and about, sentimental value, an acoustic guitar, to block out sounds, slim, to originate from somewhere, to remind someone of something/somebody*.

Explain that each person is talking about something they would hate to be without. Play the recording and get students to complete the first column. Check answers with the class, before playing the recording a second time whilst students complete the other columns. Warn students that a description is not given for every item. Play the recording again if necessary, encouraging students to compare answers after each listening.

> **ANSWERS**
>
> | | Object | How he/she describes it | Why it is important to him/her |
> |---|---|---|---|
> | 1 | Mobile phone | No description is given | Uses it to organise social life, by sending texts and calling people when out and about |
> | 2 | Alarm clock | Battery-operated; in the shape of a soldier wearing a uniform and helmet | Sentimental value, given by friends at university twelve years ago |
> | 3 | Guitar | Six string acoustic guitar | Has had for over twenty years, plays it almost every day |
> | 4 | Computer | No description is given | Uses it to store addresses, phone numbers and other information, as well as to search the Internet and e-mail friends and family. |
> | 5 | CD Walkman | Grey, quite slim | Uses it on trains to block out other noise, has had it for six years since living in Japan |
> | 6 | Ring | Silver, with a heart in the middle, held by two hands, from Ireland | Sentimental value; a reminder of Irish grandmother |

Task: speaking

1 Give students time to think of five things they already own. Tell them that they can be large or small, expensive or cheap, and refer them to the suggestions in the box.

2 Give students ten minutes to make notes using the prompt questions. Circulate, supplying vocabulary. Before starting the talks, refer students to the Useful language box.

3 Students work in groups of about four. Circulate, making notes about and errors for correction later on.

4 Spend a few minutes asking each group to report back on any interesting objects.

Real life (PAGE 88)

Buying things

1 **a** Focus students' attention on the photos. Students discuss the questions in groups and then as a whole class.

> **ANSWERS**
> 1 a market   2 catalogue / home shopping
> 3 supermarket   4 in-store shopping

b [icon] [8.7] Before listening, emphasise that students only have to identify which photos the conversations relate to.

> **ANSWERS**
> **Conversation 1**: picture 4   **Conversation 2**: picture 2

c Pause the recording after the first conversation to give students time to write. Check answers as a whole class.

> **ANSWERS**
>
> | | Conversation 1 | Conversation 2 |
> |---|---|---|
> | Item | TV | A pair of trousers |
> | Reference number | – | RZ1 224BL |
> | Cost of item | €349.99 | €39.99 |
> | Cost of delivery | €20 | €2.50 |
> | Pay by credit card? | Yes, Mastercard | No, asked for a statement |
> | Other useful information | The receipt is also a guarantee for 2 years' parts and labour | Delivery is within 3–5 working days, and goods can be returned within 7 days with free collection. |

2 **a** Students work in pairs to match sentences and responses, using their *Mini-dictionaries*. Check the pronunciation of *receipt* /rɪ'siːt/ and *guarantee* /ˌgærən'tiː/. There is no need to check answers at this stage.

b [icon] [8.7] Play the recording, then check answers with the class. Drill chorally. Students practise in pairs.

> **ANSWERS**
> 1 C   2 I   3 F   4 B   5 E   6 A   7 H   8 D   9 G

3 Put students into pairs and explain that they will write and act a similar dialogue. Emphasise that they should use the phrases from exercise 2a. Students perform their dialogues.

Writing (PAGE 89)

Saying thank you

1 Check that students understand *offended*. Students discuss the questions in pairs.

2 **a** Explain that students will read four examples of written thanks. Emphasise that the first time they read they only have to find out what each person is saying thank you for.

> **ANSWERS**
> 1 being lent a leather jacket
> 2 lunch cooked at somebody's home
> 3 a present (a Manchester United football shirt)
> 4 staying at somebody's house for the weekend

b Students read again, putting a sentence in each gap before comparing ideas in pairs. Check answers with the whole class.

> **ANSWERS**
> a   Just what I needed for the party.
> b   We haven't eaten so much for ages.
> c   I've worn it lots of times already.
> d   We thoroughly enjoyed ourselves.

c Students discuss the questions in groups. Check answers with the whole class, asking students to justify their ideas.

> **POSSIBLE ANSWERS**
> 1 20s, friends
> 2 40s or 50s, future parents-in-law
> 3 8 to 16, relatives
> 4 any age, friends

3 **a** Students work individually before checking answers with the whole class.

> **ANSWERS**
> (*Numbers relate to the numbers of the texts.*)
> 1 Thanks a million for …
> 2 Just a quick card to say thank you so much for …
> 3 Thank you very much for …
> 4 Just a quick line to say thank you so much for … ; thanks again.

b Explain that students have to look for general areas which make the texts more or less formal, rather than specific language. Go through an example – the salutations (opening greetings) set the level of formality. Students discuss the questions before checking answers with the class.

> **ANSWERS**
> The least formal is from Anna, the most formal is from Pat and Alec.
> The salutations, the signing-off (closing phrase) and the use of language/abbreviations all indicate formality.

c Discuss this as a whole class.

4 Emphasise that students have to write just a note or an e-mail. Give them a few minutes to decide who they will write to and encourage them to use the phrases from exercise 3 to help them. Circulate, supplying vocabulary and noting useful language and corrections to focus on later.

Consolidation modules 5–8 (PAGES 90–91)

A Future forms / Future time clauses

Focus students' attention on the title of the text and check the meaning of *hot gossip*. As a class, students predict what the text will be about. Check the meaning of *to hand something over*, *to feature*, *to convert something into something else*. Students work in pairs before checking answers with the class.

ANSWERS
1 to get married   2 once   3 won't give   4 until
5 to get married   6 is to   7 will start   8 returns
9 going to feature   10 to do   11 to recognise
12 to buy   13 planning   14 of converting
15 until   16 to have   17 is holding
18 to invite   19 arrive   20 they'll all have

B Vocabulary: Megamemory

1 Students work in pairs, checking the meaning of any words they do not remember in their *Mini-dictionaries*. Check answers with the whole class.

ANSWERS
a   **Names of jobs:** a firefighter, a cook, a plumber
b   **Adjectives that describe a job:** badly-paid, challenging, stressful
c   **Phrases you might use on the telephone:** Hello, it's Lawrence; I'll call you back; Thanks for calling
d   **Adjectives to describe negative feelings:** annoyed, furious, jealous
e   **Types of TV programme:** a cartoon, a documentary, a soap opera
f   **Things you might do in the evening:** arrange a night out, go for a run, go to sleep
g   **Machines you might have in your home:** an answering machine, a dishwasher, a freezer
h   **Things you might do with a machine:** switch off, plug in, switch on

2 Allow students five minutes to learn the words, then see which pair can remember the most.

3 Students work in small groups or as a whole class to add words and phrases to each category.

C Listening: Famous firsts

[C1] Do the first example with the whole class, by asking students the following questions: *Do we know who gave permission? Should this sentence be active or passive?* Students work in pairs before listening to check their answers. Play the recording again if necessary.

ANSWERS
a   1 was given 2 became 3 was given 4 been known
b   1 be elected 2 was murdered 3 decided
     4 was elected 5 died
c   1 became 2 was launched 3 be brought
     4 died 5 is named

D Speaking: Asking favours

1 Put students in pairs. Give them time to read through the boxes and check that they understand how the activity works. Circulate, giving help.

2 As students perform their dialogues for the class, note down errors and useful language to focus on at the end.

3 [C2] Students listen and answer the questions before checking their ideas in pairs. Check answers with the class.

ANSWERS

	Conversation 1	Conversation 2
Who are they?	Friends	Father and daughter
Where are they?	On the phone	At home
What favour does A want?	Jane wants to borrow a tent.	The daughter wants a lift to the station early on Sunday morning.
Why?	They're going camping at the weekend.	The rucksacks will be heavy and it will be difficult to get a bus so early.
What problem does B have?	Fran's sister has got the tent – she borrowed it last year and hasn't brought it back yet.	He's going out on Saturday night and will probably get home very late.
How does A try to persuade B? What happens in the end?	Jane offers to go to fetch the tent. Fran will phone her sister and try to sort something out.	The daughter pleads. The father agrees to think about it (but has probably really agreed).

Students can now do *Test two: modules 5–8* on pages 164–166.

module 9

Future society

Reading and vocabulary
(PAGES 92–93)

1 Check the meaning of *horoscope* and *prediction*. Discuss the questions with the whole class.

2 **a & b** Explain that students are first going to read a text about predictions which turned out to be very wrong. Emphasise that they have to match a topic to each prediction as they read. Check answers with the whole class, and ask students which prediction has come true.

> **ANSWERS**
> **Computers:** 3, 10. **Fashion:** 9. **Film and TV:** 2, 5, 7.
> **Music:** 8. **Science and technology:** 1, 4, 6, 11, 12
>
> Prediction 10, about the Internet, has come true.

3 Students work in pairs to find the phrases and discuss what they mean. Check answers with the whole class.

> **POSSIBLE ANSWERS**
> a become successful
> b use/importance
> c something that is stupid/ridiculous
> d sent into space
> e fixed/concentrated on
> f becoming unpopular/ unfashionable
> g refused
> h electronic items

4 Students discuss the questions in small groups before reporting back to the whole class.

5 Explain who James Martin is and that students will read some of his predictions. Before they read, they make predictions of their own in small groups, using the topics from exercise 2. Each group reports back one prediction to the class. Students read the text, using their *Mini-dictionaries* if necessary, to see if any of their predictions were the same as James Martin's.

6 Students work in pairs to answer the questions. Check answers with the whole class.

> **ANSWERS**
> a S
> b D We will still have to pay, but we will receive a bill rather than needing to use cash or cards, as the machine will know who we
> c S
> d S
> e S
> f S
> g D
> h S

7 Students discuss the questions in pairs before reporting their ideas back to the whole class.

Language focus 1 (PAGE 94)
Making predictions

See *Teacher's tips: using a discovery approach in the teaching of grammar* on page 8.

Students underline six examples of *will* or *won't*.

Analysis

1 Point out that all the predictions in the preceding exercise are with *will* or *won't* and express a definite prediction. Focus students' attention on the other phrases.

2 Explain how the line works. Without explaining the meaning of the phrases, get students to work in pairs and try to work out where they should go. Discuss answers with the whole class. As you do, contextualise the phrases in an example sentence (for example, *All housework will be done by computers*), and point out the following.
- Adverbs like *probably*, *definitely* and *certainly* go after *will* but before *won't*. Refer students to the sentences they underlined from the reading text to highlight this.
- *May* and *might* can be used in the negative form here, but *could* cannot.
- We can say *may well*, *might well* and *could well* if we want to say that something probably will happen.

Drill the phrases both in isolation and in the context of a short sentence (*Crime almost certainly won't disappear*).

> **ANSWERS AND LANGUAGE NOTES**
> a will almost certainly
> b will probably
> c is/are likely to
> d could/may well
> e may/might (not)
> f isn't/aren't likely to
> g probably won't
> h almost certainly won't
>
> Highlight the following.
> - *May not / might not*: students may ask which of these is more probable. Grammar books disagree on this – if there is any distinction, it is not significant. Intonation is more important in ascertaining how certain the person is.
> - There is a large number of other ways of expressing degrees of possibility/certainty – *It is possible that / Perhaps / Maybe*, etc. Do not deal with these unless students specifically ask.

PRACTICE

1 **a** Go over the example together and point out that students can change other parts of the sentences as well to reflect their opinions more accurately. This should be done as a spoken exercise in pairs initially, but the sentences can be written for further consolidation. When checking answers, draw students' attention to the following points.
- In sentences 3 and 8, *no* will have to be changed to *any* (*There may not be any more need for dentists*).
- All the phrases from the *Analysis* can be used with the passive (*All teaching will definitely be done by computers*).

b Put students into new pairs to discuss their opinions.

2 To start students off, give a few personalised predictions of your own – stress that these can be either long- or short-term predictions.

ADDITIONAL PRACTICE

Workbook: Making predictions with *will/won't*, *likely to*, *may*, page 67; Different ways of making predictions, page 68

Vocabulary (PAGE 95)

Society and change

1 **a** [9.1] Check the meaning of the words/phrases in the topic column. Before listening, students use their *Mini-dictionaries*. Have a discussion with the class about which change they think is actually happening in each case. Explain that students will hear the same topics discussed in news items, then play the recording. Check answers with the class.

> **ANSWERS**
> 1 is getting better   6 is deteriorating
> 2 is increasing   7 is getting better
> 3 are becoming less dangerous 8 is rising
> 4 is going up   9 is deteriorating
> 5 is falling   10 is decreasing

b Students read, underlining the key phrases before comparing answers in pairs. Check answers as a whole class.

> **ANSWERS AND LANGUAGE NOTE**
> 1 has never been in better shape
> 2 continues to grow; far more than
> 3 twenty-seven percent below the figures for the previous year, thirty-eight percent down; at their lowest levels since records began
> 4 set to rise; will go up
> 5 the lowest since; has fallen this year from
> 6 ridiculous; insult the intelligence; has reached its lowest point ever
> 7 optimistic is as good; or better than
> 8 another year-on-year increase; up by three percent
> 9 fallen dramatically; things just go from bad to worse
> 10 sixty-five percent do not attend the gym; get less exercise than
>
> The last news item may cause students problems because they also hear *more people registered ... than ever before.* Point out that this came after *Although*, and that it refers to registration for gyms, not actual participation.

Pronunciation

1 In pairs, students complete the table. Encourage them to guess words they are not sure of before using their *Mini-dictionaries*.

> **ANSWERS**
> a decrease   to decrease   decreasing
> b economy   —   economic
> c education   to educate   educated/
>   educational*

d	improvement	to improve	improving
e	increase	to increase	increasing
f	unemployment	—	unemployed

* Educated is the adjective to describe a person, but a book, for example, would be described as educational.

2 [9.2] Play the recording for students to check the forms of the words, and again to mark the stress patterns. Check answers with the class. Point out that the stressed syllable often changes in word families in English. Remind students that they can use their *Mini-dictionaries* to check which syllables are stressed in a word.

a de̍crease   to decrea̍se   decrea̍sing
b eco̍nomy   —   econo̍mic
c edu̍cation   to e̍ducate   e̍ducated/
                                 educa̍tional
d impro̍vement   to impro̍ve   impro̍ving
e i̍ncrease   to increa̍se   increa̍sing
f unemplo̍yment —   unemplo̍yed

3 Drill individual words that are difficult for your students, then put them into pairs to practise saying them.

2 Look at the examples with students. Explain that they should discuss any/all of the topics from exercise 1a. Then do one with the class to get them started. Students discuss their opinions in pairs or groups. Emphasise that they should give reasons, and remind them that we use the Present continuous to describe changing states.

Language focus 2 (PAGES 96–97)

Hypothetical possibilities with *if*

1 Explain that the article gives the results of a survey about how British people would behave in different situations. Check the meaning of *a poll*, *income*, *to drink-drive*. In small groups, students discuss the possible results of the same survey in their country. *If you teach a multinationality class*: make sure that the different nationalities are mixed up in the class.

2 Focus students' attention on the questionnaire, and explain that they have to choose an answer for each situation. Check the meaning of the following: *to hand something in*, *to charge someone too little*, *to steal*, *stationery*, *the speed limit*, *to pretend to be sick*, *to avoid paying tax*, *a disabled parking space*, *to drop litter*. Delay answering questions about the use of *would* and *if* at this stage. Students can simply use the phrase *Would you .... ?* as an expression. Students complete the questionnaire individually before comparing their answers in small groups.

3 **a** [9.3] Before playing the recording, check the meaning of *to have change* and *to hide*. Emphasise that students only need to decide which questions are being discussed. Play the recording straight through and then check answers with the whole class.

ANSWERS
2   d   Would you travel by train without a ticket?
3   e   Would you drive above the speed limit?
4   j   Would you drop litter?

b Students can try to guess the answers first, but tell them not to write in their books until they listen again. Pause the recording regularly to give students time to write. Students check answers in pairs before checking with the whole class. It would be useful to write up the complete sentences yourself at this stage for reference in the *Analysis*.

ANSWERS
2   would definitely; wouldn't feel
3   'd never; stepped; was speeding; would never
4   have to admit that I would do; would never; 'd put; weren't

Analysis

1 Check the meaning of *imaginary*. Give students a moment to think about the answer before checking with the whole class.

ANSWERS AND LANGUAGE NOTES
a   A real future situation: *I'll definitely travel by train.*
b   An imaginary situation: *I'd definitely travel without a train ticket.*
   Will is used in the first sentence, *would* in the second.

Students should be familiar with both *will* and *would*, but it is worth contrasting them briefly. Highlight:
•   the question forms (*Will you?/he?/they?*, etc./ *Would you?/he?/they?*, etc.)
•   the affirmative forms (*I/he/they*, etc. *will*; *I/he/they*, etc. *would*)
•   the negative forms (*I/he/they*, etc. *will not*; *I/he/they*, etc. *would not*)
•   the contracted forms (*I'll/he'll/they'll*, etc. and *I/he/they*, etc. *won't*; *I'd/he'd/they'd*, etc. and *I/he/they*, etc. *wouldn't*)
Do not at this stage go into the full 'second conditional' structure. Point out that *would* is very often used in sentences on its own. Particularly in speech, full conditional sentences are relatively uncommon – one 'half' of the conditional tends to be assumed.

2 Students work individually or in pairs before you check answers with the whole class.

ANSWERS AND LANGUAGE NOTES
Examples of hypothetical clauses using *if*: *If a child stepped …*; *if there weren't any litter bins around.*
These are past forms, but they don't refer to past time (they refer to present/future/general/imaginary time).
Highlight the following.
•   This is the subjunctive in English – if students have a subjunctive in their own language / are already familiar with this grammatical term, point this out to them. Stress that the subjunctive is not very widely used in English – this use after *if* is the most important one.

•   Because it is subjunctive, strictly speaking, *were* should be used rather than *was* in the first and third person. These days, though, many native speakers use *was*, so do not insist that students use *were*.
•   Again, point out that this *if* clause is very often used on its own, not necessarily in a full 'second conditional' sentence.

3 Students work individually before checking answers with the

ANSWERS AND LANGUAGE NOTES
The third sentence is incorrect.

It focuses on a common mistake – the use of *would* after *if*. The correct sentences illustrate the following points:
•   the use of *was* or *were* rather than *would be* (*If the ticket office was closed …* ; *if the ticket office were closed*)
•   the fact that either clause can begin the sentence
•   the fact that *might* can be used instead of *would* if you are not sure what you would do.

PRACTICE

1 Students work individually or in pairs before checking answers with the whole class. Students should use contractions where possible as this is more natural.

ANSWERS
1   'd definitely hand in   10 caught
2   found   11 'd definitely tell
3   'd be   12 hadn't charged**
4   ever lost   13 'd take
5   would hand   14 was/were
6   'd probably steal   15 'd feel
7   knew   16 'd park
8   did*   17 was/were
9   'd be   18 wouldn't do
* The Past continuous *were doing* is also possible here. Make sure that students realise that the Past simple is not the only possible tense.
** The Past perfect is used here to show time sequencing.

2 a Check students understand the questions in *Never say never*, and the following phrases: *under what circumstances, to lie to someone, to walk out of your job, to drop out of college, to give someone a lift, to hit someone.* Explain that students should think of all the possible circumstances in which they might do these things.

b Look at the examples with the class. Students work in small groups, comparing ideas. Circulate and make a note of any useful language and errors for analysis and correction later.

3 a Go through the examples with the whole class, and discuss whether they are real or imaginary. Students work in pairs to complete the exercise before checking answers with the whole class. Point out that not all the questions include an *if* clause.

ANSWERS AND LANGUAGE NOTE
1 (imaginary) *If you could live anywhere in the world, where would you live?*
2 (real) *What will you do if you have some free time this evening?**
3 (imaginary) *If you could become a famous person for a day, who would you be? Why would you choose that person?*
4 (real) *If you go shopping this week, what will you buy?**
5 (real) *Where will you go if you have a holiday next year? Who will you go with?**
6 (imaginary) *How would your life be different if you were a millionaire? What would be the best and worst things about it?*

In theory, all the sentences in this exercise could be either real or imaginary, but in most cases it is much more likely to be one than the other. For those sentences marked *, students may be able to make a good case for using a hypothetical form (if, for example, they have no spare time or money). Do not go into this, however, unless students ask.

b Focus on the example answers, pointing out the use of *probably* with *would* as well as *will* (*definitely* and *certainly* can be used in the same way). Remind students of the correct word order – *I'd probably*, but *I probably wouldn't* … Circulate and make notes of errors for analysis and correction later on.

Pronunciation

1 [9.4] Play the recording as many times as necessary. Students may find this difficult, as contractions are not usually stressed. However, it is important listening practice.

ANSWERS
1 'll   2 'd   3 'll   4 'd   5 'll   6 'll   7 'd   8 'll
9 'd   10 'd

2 Get students to repeat the sentences individually and chorally, then in pairs. If they are having problems with the pronunciation of *I'll*, suggest they insert a small /j/ sound: *I-y-l* /aɪjl/.

ADDITIONAL PRACTICE

RB **Resource bank:** *Election night special* (hypothetical possibilities with *if* –'second conditional'–), page 146; *How would your life be different?* (hypothetical possibilities with *if* (–second conditional'–), page 147

Workbook: Hypothetical possibilities with *if*, page 70; Real and hypothetical possibilities with *if*, page 70; *If* sentences in social situations, page 71

Wordspot (PAGE 98)

make

See *Teacher's tips: working with lexis* on pages 9–10.

Wordspot (make): **language notes**

Students may ask about the difference in meaning between *make* and *do*. The usual explanation is that *make* relates to 'creating' something (*make a cake*) and that do relates to 'completing' tasks or duties (*do your homework*). This explanation is basically true, but does not account for many common fixed phrases. We have not brought the two verbs together here as we believe this could make it more difficult to remember phrases with both. However, it may be helpful to give the simple explanation above to convey an idea of the difference, especially for students who have only one such verb in their first language.

Note also that *make* meaning 'to force' (*She made them eat all their dinner*) is not included here as we do not believe it is helpful to view it in terms of fixed phrases. If you make a poster of the uses of *make*, you could include a separate section for this.

1 Check the meaning of *to lock a door* and *a hole*. Students work individually or in pairs.

ANSWERS
a 6   b 5   c 7   d 4   e 1   f 2   g 3

2 [9.5] Play the recording straight through and check answers with the whole class. Drill the following phrases: *to make up your mind, to make it worse, to make the dinner, to make a noise, to make sure.* Put students into pairs to practise the dialogues.

3 Check the meaning of the section headings in the diagram. Students work in pairs before checking answers with the whole class.

ANSWERS
(*section of diagram in brackets*)
making that strange noise (b)
make a better suggestion (b)
make it worse (d)
make the dinner (a)
it's made of cotton (a)
make up your mind (e)
make sure (e)

4 Put students into pairs and refer them to page 143. Make sure that students understand that each square represents a letter, and that they need clues (as in a crossword) to complete it. As an example, get one student to read out the first clue and work out the answer as a class. Circulate and prompt with extra clues if students are having difficulties.

ANSWERS
1 make a sandwich   7 make a profit
2 made of leather   8 make you cry
3 make a mess   9 make it clear
4 made in Japan   10 make an appointment
5 make a mistake   11 make a cup of coffee
6 make a noise   12 make you angry

The hidden message is: What makes you laugh?

71

Task: Decide how to spend lottery money (PAGES 98–99)

See *Teacher's tips: making tasks work* on pages 13–14 and *Responding to learners' individual language needs* on pages 11–12.

Preparation: listening

1 **a** Check the meaning of *lottery*. Discuss the questions in pairs/groups or with the whole class.

b Focus students' attention on the map and statistics (St Ambrosia is an imaginary island in case students are in any doubt!). Read through the information together as this is important background information for the task. Students read about the St Ambrosia state lottery before checking the answer to the question with the whole class.

> **ANSWER**
> SA$10 million

2 [9.6] Focus students' attention on the photos and explain what they are going to hear. Check they understand what each of the organisations are. Play the recording, emphasising that they only need to make notes. Students compare answers in pairs before listening again if necessary.

> **ANSWERS**
> 1 The St Ambrosian Hotel and Tourism Association needs SA$4 million, a new luxury hotel and golf course.
> 2 The St Ambrosian Sports Association needs SA$6 million for a National Sports Centre.
> 3 The University of St Ambrosia needs SA$4.5 million for new equipment for the Computer Science and Technology Department.
> 4 The St Ambrosian Children's Hospital needs SA$3.5 million for beds and medical equipment to keep the hospital running for another year.
> 5 The International Petroleum Incorporated needs SA$8 million for looking for large oil deposits.

3 **a** Students work in pairs to check the meaning of the new words and decide which organisation said each.

b Students check their answers. Students will need the vocabulary from this activity for the task; drill the sentences chorally and individually.

> **ANSWERS**
> 1 the St Ambrosian Sports Association
> 2 International Petroleum Incorporated
> 3 the University of St Ambrosia
> 4 the St Ambrosian Hotel and Tourism Association
> 5 the St Ambrosian Hotel and Tourism Association
> 6 the St Ambrosian Children's Hospital
> 7 the St Ambrosian Sports Association
> 8 International Petroleum Incorporated

Task: speaking

1 Pre-teach budget and emphasise that the money can be divided between the different organisations. Give students a few minutes to decide how they want to spend the money, plan what to say and think about any words or phrases they need.

2 Put students into groups to agree together on a budget. Check through the phrases in the Useful language box together. Highlight the following points at this stage, or wait until the correction stage after the task.

- Negative opinions are expressed with *I don't think* …
- *Agree* is an ordinary Present simple verb (not *I am agree*).

3 This presentation stage can be 'formal', with representatives of each group standing up to present their budget to the rest of the class. Make it clear that if students have not reached a final solution, they should explain why, and what they agreed/disagreed about. Write up the following phrases: *We all think* … , *None of us think* … , *We couldn't agree about* … If students are still interested once everyone has presented their budgets, try to agree on a budget together as a class.

> ### *Task*: alternative suggestions
>
> a *If you are short of time or have a class with weak listening skills*: miss out *Preparation: listening* and give out all the information about the different organisations yourself. If possible, spend time creating interest in St Ambrosia and its lottery.
>
> b *If you cannot finish the task in one lesson*: get students to do *Task: speaking*, exercise 1, as homework, before moving on to the group/class discussion in the following lesson.
>
> c *If you don't think your students will be very motivated by discussing an imaginary island*: create a 'parallel' task, using the students' own country or region. Either invent the organisations bidding for lottery money yourself, or get students to invent them.
>
> d *If you prefer to do the task as a role play or simulation*: instead of playing the recording, get some students to take on the roles of the representatives of the organisations, while others take on the role of Lottery Commission members.

Real life (PAGE 100)

Ways of saying numbers

1 [9.7] Get students to guess how the numbers are said before playing the recording. Pause after each number for students to repeat. Drill any problem numbers.

2 **a** Check the meaning of: *proportion* and *estimate/estimated*. Students try to guess in pairs.

b [9.8] Students listen to check their ideas. Pause recording if necessary to allow writing time. When checking make sure students read out the full numbers correctly.

> **ANSWERS**
> 1 71%   2 −89°C   3 €27,753   4 55,680,000 km
> 5 6.3 billion   6 300,000 km/sec   7 126,000,000
> 8 483,080 m²   9 7%   10 199,859

3 a Put students into pairs and refer them to the appropriate page at the back of the book. Check that students understand the categories for the numbers given.

b Do the first example on each chart together and check that students can form the questions correctly. When students have finished, discuss any surprising numbers as a whole class.

ADDITIONAL ACTIVITY

RB **Resource bank:** *Hear … Say!* (ways of saying numbers), page 148; *Vocabulary extension* (talking about numbers, amounts and ages without being exact), page 149

Workbook: Real life: Saying numbers, page 73

Study … (PAGE 100)

English outside the classroom (2): Using the Internet

1 This activity could be done for homework or in class. If it is done in class time, students work in small groups and compare which of the tips they have already tried to use and any additional ideas they have.

2 *If you have Internet access for students where you teach*: this could be done in class time or set for homework as self-study. *If you do not have student Internet access, but you have access to the Internet*: print out some of the pages from the *Cutting Edge* website. Students 'surf' the pages as a reading activity instead.

Practise … (PAGE 101)

1 Making predictions

If this activity is done in class time, students work in pairs. For each word or phrase they cross out, they should discuss the reason why. Check answers with the whole class.

ANSWERS
a may b could c may definitely
d is likely e is definitely f may be

2 Hypothetical possibilities with *if*

If this activity is done in class, have each phrase written on a separate piece of card. Students work in pairs to match.

ANSWERS
a 3 b 5 c 2 d 6 e 1 f 4

3 Real and hypothetical possibilities

If this activity is done in class, get students to cover the words in the box, and work in pairs to try to guess what they are.

ANSWERS
a had b will c were d would e might f could

4 Phrases with *make*

Set this activity up as a competition. The winner is the first

student correctly to identify the phrases not used with *make*. Offer bonus points to the first student who gives you the correct verbs to go with these phrases. Give students a time limit and see which pair can remember the most phrases.

ANSWERS
The phrases not used are *a party* and *a risk*. The correct collocations are *to have a party / to go to a party* and *to take a risk*.

5 Describing trends

If this activity is done in class, get students to cover column B and guess the opposites before matching.

ANSWERS
a 4 b 2 c 1 d 6 e 3 f 5

6 Saying numbers

ANSWERS
a	six thousand	d	six point six
b	six million	e	six percent
c	six thousand million	f	sixty-six square kilometres

Pronunciation spot

a Students work in pairs to complete the missing letters.
b [9.9] Play the recording, pausing to give students time to decide which sound they heard. Point out the different positions of the lips and teeth when producing these sounds (encourage students to bite their bottom lip with their top teeth to produce /v/).

ANSWERS
a	v	no military value
b	b, v	the problem with television
c	v	the average American family
d	b, v	maybe five computers
e	b	You'd better learn secretarial work.
f	b, v	has been invented

Remember! (PAGE 69)

After looking back at the areas they have practised, students do the *Mini-check* on page 158. Check answers as a whole class, and ask students to tell you their scores out of 20.

ANSWERS
1 will almost certainly	11 wouldn't lend
2 is likely to	12 economical
3 There definitely won't	13 educated/educational
4 may not get	14 predict
5 You may well	15 unemployment
6 doesn't start	16 make
7 'll definitely fail	17 million
8 gave	18 rising
9 would you do	19 taking
10 were	20 had

module 10

An amazing story

Vocabulary and speaking
(PAGE 102)

Types of story

1 **a** Focus students' attention on the photos and ask if they recognise any of the stories. Put students into pairs to match the photos to categories. Emphasise that each story may fit more than one category. Note: photos a–e show, respectively, the following stories: *Gone with the Wind*, *Beauty and the Beast*, *Pirates of the Caribbean*, *Lord of the Rings* and *Theseus and the Minotaur*.

> **ANSWERS**
> a 7 b 6, 7 c 1 d 3, 4 e 3

b Students discuss the questions. Round off by finding out which types of story are the most and least popular in the class.

2 **a** Students work in pairs, using their mini-dictionaries if necessary. Check answers as a whole class.

> **POSSIBLE ANSWERS**
> 1 detective and crime stories; myths and legends; science fiction and fantasy – negative
> 2 adventure stories; myths and legends; science fiction and fantasy; fairy tales; romances; ghost stories – negative
> 3 myths and legends; romances – negative
> 4 comedies; fairy tales – positive
> 5 fairy tales, romances – either
> 6 detective and crime stories; science fiction and fantasy; comedies – positive
> 7 myths and legends; fairy tales; romances – positive
> 8 detective and crime stories; science fiction and fantasy; ghost stories – either
> 9 myths and legends; science fiction and fantasy; fairy tales; ghost stories – positive
> 10 myths and legends; fairy tales – either

b Discuss this as a class. Note that some of the phrases are direct opposites, but others are not (for example, it's not possible to describe a story as *fast*).

> **ANSWERS**
> 1 very simple 2 very realistic 3 fast-moving
> 4 sad ending 5 made me laugh 6 really stupid

3 Emphasise that students do not have to explain the plot, just say why they like it.

Language focus 1 (PAGE 103)

Past perfect

1 Check the meaning of *lateral thinking*, *scarf*, *coal*. Students read the story and work in groups to find a solution. If any students obviously know the answer,

discourage them from telling the others, but allow them to provide clues. Circulate to see if any students use the Past perfect in the discussion, but do not comment on this.

2 🔊 [10.1] Explain that students will hear some people discussing a story. Emphasise that they have to see if the same solution is found. Check answers with the class.

Analysis

1a Give students a few minutes to identify the different verb forms, then check answers with the whole class.

> **ANSWERS**
> Past simple: *lay*   Past perfect: *had put*

1b Check the form of the Past perfect on the board, highlighting:
- the form (*had* + past participle for all persons)
- the question and negative forms
- the contractions *'d* and *hadn't*.

> **ANSWERS**
> the Past perfect; *had* + past participle

2 Students discuss the two options in pairs before checking answers with the whole class.

> **ANSWERS AND LANGUAGE NOTES**
> The second rule is correct; we use the Past perfect when we are talking about an event in the past and we want to explain something that happened earlier. For many students the concept of the Past perfect will cause few problems since it will be similar in their own language.
>   The incorrect rule highlights a common misconception about the Past perfect. Point out that the Past perfect is only used in reaction to a Past simple action to show that it came first. If you are talking about a single action in the past, however long ago, you use the Past simple (*Dinosaurs died out millions of years ago*). The relationship between two past events means the Past perfect is commonly found in the following constructions:
> - after verbs like *knew* (*When she saw Peter's face, Fiona knew that she had made a mistake*), *thought* (*He thought I'd told everyone*) and *remembered* (*He remembered that he hadn't locked the door*)
> - with time words like *when* (*When she got home, she'd spent all her money*), *after* (*After he'd spoken to her, John realised it was Janet's birthday*) and *before* (*Before he was a doctor, Fred had been an artist*).
> Students may confuse the Past perfect with the Present perfect. The Present perfect always relates a past action to the present; the Past perfect relates a past action to one further in the past (it describes the 'time before the past'). Draw students' attention to the timelines on page 151 of the *Language summary* to make this clear.
>   Make sure that students are clear about the difference between the way the Present perfect and Past perfect are formed. Point out that many of the same words are used with both (for example, *already*).

PRACTICE

1 Work though the examples with the class. Check the difference between *because* (the reason) and *so* (the result). Students work in pairs before checking with the class.

ANSWERS
1 f
2 h
3 g My uncle didn't want to move because he had lived in the same house for forty years.
4 d There was no food in the house because I had forgotten to go to the supermarket.
5 b My grandparents had never flown before so they were nervous when they got on the plane.
6 c When I got home my father was angry because I hadn't phoned him.
7 a They'd already sold all the tickets so we didn't get into the concert.
8 e We didn't have to queue in the restaurant because my uncle had reserved a table.

Pronunciation

1 [10.2] Point out that students will need to listen very carefully. Pause the recording after each sentence to allow students time to discuss their answers. Students may find this challenging as the contraction ('d) is difficult to hear, being unstressed. Play the recording again if necessary, rather than giving the answers.

ANSWERS
1 PS   2 PP   3 PS   4 PS   5 PP   6 PP   7 PP   8 PS

2 Check the difference in meaning, if necessary, between *I'd left my umbrella at home* and *I left my umbrella at home* to show students how important this practice is. Students work in pairs to practise.

2 **a** Explain that there are two more puzzles to solve, like the one in *Language focus 1*, exercise 1. Put students into pairs and get them to read the relevant puzzle, using their mini-dictionaries. Then refer them to the appropriate page at the back of the book to read the solution to their partner's puzzle. Circulate, suppling any necessary vocabulary definitions.

b Circulate as students work, noting down any useful language, especially in the use of the Past perfect, to focus on later.

Reading and vocabulary
(PAGES 104–105)

1 Students discuss the questions in small groups followed by brief feedback to the class.

2 **a** Students work individually, then in pairs to establish a logical order, before checking answers with the class. Check pronunciation of the words in bold.

ANSWERS
A serious crime is attempted.
The police suspect someone.

The suspect is followed.
He is arrested.
He is questioned by the police.
The suspect is charged.
He appears in court.
He pleads innocent or guilty.
He is found guilty.
He is sentenced.

b Students may be able to guess the difference between the crimes, especially if they have similar words in their first language. Encourage them to guess in groups before checking in their mini-dictionaries and then with the class.

3 Emphasise that students only need to read the beginnings of stories 1–3 at this stage, not the endings A–D. Point out that the photo on page 105 shows the Millennium Dome, which was built in 1999 to mark the new millennium.

ANSWERS
1 theft; more than €3 million
2 mugging and fraud; £5,000
3 robbery; diamonds worth approximately $350 million

4 Focus students' attention on the words and phrases in the box, checking the meaning of *a cargo crate*, *a JCB digger*, *a smoke bomb*, *a speedboat*. Students read and discuss the answers in pairs before checking with the whole class.

ANSWERS
1 Martin Dempsey hid in a cargo crate on a plane, then used a pocket knife to cut his way out.
2 Toby Williams used a photo from a driving licence and wore women's clothes to look like Mrs Walsh. He wanted to cash a cheque written to her.
3 A gang of professional thieves crashed a JCB digger into the Millennium Dome, threw smoke bombs and planned to escape in a speedboat.

5 **a** Explain that none of the crimes was successful. Students cover the texts and work in pairs to guess the endings. Write some of their suggestions on the board.

b Emphasise that there is one extra ending. Get students to read the endings and check in pairs before going through answers with the class. Ask if anyone guessed correctly.

ANSWERS
1 C   2 A   3 B   D is the extra ending.

6 **a** Do the first example as a class. Explain that for the first one there are two different words. Students identify the text, then the sentence or line in the text most likely to contain the meaning given, and then decide which word expresses that meaning. Check the answers with the class.

ANSWERS
1 snatched, grabbed   2 ingenious   3 foiled
4 priceless   5 smashed   6 yelled   7 astonished
8 leapt   9 horrified   10 desperate

b Discuss the question as a whole class.

ANSWER

The writers chose these words for dramatic effect, to make the stories sound exciting.

Pronunciation

1 [10.3] Give students time to read the sentence. Point out the stressed words and weak forms, and get students to think about how the sentence is pronounced. Play the recording, more than once if necessary.

2 [10.4] Play the sentence several times so students get familiar with the rhythm. Once they have marked the stressed syllables, identifying the weak forms is easier.

ANSWERS

Spanish police yesterday **told** the story of **how the** /ə/ /ə/ /ə/

forty-year-old **man, Martin Dempsey** from **Manchester,** /ə/

was **caught.** /ə/

3 Drill the sentences chorally before students practise individually. If your students tend to stress the weak forms, first drill each phrase saying only the stressed words, to establish the rhythm, for example, *Martin Dempsey Manchester caught.* Then, keeping the same rhythm, get students to squash the weak forms into the sentence.

7 After the discussion in pairs, have a brief class discussion.

Language focus 2 (PAGES 106–107)

Reported speech

1 Check the meaning of *to be separated, a tattoo, an owl, to phone in sick.* Students work in pairs before checking answers with the whole group. Make sure that students are clear which brother is which, to avoid confusion later.

ANSWERS

a They were brothers who were separated when they were children.

b Michael remembered that Harry had an owl tattooed on the back of his hand.

c Because she was off sick and he wanted to know what appointments he had. He found a number with the name 'Bell' and 'URGENT' written next to it.

2 **a** Students work in pairs before checking answers with the whole class. As you check answers, copy the story in the correct order onto the board, leaving space between each sentence to write the direct speech version later on.

ANSWERS

1 Michael asked if he could speak to Mr Bell.

2 The woman said she was sorry, but she had only just started working there, and she didn't know who Bell was.

3 She asked him to ring back later when her boss, Mr Findlater, was there.

4 Michael said he would ring back later, and asked her if Mr Findlater's name was Harry.

5 The woman said that it was.

6 Becoming excited now, Michael asked her whether she had ever noticed a tattoo on the back of Mr Findlater's hand.

7 She told him that he had a tattoo of an owl on his hand.

8 When Michael's secretary came back to work, he asked her who had given her his brother's number.

9 The secretary told him it wasn't a phone number, it was a bank account number for Mr Bell, one of their customers.

10 Thanks to this amazing coincidence, Michael had found his brother at last.

b Write in the direct speech version of the beginning of the conversation, under the reported version, in a different colour if possible. Students do the rest in pairs or small groups.

c [10.5] Play the recording, pausing after each line of the dialogue. Write up the rest of the direct speech version under the reported version on the board as above.

ANSWERS

See tapescript for recording 5 on page 173 of the *Students' Book.*

Analysis

1 Give students a few minutes to compare the texts individually before checking answers with the whole class. (Only a few tenses are covered here – others are covered in the *Language summary*, so you may wish to refer to it at this stage to give students a fuller picture of tense-shift patterns.)

ANSWERS AND LANGUAGE NOTES

a In reported speech, the tense moves back into the past.

b

Direct speech	Reported speech
Present simple *I don't know who Mr Bell is.*	Past simple *She said she didn't know who Mr Bell was.*
Present perfect *I've only just started working here.*	Past perfect *She said (that) she had only just started working there.*
Past simple *Who gave you my brother's number?*	Past perfect *He asked who had given her his brother's number.*
will *Yes, I will.*	*would* *She replied that she would.*

Time words in reported speech have to reflect the past time frame (for example, *the next day* rather than *tomorrow*). This is logical, and should not cause problems if students are using reported speech in a natural context.

2 Students to underline the reported questions in the text and discuss the questions in pairs. Check answers with the class.

ANSWERS AND LANGUAGE NOTES
a The five reported questions including sentence numbers from *Language focus 2, exercise 2a)* are:

1 Michael asked if he could speak to Mr Bell.
3 She asked him to ring back later when her boss, Mr Findlater, was there.
4 Michael ... asked her if Mr Findlater's name was Harry.
6 Becoming ... Michael asked her whether she had ever noticed a tattoo on the back of Mr Findlater's hand.
8 When ... he asked her who had given her his brother's phone number.

The verb *asked* introduces each one. (*Wonder* is also a commonly used verb in reported questions.)
b There is no inversion of subject and verb in reported questions. Again, this is perfectly logical, because reported questions are not true questions.
c If and *whether* are used with *yes/no* questions (*Michael asked if he could speak to Mr Bell*).

There is no difference in meaning between *if* and *whether*, and they are not needed in *wh-* questions where the question word acts as a conjunction (*he asked her who had given her his brother's number*.)

PRACTICE

1 a Remind students who Harry and Michael Findlater were and what happened to each of them. Students decide who said which things.

ANSWERS
1 Michael 2 Harry 3 Michael 4 Harry
5 Michael 6 Michael 7 Harry 8 Michael

b Students write sentences either individually or in pairs before checking answers with the whole class.

ANSWERS AND LANGUAGE NOTE
1 Michael said (that) he couldn't believe he'd finally found Harry.
2 Harry asked how Michael had got his phone number.
3 Michael asked if Harry would show him his tattoo.
4 Harry said (that) Michael was certainly taller than when he last saw / had last seen him.*
5 Michael said (that) he had spent nearly thirty years looking for Harry.
6 Michael asked if Harry had ever tried to look for him.
7 Harry said (that) it was luck that Harry's secretary was / had been off sick that day.*
8 Michael said (that) he thought he'd give her a pay rise!

Some verbs are not changed, as in the sentences marked*. This is because they relate to more background information – in both cases, part of the sentence shifts to show that speech is being reported. The tenses can change, and for weak classes it may be simplest to follow the same pattern.

2 Allocate roles A and B. Put students into groups so that As and Bs work together to prepare for the role play. Circulate, supplying vocabulary and useful language. After a few minutes, regroup students into pairs of A and B. A interviews B. Circulate and note down any errors and useful language to focus on at the end of the activity.

3 Look at the examples with the class. Unless your class is very strong, get students to write out the reported-speech versions before feeding back to the class. Alternatively, get them to feed back orally, then write up the results of their questionnaire in reported speech for homework.

ADDITIONAL PRACTICE

RB **Resource bank:** *Jungle survivors* (reported speech), page 151; *Vocabulary extension* (verbs to use instead of *say*), page 152

Workbook: Reported speech, page 79; Reported questions, page 80

Wordspot (PAGE 107)

say and *tell*

1 [10.6] Check the meaning of *the truth, a lie, a prayer, a joke*. Students work in pairs before listening to check their answers.

ANSWERS
a say b tell c tell, tell d tell e say f tell
g tell h tell i say j tell k say

2 Do the first two examples together, then get students to underline the phrases and complete the diagram.

ANSWERS
say: sorry, a prayer, yes or no
tell: someone what to do, a joke, (someone) the truth, someone something about, lies, someone off, the difference between two things

3 Demonstrate a question with a student. Students work in pairs. Round off with brief feedback, asking students about the most interesting/unusual answers they heard.

Vocabulary (PAGE 108)

Adverbs for telling stories

1 Check the meaning of *to search, to lose touch, evidence*. Students match the sentences individually or in pairs before checking answers as a whole class.

ANSWERS
a 5 b 1 c 8 d 6 e 4 f 2 g 7 h 3

2 Do the first example as a class, making it clear that students must continue the sentences logically, according to the meaning of the adverbs. Students work in pairs. Do this as a spoken exercise initially, and then get students to write sentences. Circulate as students write, noting down any problems with the use of adverbs to focus on later.

Task: Tell a ghost story

(PAGES 108–109)

Preparation: speaking

1 Focus students' attention on the pictures and emphasise that they all relate to a story called *The Guests* which they will hear later. Students check the meaning of the words in the box and match them to the pictures. Discuss answers with the class.

> **ANSWERS**
> Picture 1: a burned-out house, some ruins
> Picture 2: a newspaper headline
> Picture 3: someone offering to pay
> Picture 4: an isolated house
> Picture 5: an envelope
> Picture 6: an elderly couple
> Picture 7: thick fog
> Picture 8: an envelope
> Picture 9: a restaurant owner

2 Put students into pairs to do this.

Task: speaking and listening

1 Put students into groups of three or four. Read through the questions and give them time to think before discussing the answers in groups. Emphasise that students are going to tell their story to another student so it needs to be comprehensible. Focus on the *Useful language* box, drilling the phrases and checking any problems. Tell students they can make notes if they want, but they should not write out the whole story. While students practise telling their stories, circulate and provide vocabulary.

2 [10.7] Students listen and answer the questions before working with a new partner. They discuss how close their stories were to the original one.

> **ANSWERS**
> a to visit the man's mother
> b They had started their journey late and it was getting dark and the fog was getting thicker.
> c They had coffee, ate cake and talked for a while with the old man and woman.
> d They offered to pay for their accommodation.
> e an envelope with money for the room
> f Because the house they said they had stayed in was actually no longer there.
> g The house had been burned to the ground a month before.
> h Their envelope was on the badly burned table.

Task: **alternative suggestions**

If you have a creative group: they may prefer to tell their own frightening stories, right from the beginning. However, it would still be useful to provide a model.

- Tell a story yourself about a mysterious/frightening event.
- As a task you could write a list of key words from your story on the board, then tell students to listen and order them or explain their significance in the story.

The next stage is to get the students to tell their own stories. It is simplest if each student works individually. The following framework should help:

- Give them time to think of a story, suggesting possible sources (films, personal experiences, etc.). The story does not have to have a supernatural element – it could be frightening, for example, because they were in danger.
- Give students 15–20 minutes to plan their stories.
- If you think they need additional practice, get them to tell their stories in pairs before telling the class.
- If you have a large class, instead of listening to everyone's story as a class, get students to tell their stories in groups. Alternatively, you could spread the story-telling over the next few lessons.

Writing (PAGE 110)

A narrative

1 Students work in small groups to categorise the time phrases before checking answers with the whole class.

> **ANSWERS**
> **Probably from the beginning of the story**: once there was a man; one day, many years ago
>
> **Probably from the middle of the story**: then; the following night; a few weeks passed; a few days later; later that day; after a while
>
> **Probably from the end of the story**: at last; eventually; finally; in the end

2 Explain that students are going to write a scary story, and make the different options clear to the class. Give students a few minutes to decide.

3 Set a time limit of ten minutes. Students work individually on their first draft. Circulate, providing any useful language or vocabulary the students need.

4 Elicit examples of some of the language listed. Students work individually through the proofreading tasks for ten to fifteen minutes. Circulate and provide feedback.

5 Collect the final versions of the stories, and either display them around the walls or distribute them amongst the students to read. Discuss the stories as a whole class.

Study ... (PAGE 110)

Making the most of graded readers

Students read about graded readers and, as a class, discuss advantages they have read about. *If you have access to graded readers where you teach*: take some along to the class to show the students. *If you have Internet access for students where you teach*: students look at the Penguin website in class time or set it for homework as self-study.

Practise ... (PAGE 111)

1 Past perfect

If this activity is done in class, students work in pairs. For each verb they circle, they should discuss the reason why. Check answers with the whole class.

ANSWERS
a had gone   b had ever spent   c had done
d had known   e had left   f had threatened

2 Reported speech

Reveal the sentences one by one. As you reveal each sentence, ask students to put up their left hand if the sentence is correct, and their right hand if the sentence is wrong. Students are awarded a point for each time they raise the correct hand. Anybody who raises the wrong hand loses a point.

ANSWERS
a incorrect   b correct   c correct   d incorrect
e correct   f incorrect   g incorrect   h correct

3 Reported questions

If this activity is done in class, put the sentences onto card, with each word on a separate piece of card. Students work in pairs to put each sentence into the right order.

ANSWERS
a   The teacher asked me why I was late.
b   He asked us if we were going home.
c   They asked her where she was going.
d   My brother wanted to know where I was.
e   I didn't ask him how he was.

4 Adverbs

Get students to cover column B with their hand and to try to give the conclusions that relate to each adverb, before uncovering and matching to check that they were right.

ANSWERS
a 2   b 6   c 1   d 4   e 5   f 3

5 Crime

After students have successfully matched the explanations and crime words, they try to write one more question for their partner, to test them on the meaning of another crime word.

ANSWERS
a   think
b   He got money dishonestly.
c   admits
d   taken to the police station
e   find out his punishment

6 *say* and *tell*

Set the activity up as a competition. The winner is the first student to correctly identify the *say/tell* phrases. Then see who can remember the most other phrases in five minutes.

ANSWERS
say: yes, sorry, thank you
tell: a lie, the truth, someone off, a joke, someone what to do

Pronunciation spot

a Students work in pairs, taking turns to read out the sentences while their partner listens to see how many /h/ sounds there are, and how many are silent.

b 🖭 [10.8] Play the recording, pausing after each sentence to give students time to decide how many /h/ sounds they heard. Then students work in pairs, practising reading the sentences to each other. If your students have problems forming the /h/ sound, ask them to hold a tissue in front of their mouth. When they say words containing the /h/ sound, the piece of paper should move slightly as air is expelled from their mouth.

ANSWERS

Said	Silent
1 two	none
2 two	none
3 two	one (hour)
4 two	one (ghost)
5 one	one (honest)
6 two	none

Remember! (PAGE 69)

After looking back at the areas they have practised, students do the *Mini-check* on page 158. Check answers as a class, and ask students to tell you their scores out of 20.

ANSWERS
1 arrived
2 had been
3 hadn't had
4 ate
5 were
6 hadn't flown
7 found
8 when/if/whether
9 him
10 In
11 him where he lived
12 (that) she was leaving the next day
13 the waitress (that) I'd never eaten snake before
14 (me) if I had enjoyed the film
15 her friends (that) she'd just got engaged
16 cry
17 tell
18 By
19 off
20 plead

module 11

Rules and freedom

Language focus 1 (PAGES 112–113)
Obligation and permission in the present

See Teacher's tips: using a discovery approach in the teaching of grammar on page 8.

1 Check students understand *rules* and the places in the box. Elicit an example before students work in pairs. You could allocate different places to each pair to get a wide range of sentences. Discuss ideas with the whole class. Do not focus explicitly on modals of obligation at this stage. Circulate and make notes on how well students are using them. In particular:
- are they only using *must* or are they using *have to* and *have got to* as well?
- do they seem to understand the difference between *must* and *should*?

Make a note of useful errors for correction after the *Analysis*.

2 Check the meaning of *sign* and focus students' attention on the pictures. Check the meaning of *cricket*, *wet paint*, *boarding card*, *inspection*, *staff*, *diving*, *a cyclist*, *a pedestrian*, *denims*, *smart-casual*. Students discuss the questions in pairs before checking answers with the whole class. As you check answers, focus on the meaning of the signs rather than the students' use of the modal verbs – this will come later.

ANSWERS

	Where?	Meaning?
1	Most places where you can buy something	We accept all major credit cards.
2	Parks	Dogs, football and cricket are not allowed here.
3	Hospitals, libraries, planes, classrooms	You cannot use your mobile phone here.
4	Anywhere that is being or has just been decorated	Be careful of the wet paint.
5	Airports, train stations	You can smoke here.
a	Any place of work – airports, bars, pubs, hospitals, libraries, museums, nightclubs, public swimming pools, train stations	Only staff can go in to this area.
b	Airports	Somebody is going to check your boarding card and passport.
c	Beaches	Swimming is not allowed here, because it is dangerous.
d	Public swimming pools	Diving is not allowed here.
e	Bars, pubs, nightclubs	You can wear smart-casual clothes here, but not denims or T-shirts.
f	Roads	You cannot park here.
g	Parks and roads	Only cyclists and pedestrians are allowed here.

3 Explain that there may be one or two sentences that are not true about each sign. Look at the first example together before getting students to do the rest. Check answers with the class.

ANSWERS AND LANGUAGE NOTES
The verbs below mean the same as the signs; the other verbs do not.

a Sign 1 *can* (*Must* and *have got to* would have the opposite meaning, leaving no choice to pay by any other means.)

b Sign 5 *Are allowed to / can* (The meaning of *can* and *are allowed to* is basically the same.)*

c Sign 3 *mustn't/can't* (*Shouldn't* is also possible, but not correct here because the sign has a stronger meaning. *Shouldn't* means 'It isn't a good idea to …')

d Sign 2 *are not allowed* (There is a very clear relationship between a sign or rule which says 'no' and *not allowed*.)

e Sign 4 *ought to* (*Have to* is too strong here; the sign gives a warning rather than stating an emphatic rule. *Ought to* is very similar in meaning to *should*. It means 'it's a good idea, it's the right thing to do'. *Don't have to* means 'it's not necessary, but you can if you want', which would imply that there is no wet paint.)**

*Be *allowed to* has a narrower meaning than *can* since it is only used to refer to rules/things that are officially authorised in some way (this point may be too complex for students unless there is a precise translation in their own language).

**grammar books disagree about whether or not there is a difference between these *ought to* and *should*, but at this level, where *ought to* is only likely to be for passive recognition, there is no need to worry about any difference.

Analysis
If you have already dealt with the differences in meaning above, students should be able to categorise the verbs. Check answers with the whole class, highlighting the problems of form below. The phrases can be drilled, although pronunciation is dealt with later as part of the practice.

Highlight the following if you think they might present problems:

Meaning

- Although *must* and *have to* have very similar meanings, *mustn't* and *don't have to* do not. *Mustn't* means the same as *can't* ('there is an obligation not to do something; there is no choice'). *Don't have to* means 'it isn't necessary to do this, but there is a choice – you can if you want to'.

- *Must* and *have to* are very similar in meaning, but not the same. With *must* the obligation comes from the speaker, with *have to* the obligation comes from someone other than the speaker, from outside. For example, a teacher to a student: *You must finish the homework by Friday*. The student explaining to an absent student later: *You have to finish the homework by Friday* (i.e. that is what the teacher says), not *You must finish the homework by Friday*. Although this is still clear, it sounds too authoritarian, as if the obligation is imposed by the student.

Form

- The bare infinitive is used after *can*, *must* and *should*.
- The infinitive with *to* is used after the other verbs.
- *Be allowed to* is a passive form and therefore needs the verb *to be*.
- Negatives and their contractions are formed like this : *can't / mustn't / shouldn't / oughtn't to / don't have to / haven't got to*. Note that *oughtn't to* is not very commonly used.
- Questions are formed like this: *Can I ...? / Must you ...? / Should we ...? / Ought we to ...?* / *Do you have to ...? / Have we got to ...? / Are they allowed to ...?* Note that *Ought we to ...?* is not very commonly used.
- *Can*, *must*, *should* and *ought to* do not change forms in the third-person singular, but we say *Does he have to ... ?* And *Has he got to ... ?*

PRACTICE

1 **a** Emphasise that students have to complete the sentences to make them mean the same as the signs. Students work in pairs and write their answers. Don't go through the answers with the class yet.

b [11.1] Students listen before checking answers with the class. Replay the cassette if students have problems distinguishing between positive and negative sentences, rather than telling them the answers yourself.

Pronunciation

1 [11.2] Pause the recording after each sentence, and drill chorally and individually. Pay particular attention to the following.
- *Can* is weak and unstressed, whereas *can't* is stressed.
- *To* is in all cases where it is used before the infinitive weak and unstressed.
- The 'v' in *have to* and the 's' in *has to* are pronounced /f/ and /z/ (in contrast to *have* used as a verb on its own).
- *Mustn't*, *should*, etc. contain silent letters. (You could also mention the pronunciation of *ought to* /ɔːťʊ/ here.)

2 Students continue to practise in pairs, saying first the verb, then the full sentence. Encourage them to pay attention to stress and weak forms.

2 Emphasise that students have to complete the sentences to make them true. Before starting, check the meaning of: *a pedestrian crossing, a seat belt, a motorway, to pay a fine*.
   This can be done as a spoken or written exercise, with students working in pairs or groups. As you check answers, encourage students to give alternative suggestions as there is not necessarily one correct answer. For example, students might want to say any of the following:

Lorries are allowed to drive through the city centre. (There's no law against this.)
Lorries shouldn't drive through the city centre. (It's not a good thing – it causes pollution.)
Lorries don't have to drive through the city centre. (There is a ring road they could use.)

The important thing is that students know why they are using the form they have chosen. Get them to explain their sentence when there is any doubt.

3 **a** Students work individually to write rules. Allocate places to each student if you want a range of different places to be covered. Circulate as students work, noting down errors and useful language to focus on later.

b Emphasise that as students read out their rules, they should not say which place they are talking about.

ADDITIONAL PRACTICE

Workbook: Obligation and permission, page 83; *Must* and *have to*, page 85

Listening (PAGE 114)

Annoying rules

1 a Focus students' attention on the photo and elicit that the driver has broken a parking rule. Check the meaning of *a wheel clamp*, *to be clamped*, *to have your car clamped*. Discuss the questions with the class.

b Students work in small groups to brainstorm. Write their ideas on the board.

2 [11.3] Students listen just to note the topic of each complaint. They check answers in pairs before checking with the whole class.

> **ANSWERS**
> a aeroplane safety announcements
> b paying before you board buses
> c dress codes at work
> d women changing their surname when they get married
> e hotel checkout times
> f paying to use a public toilet

3 a Students work in pairs to match halves of phrases, before listening again to check.

> **ANSWERS**
> 1 One rule I find really annoying is …
> 2 totally unnecessary
> 3 I find this really annoying.
> 4 A rule that does annoy me is …
> 5 One rule that really annoys me is …
> 6 an unwritten social rule
> 7 What really annoys me in a hotel is …
> 8 One thing I find really annoying is …

b Students work in small groups to discuss the same topics.

4 Give students time to think of ideas and make notes. Students work in groups to write a list of annoying rules, using the phrases from exercise 3a. Ask a few groups to report back to the class.

Language focus 2 (PAGES 114–115)

Obligation and permission in the past

See *Teacher's tips: using a discovery approach in the teaching of grammar* on page 8.

1 Check that students understand the difference between *a rule* and *a law,* and the meaning of *a beard, a nobleman, to pay tax, male, female, to resign from your job, a vehicle, a flag, to solve a problem.* Students work individually or in pairs before checking answers with the whole class.

> **ANSWERS**
> a 2 b 4 c 3 d 1 e 5

2 At this stage, students will need to use past forms of verbs of obligation. Either correct them as necessary and use the *Analysis* simply as a summary of the forms, or leave mistakes uncorrected until you get to the *Analysis*. Discuss answers with the whole class.

> **ANSWERS**
> The laws in each case (including example numbers from exercise 1) are as follows.
> a Noblemen had to pay tax to have a beard.
> b People had to pay tax on the number of windows they had.
> c Female teachers were not allowed to get married or go out with men.
> d If you were driving a car, someone had to walk in front of you waving a red flag.
> e People were not allowed to eat ice-cream soda on Sunday.

Analysis

1 Students work individually, working out the forms, before checking answers with the whole class. Check the pronunciation of *could* /kʊd/, *couldn't* /kʊdnt/, *were allowed to* /wə əˈlaʊd tuː/.

> **ANSWERS AND LANGUAGE NOTES**
>
> | | |
> |---|---|
> | can | could |
> | can't | couldn't |
> | have to | had to |
> | don't have to | didn't have to |
> | must | had to |
> | mustn't | wasn't/weren't allowed to/ couldn't |
> | have got to | had to |
> | is / are allowed to | was / were allowed to |
> | isn't/aren't allowed to | wasn't/weren't allowed to |
>
> Highlight the following.
> - *Must* has no past form, so *had to* is used instead. In the negative form we use *couldn't* or *wasn't/weren't allowed to*. Students may find this confusing.
> - *Had got to / hadn't got to* are not standard English, *had to / didn't have to* are used in the past form instead.
> - The past form of *should* is dealt with in Module 12.

2 Students work individually, underlining the past forms of the modal verbs in the laws, before checking answers with the whole class.

> **ANSWERS**
> (*including numbers of laws from* Language focus 2, *exercise 1*)
> a weren't allowed to, had to
> b had to, didn't have to
> c couldn't, had to, could
> d had to, couldn't
> e were not allowed to

PRACTICE

1 [cassette] [11.4] Check the meaning of *a servant*, *his master*, *to vote*, *a theoretical test*. Emphasise that there is sometimes more than one possibility. Students work in pairs before playing the cassette to check answers.

> **ANSWERS**
> a couldn't/weren't allowed to; had to
> b couldn't/weren't allowed to; had to
> c couldn't/weren't allowed to
> d couldn't/weren't allowed to; were allowed
> e could/was allowed to; didn't have to; had to

2 Students discuss the questions in small groups and then briefly as a class.

ADDITIONAL PRACTICE

Workbook: Obligation and permission in the past, page 84.

Task: Present your opinions
(PAGES 116–117)

See *Teacher's tips: making tasks work* on pages 13–14 and *Responding to learners' individual language needs* on pages 11–12.

> **Task: a note on controversial topics**
>
> We have included controversial topics for discussion in this section, so the students can present their own opinions. However, there is a possibility that some students may find some of the topics uncomfortable for classroom discussion. For this reason, in *Preparation: vocabulary*, exercise 3b, students are asked to consider carefully which topics they are not happy to discuss. It is important that you emphasise this choice.

Preparation: vocabulary

1 **a & b** Create interest by focusing students' attention on the photos and discussing briefly what issues they deal with. Check the meaning of a *strict law* and *rights*. Work through the first example as a class before putting students into pairs to categorise the phrases and the sentences that describe them, using their mini-dictionaries if necessary.

> **ANSWERS**
> **1a More rights**
> It should be made legal (for people to …).
> People should have the right to do this.
>
> **Stricter laws and fewer rights**
> It should be against the law (to …).
> It should be made illegal (for people to …).
> It should be banned.
> People shouldn't have the right to do this.
> People should be fined / sent to prison (for doing this).
> There should be capital punishment.
>
> **1b** It's fair. +   It's ridiculous. –
> It's too harsh. –   It's sensible. +
> It's too liberal. –   It's unfair. –

2 Check the meaning and stress of *controversial* and *controversy*. Note that the noun can be pronounced *controversy* or *controversy*. Explain that students will read 14 controversial statements. Emphasise that they will not have to express their own opinions at this stage, but only read and say which are already law in their country. Check answers as a class.

3 Check the meaning of the following: *hunting*, *to smack*, *to be terminally ill*, *to carry a gun*, *permission*, *to be banned*, *capital punishment*, *military service*, *to be compulsory*. Students work individually. Emphasise that students don't have to discuss any topic which they don't want to.

Task: speaking

1 **a** Put students into groups of three to five (try to include a mix of quieter and more opinionated students in each group). Emphasise that students should not discuss the topics yet, but that they have five minutes to agree on three topics they would like to discuss.

b Refer students to *Useful language*, section a, and give them up to five minutes to think about their opinions and how to express them. Circulate, supplying any vocabulary they need.

2 Students work in their groups. Make it clear that if they agree very quickly or do not have very strong opinions about any of the laws, they should move on to other issues. Focus their attention briefly on *Useful language*, section b. You may choose to drill and practise these phrases in short sentences, or wait until after the task, rather than interrupt the flow of students' thought at this stage. If some groups finish before others, ask them to choose one more topic to discuss, or to prepare how they will summarise their group's opinion.

3 Focus students' attention on *Useful language*, section c. The summarising stage can either be formal, taking everyone's opinion into account, or an opportunity for more free discussion now that students have formulated and rehearsed their views. If students are still very keen to discuss the issues, do not structure this stage too much. If students have less to say, put the emphasis on describing different points of view and reasons for them, and look at useful language points that have come out of the task.

> **Task: alternative suggestions**
>
> a *If you are short of time*: adapt the task in one of the following ways:
> • Set *Preparation: vocabulary* for homework the previous lesson, then start with *Task: speaking*.
> • Do the *Preparation: vocabulary* in one lesson, then get students to prepare their opinions for homework, thinking about any vocabulary they need to express what they feel. In the next lesson, circulate and supply the vocabulary they need, before moving on to *Task: speaking*.
>
> b *If you think your students will find the discussion work difficult for any reason*: adapt the task in one of the following ways.
> • Replace some/all of the issues with ones you know are topical for your students. Present these in the form of provocative statements for students to

agree/disagree with (like the controversial statements in the task).

- Some students, particularly younger ones, may respond better to these issues if they are reformulated in more personal terms, for example:
  If I had incurable cancer, I would want to be able to choose whether or not to die.
  I am / would be happy to do military service for a year or two.

- Some students may have cultural problems with the possible conflict of ideas that this kind of discussion may provoke. In this case, change the focus of the task by asking students to think about all the possible arguments for and against each law (or each group can do this for one or two of the laws). Do the first example together, making a list of points on the board, for example:

  For
  Your life may be completely miserable if you are in terrible pain.
  It is a waste of money to keep people alive who will never get better and who don't want to live.

  Against
  No one has the right to end a human life.
  Relatives or the state may try to persuade people to die for financial reasons.

  Students extend these lists in the group discussion and present them to the whole class. If students want to discuss their own opinions, they can still do this as part of the class discussion at the end of the task.

Reading and vocabulary
(PAGES 118–119)

1 Check that students understand the meaning of *to sue* and *compensation culture*. Discuss the questions as a class.

2 Students work in pairs using their mini-dictionaries before discussing ideas with the whole class. Write students' predictions on the board.

3 Check the meaning of the following: *to twist your ankle*, *to break your ankle*, *a toddler*, *to get rich quick*, *someone's fault*, *spilt*, *a soft drink*, *a payout*. Students work in pairs before checking answers with the whole class. As you check answers, refer back to students' predictions, too.

ANSWERS

Information about the person/people suing	Name/Type of organisa-tion sued	Amount of money they received	Reasons for suing
Roslyn Darch	A furniture store	$780,000	Tripped over a child and broke her ankle
Hundreds of smokers	Tobacco companies	Millions of dollars	Responsible for terminal illnesses developed because of smoking
Overweight New York teenagers	A fast-food company		Not enough warning that their products would make them fat
The parents of a 19-year-old English schoolgirl	A school	€42,000	She didn't get a top grade in her university entrance exam.
Sandra York	Restaurant in Philadelphia	$113,000	Slipped on a spilt soft drink

4 Students discuss the questions in small groups. Encourage them also to talk about any extreme cases they have heard or read about.

Writing (PAGE 119)
Linking words

1 Do a couple of examples together before getting students to do the rest individually or in pairs. If necessary, give examples from the *Language summary* as students do the exercise, rather than waiting until the end. Read through the *Language summary* together as a class while checking answers, particularly the information on word order. Highlight the use of commas, too.

ANSWERS
Similar meaning to *and*: also, besides, what's more
Similar meaning to *but*: although, despite this, however
Similar meaning to *so*: for that reason, as a result, therefore

2 Check the meaning of *to prevent*, *to control your weight*, *unhealthy*, *to be depressed*, *a cure*, *a disease*, *heart disease*, *the common cold*. Do an example together, showing students how they can start with *and*, *but* or *so* to help them choose the right word, and highlighting the punctuation. Elicit different possibilities for b, focusing on punctuation again.

ANSWERS
a • What's more, / Also, / Besides,
   • Despite this, / However,
b • For that reason, / Therefore,
   • What's more, / Also, / Besides,
c • What's more, / Also, / Besides,
   • As a result, / For that reason, / Therefore,
d • Despite this, / However, / although
   • However, / although
e • As a result, / For that reason, / Therefore,
   • However, / Despite this,

If we use *although* we do not need a new sentence or a following comma, as it is a conjunction not an adverb.

3 Either for homework or in class time, students work individually to write about the topics from the task.

Wordspot (PAGE 120)

do

See *Teacher's tips: working with lexis* on pages 9–10.

1 Focus on the diagram and check that students understand the section headings. Students work individually or in pairs/groups before checking answers with the whole class. Drill the phrases as you check them.

> **ANSWERS**
> (*section of diagram in brackets*)
> do badly (d), do your best (d), do a course (a), do economics (at university) (a), do your homework (a), do the ironing (e), do overtime (at work) (b), do the shopping (e), do the washing-up (e), do some work (a/b), do yoga (c)

Note: We have not contrasted *do* with *make* here, but they are contrasted in the *Consolidation* at the end of Module 12.

2 **a** 🔊 [11.5] Explain that students are going to hear twelve questions containing expressions with *do*. Emphasise that students should only write single words or phrases. Pause the recording after each question, explaining if necessary and allowing students time to write.

b Refer students to the tapescript and drill each question before students spend three minutes memorising them.

3 Demonstrate the activity by asking a few students some of the questions. Put students in pairs to ask and answer.

Study ... (PAGE 120)

Checking your written work

1 This activity could be done for homework or in class. If it is done in class time, it could be done as a discussion. Students work in small groups and compare which of the tips they already use and any additional ideas they have (for example, doing their written homework on the computer, and using the spelling and grammar checker).

2 Students do the corrections individually, before checking answers with a partner and then the whole class.

> **ANSWERS AND LANGUAGE NOTES**
> a Relating to study: do a course, do economics (at university), do your homework, do some work
> b Relating to jobs/duties: do overtime (at work), do some work
> c *do* + activity (usually in a class): do yoga
> d Other phrases: do badly, do your best
> e *do* + a domestic task: do the ironing, do the shopping, do the washing-up

> ***Study ...: additional suggestion***
>
> *If your students are enthusiastic about improving their writing skills*: agree on a correction code which you can use to mark their written work. Write one of the texts from exercise 2 and, as you check answers with the class, decide how you could indicate on a piece of homework where the mistake it is and what type of mistake it is, so that students can try to self-correct. For example, write in the margin the following prompts: *word missing, s* (for third-person 's'), *tense, spelling, punctuation.*

Practice ... (PAGE 121)

1 Obligation and permission in the present

If this activity is done in class time, put the sentence halves on to different pieces of card. Students work in pairs to match them.

> **ANSWERS**
> a 2   b 3   c 1   d 4   e 5

2 Obligation and permission in the past

If this activity is done in class time, set it up as a spoken activity. Reveal the sentences one by one. As each sentence is revealed, a student volunteers to put it into the past. The other students decide if they are right or wrong. If they think they are wrong, another student tries. Students write the sentences for further consolidation if necessary.

> **ANSWERS**
> a We weren't allowed to / couldn't take our jackets off.
> b I couldn't understand every word.
> c We had to leave early.
> d We were allowed to invite who we wanted.
> e I didn't have to go to work.

3 Rights and freedom

If this activity is done in class time, students work in pairs. For each pair of sentences which have different meanings, they have to discuss why they are different. Check answers with the whole class.

> **ANSWERS**
> a same
> b same
> c different – the first sentence means you can vote if you want to; the second means that voting is compulsory.
> d different – the first sentence means that you only pay a penalty.
> e same

4 Linking words

If this activity is done in class time, students work in pairs. After choosing the correct alternative, they write a sentence which correctly uses the other alternative. Emphasise that they may need to change the punctuation. Check answers with the whole class.

ANSWERS
a As a result
b Even though
c also
d Besides
e In spite of this
f what's more

5 Presenting your opinions

If this activity is done in class time, write the sentences on the board in two places, including the extra words. Students work in two teams. Reveal the first sentence. A member of each team runs to the board and rubs out the extra word, as directed by their team. The first team to erase the correct word is awarded a point. Reveal the second sentence, and so on.

ANSWERS
a is   b is   c am   d about   e for   f have

6 Phrases with *do*

If this activity is done in class time, set it up as a competition. Students work in pairs. The winning pair is the first correctly to identify the *do* phrases. For a further point, see which pair can correctly identify the verb which collocates with the other phrases (*make*). Finally, see which pair can remember the most other *do* phrases in five minutes. Award one point for each correct phrase. The pair with the most points wins.

ANSWERS
do: the housework, overtime, military service, nothing, some exercise, your best, the ironing

Pronunciation spot

a Students work in pairs, taking turns to say what the different sounds are, and checking the ones that they can't remember in their mini-dictionaries.
b Students work individually or in pairs.
c [11.6] Play the recording, pausing after each word to give students time to decide if they have written the correct symbol and to repeat the word.

alth<u>ou</u>gh	/əʊ/
c<u>a</u>tegory	/æ/
comp<u>e</u>nsation	/e/
d<u>o</u>gs	/ɒ/
gr<u>ee</u>d	/iː/
<u>h</u>arsh	/h/
ha<u>v</u>e	/v/
l<u>i</u>beral	/ɪ/
li<u>b</u>rary	/b/
m<u>u</u>st	/ʌ/
<u>ou</u>ght	/ɔː/
pa<u>th</u>	/θ/
<u>th</u>ere	/ð/
<u>w</u>ashing	/w/

Remember! (PAGE 69)

After looking back at the areas they have practised, students do the *Mini-check* on page 158. Check answers as a whole class, and ask students to tell you their scores out of 20.

ANSWERS
1 We didn't have to
2 are allowed to
3 You should
4 Do I have
5 You aren't allowed
6 You're allowed
7 As a result
8 although
9 Even though
10 Besides
11 also
12 a mess
13 a mistake
14 a suggestion
15 a profit
16 to make
17 make
18 be made
19 making
20 to make

module 12

Dilemmas

Language focus 1 (PAGES 122–123)

could have, *should have*, *would have*

See *Teacher's tips: using a discovery approach in the teaching of grammar* on page 8.

1 **a** Focus students' attention on the photos and the headline of the story. Check the meaning of *tough*, *to row*, *a journey*, *a shift*. Students work individually then compare in pairs before checking answers with the whole class.

> **ANSWER**
> It was a 60-day race over 5,000 km.

b Get students to discuss their ideas with the whole class. Write their guesses on the board.

2 [12.1] Students work in pairs to check the meaning of the words in the box. Refer them to the questions before they listen. When you check answers, discuss which of the students' guesses were closest before going through the comprehension questions.

> **ANSWERS**
> a Andrew was very experienced and had won international competitions; Debra had only learned to row the year before.
> b Andrew suffered from acute anxiety, developing an irrational fear of the ocean.

3 [12.2] Get students to discuss their ideas with the whole class. Write their ideas on the board. Refer students to the questions before they listen to the next part. As you check answers, discuss which of their ideas were closest before going through the comprehension questions.

> **ANSWERS**
> a yes
> b collision with huge oil tankers; sharks; extreme weather conditions; a lack of fresh food
> c around Christmas time, after more than three months alone at sea
> d She unexpectedly met a yacht and was given fresh bread, some biscuits and ten minutes of conversation.
> e 26th January 2002
> f 70 days

4 Students work in pairs to discuss which statements they agree with. Find out which statement most students chose.

Analysis

Students work in pairs before checking answers with the whole class.

> **ANSWER**
> 1 refers to the past; explanation c.
> 2 refers to the past; explanation b.
> 3 refers to an imaginary situation and to the past.

Focus students' attention back on sentences 1 to 3 and point out the constructions used in each case, including the negative forms:

could / should / would + have + past participle.
couldn't / shouldn't / wouldn't + have + past participle

Point out that *would* can be contracted to *'d*.

PRACTICE

1 **a** Check the meaning of the following: *to take a risk, a phobia, risky, to cheat, brave, bravery*. Students work in pairs. If necessary, refer them to the list of irregular verbs on page 155 to check any past participle forms.

b [12.3] Explain that students will just hear the answers, not the complete sentences. Encourage students to listen again if they find it difficult to hear the answers, rather than telling them yourself. Pause after each one to check with the class.

> **ANSWERS**
> 1 should have learned
> 2 wouldn't have entered
> 3 shouldn't have entered
> 4 could have died
> 5 wouldn't have survived
> 6 shouldn't have taken
> 7 would have found
> 8 would have given
> 9 could have attacked
> 10 should have given

Pronunciation

1 Point out the weak pronunciation of *have* and the vowel sound /ə/ in the verbs (/kʊdəv/, /ʃʊdntəv/). Drill the forms as isolated phrases including the negative forms.

2 [12.4] Students listen and practise the phrases. If your students find this difficult, model the phrases yourself, slowly at first and gradually speeding up to normal speech.

2 **a** Check the meaning of *to burgle* and *a vase*. Students
read, then compare in pairs, before checking answers with
the whole class.

> **ANSWERS**
> There was a burglar in the house with a gun. Olivia hit
> him over the head with a vase.

b Students work individually or in pairs to write sentences.
Circulate, supplying vocabulary before checking answers with
the whole class. As you check answers, ensure that students
are using weak forms of *have* and contractions where
appropriate.

> **POSSIBLE ANSWERS**
> She could have phoned the police.
> In my opinion, she shouldn't have gone downstairs.
> In her position, I would have tried to get help.
> Her husband could have been shot.

3 Put students into pairs, A and B. Explain that they will
read about different situations. Refer students to the
relevant pages at the back of the book, and give them five
minutes to read the story and make notes of the main points.
Circulate, explaining vocabulary if necessary.

4 Do this as a speaking activity. Circulate and note down
errors to focus on at the end of the activity.

ADDITIONAL PRACTICE

Workbook: *could have / should have / would have*, page 89

Language focus 2 (PAGES 124–125)

Imaginary situations in the past with *if*

1 Elicit one or two examples of decisions students might
have made recently, or tell students about some of your
own. Check the meaning of *instinct* and *to toss a coin*. Students
discuss the questions in small groups.

2 Check the meaning of: *dice/die, to offer someone a ride,
philosophy, manuscript*. Ask if students have heard of *The
Dice Man* or if they can guess what it is about. Students read,
then compare in pairs, before checking answers as a class.

> **ANSWERS**
> a by throwing dice
> b He introduced himself to his future wife after
>   throwing a die to decide whether or not to stop and
>   offer her a ride in his car.
> c Because he thought he made 'safe' and 'boring'
>   decisions.
> d He was a college professor.
> e His students were fascinated by the idea.
> f an English publisher, Mike Franklyn
> g They thought they were going to die in a storm.
> h some Scottish sailors

3 Even if students are not confident about the 'third
conditional' form, they should be able to attempt this as

they do not need to produce the language. Students work in
small groups to match sentence halves.

> **ANSWERS**
> a 3 b 6 c 2 d 5 e 1 f 4

Analysis

1 Check the meaning of *hypothetical*. Discuss each question in
turn as a class.

> **ANSWERS**
> a hypothetical
> b They all refer to the past. The Past perfect is used
>   (*had* + past participle).
> c Sentences a, b, c and d refer to the past.
>   Sentences e and f refer to the present.

2 Highlight both forms. First write up the following formula to
summarise the 'third conditional'.

past condition (imaginary)	➔	past result (imaginary)
If + Past perfect	+	*would/wouldn't* + *have* + past participle
If he hadn't been bored, (then)		*he wouldn't have started dicing.* (then)

Emphasise that it is not possible to use *would have* after *if*
and that both *had* and *would* can be contracted to *'d*. Leave
this summary on the board to contrast it with the 'mixed
conditional':

past condition (imaginary)	➔	present/general result (imaginary)
If + Past perfect	+	*would/wouldn't* + verb
If the book hadn't been successful, (then)		*he would still be a college professor.* (now)

Emphasise that the use of the verbs here is entirely logical. It
may be useful to translate the 'mixed conditional' to make
this clear. Students may ask you if they can mix the
conditional the other way round (a present/general condition
with a past result). This is also possible, for example:

If I didn't trust you,	*I wouldn't have lent you my car yesterday.*
(now)	(then)

Don't go into this unless students ask specifically. Refer
students to the *Language summary* for further examples of
'conditionals', and to find out about the use of *might* and
could.

Analysis: language notes

Most classes will find this Analysis challenging, so it is
advisable to work though it step by step as a class,
rather than leaving students to work it out for
themselves. We have dealt with 'mixed conditionals', as
well as 'third conditionals' because in most real-life
communicative situations these are found together.
However, your students may not be familiar with 'mixed
conditionals', and may find them difficult at first.

PRACTICE

1 📼 [12.5] Focus students' attention on the photos. Explain that each person had to make a big decision. Before listening, ask students to describe where Erin, Kieron and Margot are; guess how old they are, what jobs they might do, etc; and predict what the decision was in each case. Check the meaning of *company director*, *a nanny*, *to regret something*, *to dream of being something*, *second best*, *to work out well*. Students listen before checking answers in pairs and then as a whole class. As you check answers, find out what your students would have decided in the same situation.

ANSWERS

	Erin	Kieron	Margot
a) What was the decision?	To give up being company director and become a full-time mother	To give up a career as a professional footballer and retrain as a coach	To leave her family, friends and job to live in Greece
b) Why did they make it?	She hated leaving her baby with a nanny.	He broke his leg badly when he was nineteen and continued to have problems with it.	She met Nikos on holiday and really liked him.
c) How are their lives different now?	She has two children and less money than before.	Now he's a coach, but he's lost his dream.	She runs a restaurant on a Greek island with Nikos.

2 Students work individually or in pairs before checking answers as a class. Emphasise that answers will vary slightly if they use *might*.

ANSWERS AND LANGUAGE NOTES
a   hadn't had, would have continued
b   hadn't left, would have spent (*would spend* is also possible*)
c   would/might have*, had stayed, wouldn't be happy*
d   could/might have become, hadn't broken
e   had been able, wouldn't/mightn't have become
f   would/might be*, had fulfilled
g   hadn't gone, wouldn't have met
h   would/might have forgotten, hadn't followed
i   hadn't married, would/might still be living**
j   hadn't moved, would/might still be*

* These sentences use the 'mixed conditional' form as there is a reference to now.
** The continuous form is more natural here.

3 Give one or two personal examples of your own, before getting students to work in pairs/groups. This exercise can either be spoken or written – weaker students can write sentences first before telling other students. Circulate, monitoring and supplying vocabulary.

4 Students spend a few minutes thinking about a big decision they have made. Circulate supplying vocabulary. Students work in pairs to discuss their decisions.

ADDITIONAL PRACTICE

RB **Resource bank:** *Suzie's story* (past sentences with *if* – 'third conditional' and *shouldn't have*), page 157

Workbook: Imaginary situations in the past with *if*, page 91

Vocabulary (PAGES 126–127)
Problems and solutions

See *Teacher's tips: making the most of the* Mini-dictionary on page 12.

1 Focus students' attention on the pictures and ask them what they think they show. Elicit/explain that the pictures show the story of a problem. Point out that the sentences tell the same story, but that they are in the wrong order. Students should first check the words in bold, then order the sentences in pairs. Check answers with the whole class, going over language points relating to phrasal verbs. Drill the sentences both as isolated phrases and as longer sentences.

ANSWERS AND LANGUAGE NOTES
a 8   b 4   c 5   d 1   e 2   f 7   g 3   h 6

The phrasal verbs *think something over*, *talk something over*, *sort something out* and *make up your mind* are separable. With a noun, they can either be separated (*talk your plans over*) or joined (*talk over your plans*), but with a pronoun they must be separated (*talk it over* not *talk over it*)

***Vocabulary*, exercise 1: alternative suggestion**

Do this as a 'disappearing story' in the following way.
• As you check the order of the story, write it out on the board.
• Tell students to close their books and get a student to read the story aloud from the board, correcting pronunciation as necessary.
• Rub out one or two of the phrases in bold in exercise 1, replacing them with gaps.
• Get another student to read the story aloud, filling in the gaps as necessary.
• Repeat the process, removing one or two phrases each time, until all the target phrases are replaced by gaps. (As the reading-aloud stage gets more difficult, it may be necessary to ask other students to help, to keep up the pace.)
• Finally, get students to write out the story from the remaining prompts. Alternatively, they could write a more complete story, explaining what the problem was, either in class or for homework.

2 Students work in pairs to match phrases and definitions.

ANSWERS
a   go away
b   trouble-free

c   sort out
d   didn't have a care in the world
e   suffered sleepless nights
f   sympathetic
g   expert advice
h   helpline
i   came up
j   made up his mind
k   ignore
l   talk it over
m   concerned
n   think it over

3 Give students a few minutes to memorise the phrases and get them to close their books. Elicit/give a few suggestions of what the problem could have been, and put students into pairs to think of the whole story. Circulate, prompting ideas and supplying vocabulary. Get some students to retell the story to the rest of the class or to summarise the problem and solution they came up with. If your students have problems coming up with ideas, put up the following prompts:

He had a very good, secure and well-paid job, but he was bored to death of it. / His debts were getting worse and worse, but he couldn't stop spending money. / He was terribly in love with his boss, a married woman ten years older than himself. / He was terribly jealous of his wife/girlfriend although he had no evidence that she was being unfaithful to him.

ADDITIONAL ACTIVITY

Workbook: Vocabulary: Problems and solutions, page 92

Wordspot (PAGE 127)

think

See *Teacher's tips: working with lexis* on pages 9–10.

1 Do the first one as an example before getting students to work individually or in pairs.

ANSWERS
a 8   b 5   c 7   d 6   e 12   f 3   g 9   h 4
i 11   j 10   k 2   l 1

2 Focus on the diagram and explain the meaning of the category headings. Students work individually or in pairs before checking answers with the whole class. If you have a monolingual class, as you go through the answers, you may find it useful to translate some of the phrases into the students' first language to show that *think* can be used for a number of different verbs. If you do not speak the students' first language, or you have a multilingual class, it should still be possible for students to make the translation.

ANSWERS
(section of diagram in brackets)
What do you think of … ? (a), be thinking of + -ing (b), think the world of someone (d), Just think! (c), think up something (b), think it over (d), I think so (a), think straight (d), think for yourself (b), think back (b), I don't think so (a), I should think (a)

3 Students work in pairs before checking answers with the whole class.

ANSWERS
a   I don't think so.
b   What do you think of … ?
c   are thinking of/about …
d   think up
e   Just think!
f   I think so.
g   I should think
h   think the world of …
i   think straight
j   think for themselves
k   think back
l   think it over

Task: Find solutions to problems
(PAGES 128–129)

See *Teacher's tips: making tasks work* on pages 13–14 and *Responding to learners' individual language needs* on pages 10–11.

Preparation: reading and vocabulary

1 a Introduce the topic by asking students if they ever read problem pages in magazines or on websites, and discuss the following questions as a class:

Why do people write to columns like this? Would you ever write asking for advice? Why? / why not?

Explain that on this website people send in their opinions on someone's problem, rather than a journalist or 'agony aunt' answering.

Students just read the five titles and predict the contents of each letter in small groups. Write students' predictions on the board.

b Students read then check in pairs before going through answers with the class.

2 Students read, then compare answers in pairs, before checking answers as a whole class. As you check answers, make sure that students understand any other important circumstances, as this will affect how well they do the task.

ANSWERS
a 1   b 4   c 5   d 2   e 3   f 1   g 4   h 2   i 3

3 Get students to close their books and work in pairs to summarise each problem.

Task: speaking

1 Give students ten to fifteen minutes to work individually and brainstorm a list of options for each problem. Refer them to *Useful language*, section a. Emphasise that they do not have to give their opinion yet.

2 Put students into small groups. Refer them to *Useful language*, section b, and highlight the use of *I don't think he/she should* for negative opinions. Tell students to make a list of all possible solutions, deciding which they think is the best / the worst. Encourage students to persuade each other of their point of view if there are differences of opinion, but do not insist that they reach a common solution if this is not possible. Circulate, supplying vocabulary. Monitor and note down errors and useful language for correction and analysis later on.

3 Give students a few minutes to prepare what they will report to the class, referring them to *Useful language*, section c. Tell them to list the possible solutions they came up with before saying what they think the person should do. Collect errors and useful language as above.

Task: alternative suggestions

a *If you want to make the task shorter or split it over two lessons*: do one of the following.

- Give students a list of difficult vocabulary from the texts to check in their mini-dictionaries before the lesson.
- Read the problem letters for homework. Check comprehension before going on to *Task: speaking*. (This homework could be combined with the vocabulary work above.)
- Do *Preparation: reading and vocabulary* in one lesson and *Task: speaking* in the next lesson. This would give students plenty of time to think about solutions and how to express them in English. Start the second lesson with a brief opportunity for students to ask you about vocabulary, etc.
- Reduce the number of problems you look at in *Preparation: reading and vocabulary*. These problems have been designed to appeal to a range of ages, but you could omit those that you think your students will have problems relating to.

b *If you have a large class*: in *Task: speaking*, exercise 3, ask one group to volunteer to list their ideas for each problem. Before they give their opinion, ask the other group if they came up with any other possible solutions. After the nominated group has given their opinion, ask the other groups to say what solution they thought was the best.

c *Role play*: as a follow up to the task, get students to act out a conversation between the writer of the problem and a friend who is advising him/her what to do. Feed in some phrases for asking for / giving advice, for example:
I've got a (bit of a / terrible) problem …
I just don't know what to do.
What do you think I should do?
Perhaps you should …
Have you thought about … ?
You should definitely …
Try not to worry so much …
If students role-play different problems, they act out their conversations for the whole class.

Follow up: writing

Give students a few minutes to read through the options and decide which one they would like to do. Students work individually or in pairs. Give them plenty of time to do their piece of writing. Circulate, supplying vocabulary they need and correcting where necessary. When they have finished, get some/all of the students to read out their stories or act out their dialogues. If there is time, follow this up with a correction slot. Students could write a more 'polished' version for homework, incorporating the corrections you have gone over in class.

ADDITIONAL ACTIVITY

RB **Resource bank:** *What should I do?* (giving advice), page 158

Song (PAGE 130)

Out of Reach

1 a Focus students' attention on the photo and discuss the questions as a class.

b Students work in pairs, using their mini-dictionaries if necessary.

2 a Students work in pairs to read and predict the missing words. Ask them if they predicted the type of song correctly.

b 📼 [12.6] Play the song, let students check in pairs, then go through answers as a whole class.

> **ANSWERS**
> I was stupid for a while
> And now I feel like a fool
> Was I ever loved by you?
> I never had your heart
> We were never meant to be
> I could drown if I stay here
> I know I will be okay
> Was I ever loved by you?
> So much hurt, so much pain
> And I hope that in time, you'll be out of my mind
> Was I ever loved by you?
> You never gave your heart
> There's a life out there for me

3 Students work in pairs before checking answers with the whole class.

ANSWERS

Words/Phrases connected with sadness	feel like a fool So confused my heart's bruised despair I could drown so much pain what is lost inside
Words/Phrases connected with happiness	Swept away by you There's a life out there for me

Pronunciation

1 [⏷] [12.7] Students work in pairs, saying the words to help each other hear the vowel sounds, before listening to check. Check answers with the whole class.

ANSWERS

okay	pain
bruised	confused
far	heart
fool	you
see	reach
mind	sign

2 Drill the individual words chorally and individually, then get students to practise saying them in pairs.

Real life (PAGE 131)

Saying goodbye

1 a Focus students' attention on the pictures and, as a whole class, ask them to guess who the people are, where they are and what their relationship is.

b [⏷] [12.8] Play the recording. Students should be able to answer the questions without having any vocabulary pre-taught. Check answers with the whole class.

ANSWERS

father and son
(new) friends
teacher and students

2 Students work in pairs to complete the gaps. Refer them to the tapescript or encourage them to listen again if they have problems. As you check answers, highlight the different degrees of formality and familiarity.

ANSWERS AND LANGUAGE NOTES
(picture number in brackets)

a Sweet dreams. (1)
b Night night. (1)
c I wish you all the very best of luck. (3)
d I'll be off then. (2)
e Take care. (2)
f I'd like to thank you all ... (3)
g See you in the morning. (1)

h I'll see you around. (2)
i It's been great working with you. (3)
j Safe journey! (2)
k Keep in touch. (2)
l Do come and see me. (3)
m I'd better be going. (2)

Highlight the following.
• *Night night* and *Sweet dreams* would usually be said within a family, and especially to small children.
• *I'll be off then, See you around* and *I'd better be going* are informal phrases, for use between friends and colleagues. *See you around* would be said when no arrangement has been made to meet again.
• *Take care, Keep in touch* and *Safe journey*! are neutral phrases.

3 a Put students into pairs and give them a few minutes to decide on a context for their dialogue. Allow fifteen to twenty minutes for students to write and rehearse their dialogue. Circulate, supplying vocabulary and useful language.

b As students perform their dialogues for the class, the other students should guess what the context is. Note down corrections and useful language for analysis at the end.

Consolidation modules 9–12

(PAGES 132–133)

A Past perfect / Reported speech

Tell students that they will read a text about the world's least successful tourist. Before they read, students predict as a whole class what will be in the text.

Check the meaning of the following before students read: *a one-hour stop, modernisation, ancient buildings, to destroy something, to emigrate from somewhere, interpreter*. Students work in pairs before checking answers with the whole class. As you check answers, refer first to the students' predictions to see if any were close. Use the relevant *Language summary* to clarify any problem areas.

ANSWERS

1 decided 2 made 3 had arrived 4 got
5 spent 6 noticed 7 had destroyed 8 told
9 was 10 spoke 11 asked 12 managed
13 had emigrated 14 was able 15 had spent 16 decided 17 tried 18 wasn't 19 refused
20 was 21 had hired 22 didn't speak
23 had gone on 24 drove 25 knew 26 drove

B Possibility, obligation and permission

1 Students work in pairs, checking the meaning of any words they do not know in their mini-dictionaries.

Encourage them to discuss the reasons for their choice of verb form in each case. Check answers with the whole class.

ANSWERS
1 ought
2 have to, don't have to
3 should have
4 aren't allowed
5 didn't have to speak
6 well

C Listening: Hypothetical forms

1 [C1] Explain that students are going to hear three different people talking separately. Check that students understand *venture* and *tournament*. Students listen, then compare answers in pairs, before checking with the whole class.

ANSWERS
a Speaker 3
b Speaker 1
c Speaker 2

2 Put students into small groups and explain that they will have 'control' of the recording. Tell them that they have to listen again and make notes, and can decide when they would like you to press 'pause'. Each time they ask you to pause, make sure that students compare answers within their group. Play the recording again, if necessary.

3 Write each speaker's final sentence on the board. Students work individually and then compare their endings in pairs.

D *make/do/say/tell/think*

1 Make this a competition to see which pair can match the phrases correctly first. Check answers as a whole class.

ANSWERS
make: a suggestion, the difference, a profit, sure, up your mind
do: some exercise, a course, your best, the housework
say: yes, hello, a prayer, sorry
tell: lies, someone what to do, the truth
think: back, straight, the world of someone, something over

2 Put students in pairs. Emphasise that they need to write the dialogue and rehearse it. Circulate so that students can ask you for any vocabulary they need. As students perform their dialogues for the class, the others listen for the phrases from the box. Note down errors and useful language from the dialogues to focus on at the end. One possibility is just to focus on errors relating to phrases with *make*, *do* and *say* or *tell* and *think*.

E Speaking: Agreeing and disagreeing

1 Focus students' attention on the ten statements, and check that they understand them. Check the meaning of *compulsory*, *household chores*, *vegetarian*, *crime doesn't pay*. Students work individually to decide which they agree and disagree with.

2 Explain that students will have to talk about their chosen topics for one minute. Give them five to ten minutes to prepare. Emphasise that they should not write out what they want to say, only make brief notes. Circulate, supplying vocabulary.

3 Students work in groups. After each student has spoken, the others should give their opinions, too.

F Vocabulary: Word puzzle

Put students into pairs and show them the puzzle. Make sure that they understand that each square represents a letter, and that they need the clues (as in a crossword) to complete it. As an example, get one student to read out the first clue, then elicit the answer from the class. Circulate and prompt with extra clues if students are having difficulties.

ANSWERS
1 away   2 therefore   3 gradually   4 improve
5 likely   6 fairy   7 rise   8 mind   9 guilty
10 worse   11 touch   12 increase   13 banned
14 scary   15 talk   16 allowed   17 fraud
18 arrest   19 sort
The hidden message is *You've finished at last*!

Students can now do *Test three: modules 9–12* on pages 167–170.

ADDITIONAL ACTIVITY

RB **Resource bank:** *Preposition challenge* (revision of prepositions), pages 159–160

Resource bank
Index of activities

Activity	Language point	When to use	Time (minutes)
Learner-training worksheet 1	Being an active learner	near the start of the course	25–35
Learner-training worksheet 2	Working with monolingual dictionaries	near the start of the course	25–35
Learner-training worksheet 3	Dictionary skills race	*after Learner-training worksheet 2*	20–25
Learner-training worksheet 4	Learning about new words	near the start of the course	25–35
Learner-training worksheet 5	Recording and remembering vocabulary	near the start of the course	25–35
1A Get to know the *Students' Book*		first day of the course	25–30
1B Who am I?	Expressions of liking and disliking	after *Vocabulary 1*, exercise 3, page 8	20–30
1C Three-person snap	Short answers with *do*, *have*, *be*	after *Practice*, exercise 4, page 7	15–20
1D Vocabulary extension	Phrases for talking about people around you	after *Vocabulary 2*, exercise 3, page 10	25–30
1E Something in common	Present simple and continuous	after *Practice*, exercise 4, page 11	25–35
2A Past tense pelmanism/ What about you?	Irregular Past simple forms	any time in Module 2	15–25
2B Alibi	Past simple and continuous	after *Practice*, exercise 2, page 17	45–55
2C School reunion	*used to, still, not ... any longer / more*	after *Practice*, exercise 2, page 19	30–40
3A The best place in the world	Superlatives (and Present perfect)	after *Practice*, exercise 4, page 27	30–45
3B *100 places to visit before you die*	Vocabulary extension (word building)	after *Reading*, exercise 4, page 28	30–40
3C The City Language School	Recommending and advising	after *Task: speaking*, exercise 3, page 33	25–35
3D How do I get to ... ?	Asking for and giving directions	any time in Module 3	25–35
4A Find someone who ... lied!	Present perfect simple (for experience)	after *Practice*, exercise 3, page 39	20–25
4B How long have you had it?	Present perfect simple and continuous (for unfinished past)	after *Practice*, exercise 2, page 41	20–25
4C What sort of person are you?	Vocabulary extension (word building)	after *Vocabulary 2*, exercise 3, page 42	30–40
5A *Have you got what it takes*?	Vocabulary extension (dependent prepositions)	after *Reading and vocabulary*, exercise 4, page 49	25–35
5B The great diamond robbery	Future clauses with *if, when*, etc.	after *Practice*, exercise 3, page 53	20–35

Activity	Language point	When to use	Time (minutes)
5C Vocabulary extension	Talking about work and training	after *Vocabulary*, exercise 3, page 51	25–35
6A Passive dominoes	Passive forms	after *Practice*, exercise 2, page 64	15–25
6B Vocabulary extension	Passive verbs often in the news	after *Practice*, exercise 2, page 64	30–40
6C Adjective snap	'Extreme' adjectives	after *Vocabulary*, exercise 4, page 65	25–35
7A Vocabulary extension	Informal words and phrases	any time in Module 7	25–35
7B Doonbogs!	Making generalisations	after *Practice*, exercise 3, page 75	30–40
7C What time shall we meet?	Making a social arrangement	after *Real life*, exercise 4, page 77	30–40
8A *Machines behaving badly*	Vocabulary extension (verb–noun collocations)	after *Reading*, exercise 7, page 81	30–40
8B Relative clauses crossword	Defining relative clauses	after *Practice*, exercise 3, page 83	15–25
8C Camping holiday	Quantifiers (*a few, a lot of*, etc.)	after *Practice*, exercise 2, page 85	30–40
9A Election night special	Hypothetical possibilities with *if* ('second conditional')	after *Practice*, exercise 3, page 97	30–40
9B How would your life be different?	Hypothetical possibilities with *if* ('second conditional')	after *Practice*, exercise 3, page 97	15–25
9C Hear … Say!	Ways of saying numbers	after *Real life*, exercise 3, page 100	15–20
9D Vocabulary extension	Talking about numbers, amounts and ages without being exact	after *Real life*, exercise 3, page 100	25–30
10A Ralph and the guitar case	Past perfect, Past simple (Past continuous)	after *Practice*, exercise 2, page 103	20–40
10B Jungle survivors	Reported speech	after *Practice*, exercise 3, page 107	30–45
10C Vocabulary extension	Verbs to use instead of *say*	after *Practice*, exercise 3, page 107	25–30
11A *To sue or not to sue?*	Vocabulary extension	after *Reading and vocabulary*, exercise 4, page 118	20–30
11B In my opinion …	Agreeing and disagreeing	after *Task: speaking*, exercise 3, page 117	25–35
12A Suzie's story	Past sentences with *if* ('third conditional') and *should(n't) have*	after *Practice*, exercise 4, page 125	20–30
12B What should I do?	Giving advice	after *Task: speaking*, exercise 3, page 129	20–30
12C Preposition challenge	Revision of prepositions	at the end of the course	20–30

Instructions

The activities in the *Resource bank* are designed to consolidate and extend material covered in the *Students' Book*. The **first** point at which each activity in the *Resource bank* can be used has been indicated in the index (this has also been indicated at the appropriate point in the teacher's notes). This is to be taken as a guideline only, however – teachers may choose to do an activity in the same class as the practice activities in the *Students' Book,* in the following class as a 'warmer' or 'filler', or after a longer time space as a revision exercise.

For those activities involving cards it is a good idea to invest time in preparing class sets which can be reused again and again. Do this by cutting up the photocopied sheets, sticking each card onto thick paper or cardboard, and then covering them with adhesive film.

Learner-training worksheet 1
(Being an active learner)   *25–30 mins*

You will need: one copy of the worksheet per student

1   Pre-teach difficult phrases and answer any questions on vocabulary students have as they read through the texts. Give students time to absorb the information.
2   Get students to underline first the good habits of each learner, and then the bad habits. Encourage discussion rather than give the 'answers' yourself.
3   Pre-teach any difficult vocabulary before students read the analysis.
4a Handle this discussion sensitively, avoiding any judgemental comments, particularly about individual students. Take a positive attitude to any resolutions they make, encouraging realistic aims students can stick to.
 b Be positive about any suggestions students make. If necessary, bring up important issues yourself (such as homework, and the use of English within the lesson), and suggest that you come to some kind of agreement about them.

Learner-training worksheet 2
(Working with monolingual dictionaries)

You will need: one copy of the worksheet per student

Note: do this worksheet as soon as possible after the beginning of the course. First discuss briefly with students the value of a monolingual dictionary, and find out who has used one before. Strong students can work through the questions in pairs/groups before checking answers with the whole class. With other classes, it may be best to check answers after every question.

1   Check that students understand what a transitive/intransitive verb and a countable/uncountable noun are. Do the first example together.
2   Note that there is no definitive answer for any of these. The aim is simply to illustrate that students do not

always need to understand the definition to grasp the meaning of the word – the example can sometimes be more useful.
3   Students do the exercise individually or in pairs, before checking answers with the whole class.
4   Check that students understand what a preposition, an *-ing* form and an infinitive are. Remind them of the list of irregular verbs on page 155 of the *Students' Book*.
5   Explain the different types of information in the box before students do the exercise individually or in pairs.
6a Make sure that students understand what word stress is and how it is marked. Give more examples of your own if necessary before getting students to do the exercise individually or in pairs.
 b These words have been selected because they only contain one sound which is difficult to transcribe. If you need to teach the phonemic script, it is probably best done in short slots at the beginning of the course, covering four to six sounds per session, and incorporating lots of revision. The emphasis should be on students being able to recognise rather than transcribe the symbols.

Learner-training worksheet 3
(Dictionary skills race)

You will need: one copy of the worksheet per student

This can be done in a separate lesson from *Learner-training worksheet 2* as a useful way of consolidating skills. It can be done in pairs, groups or as a team game. If necessary, add more questions of your own.

Learner-training worksheet 4
(Learning about new words)

You will need: one copy of the worksheet per student

1   Explain the meaning **only** of the words in the box (the point of the exercise is to show that just knowing the meaning is not sufficient to be able to use a word effectively). For discussion point 1, give examples of each type of information, based as far as possible on mistakes students have made forming the sentences.
2a Give a time limit for students to look at the phrases, then ask them to cover them. Provide explanations of the phrases if students ask.
 b Emphasise that students must not look back at the phrases. Students should work individually rather than in pairs, as it is more instructive if they get some of the sentences wrong. The main point of the discussion is that common phrases tend to consist of words that students 'know' individually – they may sometimes have no difficulty in understanding them passively, but producing them correctly is often a different thing.

Learner-training worksheet 5
(Recording and remembering vocabulary)

You will need: one copy of the worksheet per student

1   Go over the different methods to make sure that students see the differences, without commenting on how effective they might be. Give students time to think about the advantages and disadvantages of each one before starting the discussion. During the discussion, avoid saying categorically that any method is always right or wrong – they are probably all appropriate for some types of vocabulary and inappropriate for others. This would be a good point at which to suggest/insist that everyone buys a separate vocabulary notebook. Spend some time together writing new words into the notebook during the next lesson. Remind students to use their vocabulary notebooks at regular intervals and check them whenever possible.

2, 3   Again the emphasis should be on trying out different methods and finding the ones that suit students best individually, rather than prescribing the 'right' one. Encourage suggestions from students and emphasise that they must take active steps of their own if they are to improve, particularly if they are not studying in an English-speaking environment.

1A Get to know the *Students' Book*

You will need: one set of cards for each pair of students

- Shuffle each set of cards. Put students into pairs. Place the sets of cards face down in piles at the front of the class and allocate one set to each pair.
- One student from each pair comes up to the front of the class and takes **one** card only from the top of his/her pile before going back to his/her partner. They write the answer to the question on the card.
- When a pair has completed a card, they take it to the teacher to check the answer. If it is correct, the student keeps the card and takes the next one from his/her pile. If the answer is not correct, he/she must return to his/her partner and find the correct answer.
- The first pair to find all the correct answers are the winners.

1B Who am I?   ✔

You will need: one copy of the worksheet per student

- **Before** giving out copies of the worksheet, write a number at the top for each student in the class. (If you have ten students, for example, write the numbers 1 to 10.) Distribute the worksheets in **random** order.
- Students complete the description for themselves, **without** writing their name. Students work individually and must not look at their classmates' papers.

- Collect the worksheets and shuffle them, before sticking them up round the classroom.
- Students work individually or in pairs reading the numbered descriptions and deciding which student in the class wrote each one. The winner is the student or pair of students who guessed the most correct answers.

1C Three-person snap

You will need: one set of Question cards *and two sets of* Answer cards *for each group of three students*

Students work in groups of three.

- Give student A a set of *Question cards*, face down in a pile. Give students B and C a complete set of *Answer cards* **each**, and tell them to spread them out in front of them, face up.
- Student A turns over the first *Question card* and reads the **question only** out loud. Students B and C try to find the correct *Answer card* as quickly as possible and give it to student A, saying the answer correctly at the same time. The first student to find the correct answer card takes both cards as a 'trick'.
- The student with the most tricks at the end is the winner. Students then do the activity again, with a different student turning over the *Question cards*.

1D Vocabulary extension

You will need: one copy of the worksheet per student

- Exercises 1 and 2: students work individually or in pairs before checking answers with the whole class.
- Exercise 3: make sure that students understand they can make changes to the questions if they want to and give a few examples of possible follow-up questions. Students mingle asking and answering questions before feeding back to the whole class.

1E Something in common

You will need: one set of role cards per twelve students (role cards 1–8 are needed to complete the activity; role cards 9–12 are optional)

- Tell students they are at a party where there are a lot of people they don't know. Elicit the following questions you could ask a stranger at a party: *Do you live near here? / Do you know many people here? / What do you do? / Are you enjoying the party? / What do you do in your spare time?* Pre-teach the expression *Me, too.*
- Give each student a role card and allow time for them to check the information. Students move around the room asking one another the questions above. **The aim of the activity is for the students to find at least four people at the party with whom they have something in common.** As they find them, they write the other students' names on their role card. Encourage students to ask suitable follow-up questions.

2A Past tense pelmanism / What about you?

You will need: one set of cards per three or four students; one copy of the What about you? *worksheet per student*

STAGE 1

- Students work in groups of three or four. Give each group a set of cards and tell them to spread them out in front of them **face down**.
- Each student turns over two cards. If they find a verb and its irregular past tense, they keep the cards as a 'trick' and have another turn. If the cards do not match, they replace them **in exactly the same place**.
- The activity continues until all the cards are matched up. The student with the most tricks is the winner.

STAGE 2

- Give each student a copy of the *What about you?* worksheet. Make sure they write their answers on a **separate** piece of paper **in random order**. They should write single words or short phrases, not complete sentences. Set a time limit of five minutes.
- Students work in pairs or small groups, and swap papers. They ask each other to explain why they have written the items on the paper. Encourage them to find out more information by asking suitable follow-up questions. Students report back to the class on the most interesting things they found out about their partner(s).

2B Alibi

You will need: two Suspect *role cards and two* Police officer *role cards per four students*

- Tell students there was a robbery at the school between 7.00 p.m. and midnight yesterday, and that all the money was stolen from the school safe. The police suspect the students from your class were responsible!
- Divide the class equally into police officers and suspects. (If there is an odd number of students, have more police officers than suspects.) Put the suspects into pairs. Give each pair *Suspect* role card A or B and send them out of the room to prepare their story.
- Put the police in pairs or groups and give them the corresponding *Police officer* role cards. Allow them time to prepare questions.
- When all the students are ready, bring the suspects back into the room. Separate them, and match them with a corresponding police officer. The police officers interview the suspects and make brief notes of the suspects' answers.
- When the interviews have finished, the police officers return to their original pairs/groups and compare notes to see if there are any discrepancies in the suspects' stories. The suspects return to their partners to discuss the answers they gave to the questions, and to see if they made any mistakes.
- The police officers report back to the whole class in turn and say if they think their suspects are guilty or innocent, giving reasons for their decision.

2C School reunion

You will need: one role card and one Find someone who ... *worksheet per student (role cards 1–8 are needed to complete the activity; role cards 9–12 are optional)*

- Tell students that they were all in the same class at Springfield High School fifteen years ago, when they were all seventeen or eighteen years old. Now there is going to be a school reunion, and they are going to meet their old classmates again.
- Give a role card to each student, and allow time for them to read and understand the information.
- Give each student a copy of the *Find someone who ...* worksheet. Students move around the room talking to their old classmates. **The aim of the activity is for them to find at least one person for each of the items on the worksheet.** When they have found someone, they must write down their name and then ask if they still do the same thing now.
- When they have finished, students check their answers in pairs/groups, using *used to*, *still*, and *not ... any longer/more*.

3A The best place in the world

You will need: one copy of the board per three/four students; one dice and three/four counters per group

- Students work in groups of three or four. Give each group a board, counters and dice. If one student has a watch with a second hand, make him/her the timekeeper.
- Students take it in turns to throw a number. When they land on a superlative square, they have to talk about the topic for thirty seconds without stopping. If you have a quiet class, allow each student fifteen seconds' thinking time before speaking.
- If a student cannot think of anything to say or stops talking before the thirty seconds are up, he/she has to move back to the original square. The student who reaches the *Finish* square first is the winner.

3B *100 places to visit before you die* vocabulary extension

*You will need: one copy of the worksheet per student; a set of monolingual dictionaries (**not** the* Mini-dictionary)

- Give each student a copy of the worksheet. Students work through the exercises individually or in pairs before checking answers with the whole class.

3C The City Language School

You will need: one copy of the advertisement per student; enough New student *worksheets for half the class; enough* Old student *worksheets A and B for the other half*

- Give each student a copy of the *Learn English for life* advertisement and ask them to decide on the **two** best things about the school.

- Divide the class into two groups – old students and new students. (If there is an odd number of students in the class, include an extra old student.) Give each new student a copy of the *New student* worksheet. Divide the old students into two groups. Give one group *Old student A* worksheets, and the other group *Old student B* worksheets. Give students time to read and understand the information on the worksheets.
- Pair one new student with one old student. The new student asks the old student for recommendations and advice, and writes brief notes in the first column.
- Rearrange the class so that each new student is talking to an old student who has the other worksheet. The new student again asks for recommendations and advice, and makes notes in the second column.
- When they have finished, allow new students a short time to decide what courses and extra classes they are going to do, etc. While they do this, old students A and B tell each other what advice they gave.
- The new students report back to the whole class on their decisions, giving their reasons.

3D How do I get to … ?

You will need: one copy of the worksheet per student

- Exercise 1: students work individually or in pairs before checking answers with the whole class.
- Exercises 2 and 3: students work in pairs, following the instructions on the worksheet.

4A Find someone who … lied!

You will need: one Liar! *question sheet and four* Liar! *cards per student*

- Give each student a copy of the *Liar! question sheet* and four *Liar!* cards. Check through the prompts on the *question sheet* with the whole class.
- Tell students that they are going to ask one another *Have you ever … ?* questions based on the prompts. Emphasise that they can ask the questions in any order they like.
- When a student is asked a question, he/she can either lie or tell the truth. The student asking the question (student A) is then allowed a maximum of **three** follow-up questions (in the Past simple) to help them decide if the other student (student B) is lying or not.
- If student A thinks the other student is lying, he/she can challenge him/her by holding up a *Liar!* card.
  - If student B **is** lying, he/she has to take the *Liar!* card from student A.
  - If student B is telling the truth, he/she can give one of **his/her** *Liar!* cards to student A.
  - If student B **is** lying, but student A **doesn't** challenge him/her, student B can give student A one of his/her *Liar!* cards.
  - If student B is telling the truth and isn't challenged, then no cards change hands.

- Students move around the class asking one another *Have you ever … ?* questions and try to give away their *Liar!* cards. The winner is the student who has the **least** *Liar!* cards at the end of the activity.

4B How long have you had it?

You will need: one copy of one question card per student

- Give each student **one** question card.
- Tell students they have to find out the answers to the questions on their card. Allow time for them to write down the two questions they will need to ask the other students (for example: *Have you got a best friend?/How long have you known him/her?*).
- Students move around the class asking their questions and making brief notes of their classmates' answers on the back of their cards or in a notebook.
- Students work out the answers to the original questions on their cards and report back to the class. (For example: *Ten students have got a best friend. / Ivan has known his best friend since he was two …*, etc.)

4C What sort of person are you?

You will need: one copy of the worksheet per student

- Exercises 1 and 2: students work individually or in pairs before checking answers with the whole class.
- Exercise 3: get students to walk around the class asking other students the questions. Follow this with a brief feedback session at the end.

5A *Have you got what it takes?* vocabulary extension

You will need: one copy of the Which preposition? *worksheet and one copy of the* Student A *or* Student B *questions per student*

STAGE 1
- Students complete the *Which preposition?* worksheet in pairs without looking at the text.
- Students scan the text to check their answers.

STAGE 2
- Divide the class into two groups. Give one group the list of questions headed *Student A* and the other the questions headed *Student B*. Students fill in the correct prepositions to complete the questions.
- Regroup the students so that one student A is sitting next to one student B. Students take it in turns to ask and answer their questions. Encourage students to ask at least one follow-up question after each answer.
- Students report back to the class on the most interesting answers.

5B The great diamond robbery

You will need: *one copy of the information sheet and one copy of the map per student*

- Give students the map of the National Museum and the accompanying information sheet. Ask them to read the information and locate the items listed.
- Check that the whole class has understood all the points on the information sheet before dividing students into pairs or groups. Each pair/group has to work out a plan to steal the diamond and escape without getting caught. Encourage students to use some future time clauses from the *Useful language* box.
- When all the pairs/groups have decided on their plans, regroup the students and ask them to explain their plans to each other, again using as many future time clauses as possible. Encourage the other students to ask questions and point out difficulties at this stage.
- At the end of the activity, the students decide which of the plans they have heard is the best. Students can write out their plan for homework.

5C Vocabulary extension

You will need: *one copy of the worksheet per student*

- Exercise 1: students work individually or in pairs before checking answers with the whole class.
- Exercise 2: students read through the advertisement – make sure that they understand what a reporter is and what the job involves. Divide the class into two groups – students A and B, and get them to look at the information on the relevant role card. They spend about five minutes preparing what they are going to say in the interview. Supply vocabulary as necessary.
- Put students into A-and-B pairs (if you have an uneven number of students, put two interviewers together). Students conduct their interviews before feeding back to the class on whether the candidate got the job.

6A Passive dominoes

You will need: *one set of dominoes for each pair of students*

- Students work in pairs. Give one set of dominoes to each pair, and ask them to share them out equally.
- One student places a domino on the desktop between them, and the other student has to make a complete sentence by placing one of his/her dominoes at either end of the first domino. The students then take it in turns to put down their dominoes at either end of the domino chain.
- If one student thinks a sentence is not correct, he/she can challenge the other student. If the students cannot agree, they should ask you to make a final decision.
- If the sentence is incorrect, the student has to take back the domino and miss a turn. If a student cannot make a sentence, the turn passes to his/her partner.

- The game continues until one student has used up all his/her dominoes, or until neither student can make a correct sentence. The student who finishes first, or who has the fewest dominoes left, is the winner.

6B Vocabulary extension

You will need: *one copy of the worksheet per student*

- Exercises 1, 2 and 3: students work individually or in pairs/groups before checking answers with the whole class.
- Exercise 4: students work in pairs/groups writing their articles. Go round helping/supplying vocabulary as necessary. When they have finished, the articles can be read out or put up round the classroom.

6C Adjective snap

You will need: *one set of adjective cards and one copy of the* Questionnaire *per student*

STAGE 1

- Students work in groups of three. If there are extra students, have one or two groups of four.
- Give each student a complete set of adjective cards. Student A places his/her cards **face down in a pile** in front of him/her, while students B and C lay their cards out **face up** in front of them.
- Student A then turns over the cards one at a time, saying the word on the card as he/she places it down on the desk. Students B and C have to look through their own cards as quickly as possible to find the matching adjective. (For example, if student A turns over *angry*, students B and C have to look through their cards for *furious*.)
- The first student to place the matching card on top of the adjective card takes the 'trick'. The winner is the student who gets the most tricks.
- Students then change over so that someone else is student A, and play the game again.

STAGE 2

- Give each student a copy of the *Questionnaire*. Students work individually and fill in the gaps with a suitable gradable or extreme adjective.
- Students then work in pairs and ask each other the questions. Encourage students to ask suitable follow-up questions where appropriate.
- Students report back to the class on the most interesting things they found out about their partners.

7A Vocabulary extension

You will need: *one copy of the worksheet per student*

- Students work through the exercises individually or in pairs before checking answers with the whole class. Supply vocabulary for exercise 3 as necessary, before getting students to act out their dialogues.

7B Doonbogs!

You will need: one copy of the worksheet per student

- Students work in pairs or groups. Give each student a copy of the worksheet, and ask them to read the introduction and the letter from the Earth President. Check they understand what kind of information they need to collect. Allow students time to gather ideas for their report from the pictures before they start.
- Students write the report in pairs/groups. Encourage them to use language for making generalisations in each sentence of their report.
- Collect the reports and put them up round the classroom. Students walk around the class reading the reports and deciding which they think is the best.

7C What time shall we meet?

You will need: twice the number of role cards as students in the class (if possible colour-code each set to prevent them getting mixed up)

- Students work in pairs and sit back to back. Give each pair of students matching role cards, and allow them a minute or two to read the information.
- Students act out the role play in their pairs and try to arrange a time and place to meet.
- When they have finished each role play, collect the role cards from them and give them another pair.

8A *Machines behaving badly* vocabulary extension

You will need: one copy of the matching worksheet and one copy of the Student A or Student B questions per student

STAGE 1

- Students complete the first matching exercise in pairs without looking at the text.
- Students scan the text to check their answers.

STAGE 2

- Students work in pairs to find the collocations and cross out the incorrect nouns, checking in English–English dictionaries, if necessary.

STAGE 3

- Divide the class into two groups. Give one group the list of questions headed *Student A*, and the other the questions headed *Student B*. Students fill in the verbs in the correct forms to complete the questions.
- Regroup the students so that one student A is sitting next to one student B. Students take it in turns to ask and answer their questions. Encourage students to ask at least one follow-up question after each answer.
- Students report back to the class on the most interesting answers.

8B Relative clauses crossword

You will need: a copy of each crossword for each pair of students

- Divide the class into two groups, A and B. Give a copy of the *Student A* crossword to students in group A, and a copy of the *Student B* crossword to those in group B.
- Students work together in their separate groups to check they know the meaning of the words on their half of the crossword. (All the vocabulary is taken from Modules 1–7 of the *Students' Book*.)
- Put students in pairs, so that one student A and one student B are working together. They are not allowed to look at each other's crossword.
- Students take it in turns to describe the words that appear on their half of the crossword to their partner, using defining relative clauses (*It's a place where you ...*, *This is a person who ...*, etc.). The partner has to guess the words, and write them in his/her own crossword.
- Students continue until they both have a completed version of the crossword.

8C Camping holiday

You will need: one copy of the Student A worksheet or one copy of the Student B worksheet per student

- Put students into pairs and give one student a copy of the *Student A worksheet* and the other a copy of the *Student B worksheet*. Allow time for students to read and understand the information.
- Students work in pairs, telling each other what they've got in their rucksack and commenting on their partner's choices, using the expressions from the *Useful language* box. **The aim is for students to make a list of what they decide to take with them.**
- When they have finished, students compare their list with other students' lists and comment on them using expressions from the *Useful language* box.

9A Election night special

You will need: one copy of the worksheet for each group of students

- Tell students there is going to be a national election. As well as the main political parties, there are also a number of 'fringe' parties, who are very unlikely to be elected, but are standing nevertheless.
- Put students into groups of three or four. Assign each group a political party from this list (or add your own): *The Animal Lovers' Party, The Sleep Party, The Sports Party, The Television Addicts' Party, The Fit and Healthy Party, The 'I hate English' Party.*
- Give each group a copy of the *Election manifesto* worksheet. Students decide what their party's policies are for each section, and finish the sentences on their manifesto using imaginary conditionals. Remind students to make their policies fit the overall aim of their party. Put the completed manifestos up round the class.

- One representative of each party stands beside their own manifesto, while the other students move round the class to read the other parties' manifestos. As they read, students ask the 'party representative' about aspects of policy they disagree with or don't understand, using imaginary conditionals where possible.
- At the end of the activity, the students vote for the party they think has the best manifesto (students cannot vote for their own party).

9B How would your life be different?

You will need: one copy of one question card per student

- Give each student a card and allow them time to complete the question.
- Students move around the class and ask each other their questions. At the end of the activity, students report back to the class on the most interesting or unusual answers to their questions.

9C Hear … Say!

You will need: one copy of each grid per group of three students

- Put students into groups of three and give each student in the group a copy of one of the grids. (If not all students can work in groups of three, put some of them in pairs to work together on one of the number grids.)
- Tell students that they have to listen to the numbers their partners say and find them in the *Hear* column on the grid. They then have to say the corresponding number in the *Say* column for the other students to listen and recognise. Demonstrate this first yourself, if necessary.
- When they have finished, get them to change over grids so that they are hearing and saying different numbers.

9D Vocabulary extension

You will need: one copy of the worksheet per student

- Exercise 1: students work individually or in pairs before checking answers with the whole class.
- Exercise 2: put students into pairs. They ask/answer the questions on their cards before feeding back any interesting information to the rest of the class.

10A Ralph and the guitar case

You will need: one set of Skeleton story cards *and one set of* Extra information cards *per group/pair*

- Divide students into pairs or groups, and, if possible, ensure that they have a large area to work in (on the floor, for example). Give each pair or group a set of *Skeleton story cards* and ask them to arrange the cards **in alphabetical order** in a column in front of them, card A at the top of the column.
- Give each pair or group a set of *Extra information cards*. These should be placed face down in a pile in front of them, **in number order**, with number 1 at the top.

- Students turn over the cards **one at a time** and try to fit them in a logical place in the story by placing them either side of the column of *Skeleton story cards*. Remind students to focus on the narrative tenses used and the punctuation. If they cannot fit the card into the story, they put it back at the bottom of the pile.
- When students have finished, they can move round the room and compare their stories with other groups.
- Students can write the end of the story for homework.

10B Jungle survivors

You will need: one copy of the newspaper article per student; one set of role cards for each pair of students

- Give each student a copy of the newspaper cutting and check they have understood the main points.
- Divide the class into two groups and give one group the *Reporter's role cards* and the other the *Survivor's role cards*. (If there is an odd number of students, include an extra reporter.) Students prepare questions and answers for the role play, following the instructions on the cards.
- Rearrange the class so that each reporter can interview a survivor individually. The reporters will need to take brief notes at this stage, in order to report back later.
- At the end of the interviews, rearrange the class so that each reporter is sitting with another reporter who was **not** his/her original partner. Place each survivor with another survivor who was **not** his/her original partner.
- The reporters and survivors tell their new partners what was said in their interviews, using reported questions and statements.
- The reporters write the article for the *Daily Planet*, while the survivors write a letter to a member of their family telling them about the interview.

10C Vocabulary extension

You will need: one copy of the worksheet per student

- Students work through the exercises individually or in pairs, before checking answers with the whole class.

11A *To sue or not to sue?* vocabulary extension

You will need: one set of cards for each pair of students; a set of monolingual dictionaries (optional)

PROCEDURE 1

- Shuffle each set of cards. Put students into pairs. Place the sets of cards face down in piles at the front of the class, and allocate one set of cards to each pair.
- One student from each pair comes up to the front of the class and takes **one card only** from the top of their pile. They go back to their partner, read the question and write the answers **on their card**, referring to the *To sue or not to sue?* text or an English–English dictionary to find the answers.

- When a pair has completed a card, they take it to the teacher at the front of the class to check the answers. If the answers are correct, the student keeps the card and takes the next card from his/her pile at the front of the class. If the answer is not correct, the student has to return to his/her partner and find the correct answer.
- The first pair of students to finish all the cards are the winners.

PROCEDURE 2

- If it is not possible for your students to move around the class freely, follow the following procedure:
  - Put students into pairs and give each pair a set of cards face down in a pile. Students turn over the cards one by one and write the answers on the cards.
  - When a pair has finished, they hand their pile of cards to the teacher for checking. The teacher gives back the cards which are not correct and the students correct their mistakes. The first pair of students to finish all the cards are the winners.

11B In my opinion ...

You will need: one copy of the board per three or four students; one set of Opinion cards *for each group; one die and three/four counters per group*

- Put students into groups of three or four, and give each group a game board, a set of *Opinion cards*, counters and a die. Tell a student to shuffle the *Opinion cards* before putting them face down in a pile in the centre of the board. If one student has a watch with a second hand, make him/her the timekeeper for the group.
- Explain the code on the *Opinion cards*:
  - \+   means *I strongly agree*
  - +/– means *I'm not sure*
  - –   means *I strongly disagree*
- Students take it in turns to throw a number. When they land on a square with a sentence on it, they pick up an *Opinion card*. They then have to talk for thirty seconds about the sentence they have landed on. They **must** begin with an expression for agreeing and disagreeing which matches their card, and then continue by giving reasons to support this opinion.
- When they have finished talking, they put the *Opinion card* at the bottom of the pile on the board.
- If the student cannot think of anything to say, or stops talking before thirty seconds are up, he/she has to move back to his/her original square. (If you have a quiet class, allow each student fifteen seconds' thinking time before speaking.) The student who reaches the *Finish* square first is the winner.

Note: If you think your class would have difficulty in thinking of ideas to support a point of view that is not their own, the above procedure can be simplified by doing the activity **without** the *Opinion cards*. When they land on a square they have to give their **own** opinion on the topic, starting with an expression for agreeing or disagreeing and continuing for thirty seconds. Again, allow fifteen seconds' thinking time before speaking, if necessary.

12A Suzie's story

You will need: one set of cards for each pair of students

- Put students in pairs and give each pair a set of cards. Tell students to put them in the correct order. Check answers with the whole class.
- Students then take it in turns to make a sentence using a past conditional form and/or a sentence with *should(n't) have* for each card in the story. For example, for card I: *If Suzie hadn't wanted to be a musician, her father wouldn't have given her a guitar*; for card E: *She shouldn't have spent so much time practising. She should have done her school work too.*
- Students continue making sentences alternately for the rest of the story.

12B What should I do?

You will need: one set of problem cards for each group

- Put students in groups and give each group a set of problem cards, which they place face down in a pile in front of them.
- Students take it in turns to turn over a card. They explain their problems to the group, and the other students have to give advice.
- The student with the problem then decides which of his/her classmates has given the best advice, and gives him/her the problem card. The student who collects the most problem cards is the winner.
- Students report back to the class on the best or worst piece of advice they received.

12C Preposition challenge

You will need: one set of Preposition cards *and one set of* Sentence cards *per three or four students*

- Put students into groups of three or four. Give each group a set of *Preposition cards* and ask them to distribute the cards equally among themselves. Tell them to hold them so that nobody else can see them.
- Give each group a set of *Sentence cards* and ask them to place the cards in front of them face down in a pile.
- Student A turns over the top card. If he/she has the correct preposition amongst his/her *Preposition cards*, he/she puts it down next to the sentence.
- If the other students agree that the preposition is correct, the cards are put to one side and removed from the game. If the preposition is not correct, the student has to take back the card and the next person may put down a preposition.
- Students take it in turns to turn over a *Sentence card* and put down a *Preposition card*. If a student does not have the correct *Preposition card*, he/she must pass.
- The winner is the person who gets rid of all his/her *Preposition cards* first, or who is left with the fewest *Preposition cards* at the end of the game.

103

Learner-training worksheet 1

Being an active learner

1 Read about three different students of English below and number them 1–3 according to how successful you think they will be in learning English (1 = most successful, 3 = least successful).

BERNARD

Bernard takes learning English very seriously. He's particularly keen on English grammar – he spends many hours at home studying grammar books and doing exercises. In class, he always has lots of questions for his teacher – in fact he knows so much about grammar that sometimes his teacher finds it hard to answer! Bernard is also keen to learn vocabulary – he always has his bilingual dictionary next to him in class, and looks up any new words he meets. He prefers this to listening to the teacher's explanations, because he likes to have an exact translation of things. At home, as well as doing his homework and studying his grammar books, he spends twenty minutes every day studying lists of new vocabulary that he has learnt. He quite enjoys his English lessons, but he feels that his teacher wastes too much time on group work. He doesn't like speaking to other students – they don't speak English well enough, and he doesn't like making mistakes that the teacher can't correct. So usually during these parts of the lesson, he reads one of his grammar books, or looks through the dictionary – he feels he's learning more this way. ☐

GABRIELA

Gabriela really enjoys her English lessons, though she's very busy in her job and doesn't always have enough time to study. She likes her teacher and her classmates, and enjoys speaking English, both with the teacher and with other students. She always tries to say as much as she can, even if the topic is not something that really interests her – it's still good practice. If there's something she wants to express or doesn't understand, she asks her teacher for the right word. She tries to correct herself and to use new words that she has learnt, but she doesn't worry too much if she makes mistakes. She knows she often gets things wrong, but she believes that you have to make mistakes in order to learn. Gabriela's fairly good at grammar – when she meets new grammar, she tries to work out the rules for herself, but of course she's not always right! Outside her lessons she doesn't always manage to do all her homework, but she does try to do it as carefully as possible, reading it through, and trying to correct the mistakes before she hands it in. Apart from that, she sometimes gets the chance to practise her English at work, when she meets English-speaking colleagues from the international offices of her company. She really enjoys this and makes a special effort to chat to them, even if she sometimes feels a bit shy about the level of her English! ☐

GLORIA

Gloria doesn't really know why she's learning English, but perhaps it'll be useful some day. Anyway, her parents are paying a lot of money for her lessons so, as she sees it, it's her teacher's job to make sure that she learns. She tries to come to most of the lessons, but she's generally a bit late because she's been out dancing the night before, and when she does arrive, she often isn't feeling too good. Her teacher always explains new vocabulary and grammar in English, but Gloria doesn't usually listen very hard to these parts of the lesson – her friend Monica speaks much better English than she does, so she normally asks her to translate what the teacher's said. Sometimes the teacher asks her questions and expects her to answer in English, but the questions often don't interest her much, and anyway she's a bit shy about speaking English, so she usually just answers in one word, or looks at the floor until the teacher asks someone else. They have to do quite a lot of group work in her class too, but for Gloria this is a good chance to find out what her friends have been doing, so they usually have a good chat – not in English, obviously! ☐

 PHOTOCOPIABLE

2 Compare answers with other students. Make a list of the habits and attitudes that you think will/won't make each student successful, and discuss the reasons why.

3 Read an analysis below of how successful the three students are likely to be. Were you surprised by anything you read?

What are their chances of success?

Both Bernard and Gabriela have some very positive attitudes. In particular they take an active approach to their studies – they understand that they will only progress if **they** take responsibility for learning. Their teacher cannot 'wave a magic wand' over them and make them learn English!

Bernard spends a lot of time studying outside the lesson, which is very good, and asks lots of questions, which is also good. Nevertheless, he may not be spending his time in the best possible way – of course, grammar and vocabulary are important, but just as important is to **use** what you know, whether in the classroom during groupwork, or outside. Perhaps he should take his nose out of his grammar books sometimes and go and see a film in English or, if possible, try to meet some English-speaking people.

In the end, Gabriela may actually be more successful than Bernard for this very reason. Although she feels that she doesn't spend enough time studying at home, she has a very positive attitude during lessons. She takes every opportunity to speak, asking for the words she needs to express what she wants to say, and trying to use the best English she can without worrying too much if she makes mistakes. She should do very well.

As for Gloria – what is there to say? Her English is never going to improve unless she changes her attitude! She may have a busy social life, but at least she could make better use of her time during her lessons! If she tries to answer questions in more than three words, starts listening to her teacher instead of her friend and makes an effort to speak English rather than her own language, she should soon enjoy her classes more, become a lot more confident **and** start to make some progress!

4 Discuss the following questions in pairs, or think about them individually.

a The article mentions the importance of an 'active approach' to learning. Is there anything you could do to take a more active approach? Make three 'resolutions' to help you to become a more successful learner of English – but remember to be realistic about what you can do!

b Are there any ways in which you would like your teacher to help you?

Learner-training worksheet 2
Working with monolingual dictionaries

The following exercises are all based on the *Cutting Edge Mini-dictionary*, but other monolingual dictionaries are organised in a similar way (for example, the *Longman Active Study Dictionary* and the *Longman Essential Activator*). The main difference is that our mini-dictionary only contains words and meanings that appear in the *Students' Book*, so it is much shorter than other monolingual dictionaries.

1 ABBREVIATIONS

Match the abbreviations in column A with a grammatical term in column B. Then write the correct abbreviation next to the words below. Use your mini-dictionary to check if necessary.

A	B
adj	uncountable noun
adv	transitive verb
n C	adjective
n U	adverb
v T	intransitive verb
v I	countable noun

a baggage ....   e naturally ....
b accident ....   f keen ....
c display ....   g matter ....
d housework ....   h wander ....

2 DEFINITIONS AND EXAMPLES

Look up the words below in your mini-dictionary, reading both the definitions and the examples. Then answer the following questions for each word.

- Do you understand from the mini-dictionary definition what it means?
- What helped you most – the definition, the example or both?

a deny *v* T   b invent *v* T   c available *adj*   d hopefully *adv*

3 WHEN A WORD HAS MORE THAN ONE DEFINITION

The words underlined in the following sentences have more than one definition in the mini-dictionary. Look up the words and write the number of the mini-dictionary definition which is being used in this example.

a Ali and Martin are such a friendly couple. ☐
b Jamie's party the other night was brilliant – it's a shame you couldn't come. ☐
c Lily's getting on well in her new job now. ☐
d I had a long chat with your mum the other day – she's really nice. ☐
e Give me a ring when you get home so that I know you're safe. ☐

4 USING THE DICTIONARY TO FIND GRAMMATICAL INFORMATION

In a monolingual dictionary you can find information about:
- **irregular verb forms**
- the correct **preposition** to use after a word
- whether a word is followed by a **gerund** or an **infinitive**
- **common mistakes** that foreign learners make when they use the word.

© Pearson Education Limited 2005   PHOTOCOPIABLE

There is a mistake in each of the following sentences. Look up the words <u>underlined</u> in your mini-dictionary, and use the information you find to correct the mistakes.

    a Robert <u>finded</u> a stranger standing in his kitchen.
    b Can you get the manager, please? I want to <u>complain of</u> the service!
    c I'm really <u>looking forward to go</u> on holiday next month.
    d Please can you <u>explain me</u> the homework again?

5 EXTRA INFORMATION YOU CAN FIND IN THE DICTIONARY

In a monolingual dictionary you can find extra information about:
- **common phrases** and **word combinations** with a word
- important **related words**
- important differences between **British** and **American English**
- whether a word or phrase is **formal** or **informal**, or only used in **special situations**.

Use the information in your mini-dictionary to answer the following questions.

    a If you look up *agency*, which common types of *agency* does the mini-dictionary give you?
    b If you look up *market*, which common phrase do you find?
    c If you look up *boiling*, what related word do you find?
    d What is the American word for a *sales assistant*?
    e If you look up *guy*, what do you find out about the way people use it?
    f If you look up *love-lorn,* what do you notice about the way it is used?

6 USING THE DICTIONARY TO FIND OUT ABOUT PRONUNCIATION

a) Word stress is marked like this in the mini-dictionary:

      agree /əˈgriː/ *v*

Look up the the following words in the mini-dictionary and underline the stressed syllable, as in the example.

    For example: a<u>gree</u>

    • cathedral   • meanwhile   • percent   • populated

b) The mini-dictionary also gives you the phonemic spelling of a word. (If you do not know the phonemic symbols, there is a pronunciation table on the inside front cover of the mini-dictionary to help you.) Use the mini-dictionary to find the pronunciation of the following words.

    • guilty *adj*   • bow *v* I   • knife *n* C   • fall *v* I

    © Pearson Education Limited 2005

Learner-training worksheet 3

Dictionary skills race

Work in pairs. Answer the following questions using your mini-dictionary as quickly as possible. (You **must** use your mini-dictionary to check even if you think you know the answer!) The first pair to finish are the winners!

Race:
TEST YOUR DICTIONARY SKILLS!

1 Look up the word <u>underlined</u> to find the mistake in this sentence.

• My brother always makes his <u>homework</u> before he has dinner.   *(1 mark)*

2 Use your mini-dictionary to find out:

a what a *campaign* is   *(1 mark)*
b two types of *campaign*.   *(2 marks)*

3 Use your mini-dictionary to complete the following common expression with *average*.

• .... average, we sell fifty cars a week.   *(1 mark)*

4 Look up the phonemic spelling of *rise* in your mini-dictionary and circle the word below which it rhymes with.

• nice   • prize   • niece   *(2 marks)*

5 What is the American English spelling of *neighbour*?   *(1 mark)*

6 Which syllable is stressed in the following words? <u>Underline</u> it.

• increase *v* I, T   • increase *n* U   *(2 marks)*

7 Use your mini-dictionary to choose the correct form in the following sentence.

• He insisted *to see / on seeing* the hotel manager.   *(1 mark)*

8 Use your mini-dictionary to find two words related to *cousin*.   *(2 marks)*

9 Use your mini-dictionary to complete the gap in the following sentence.

• Well, I'm not really sure – it depends .... the individual situation.   *(1 mark)*

10 Use your mini-dictionary to find the Past simple and past participle of the irregular verb *leap*.   *(1 mark)*

TOTAL 15 MARKS

Learner-training worksheet 4

Learning about new words

1 WHAT YOU NEED TO KNOW ABOUT NEW WORDS TO USE THEM

If necessary, check the meaning of the following words with your teacher. Then make sentences with the words, using the prompts and completing the gap in d.

suggest	improve	jealous	mug	bring up

a Jack / jealous / his younger brother
b I suggest (you) / take / the fast train / 9.45
c Your school work / show / a big / improve
d Last month a twenty-year-old man / assassinate .... *(write in who)*
e After / his parents / die / Pete's grandparents / bring / him up

---

Discussion point 1
Read out to your teacher the sentences that you wrote for him/her to correct. In which of the following areas did you need more information before you could use these words properly?
• pronunciation / word stress
• irregular forms
• other forms of the word (for example, the noun/adjective form)
• prepositions that follow the word
• the grammatical construction that follows the word
• when you can/cannot use this word.
Where can you get this information?

---

2 PHRASES AND WORD COMBINATIONS

a) Look quickly at the phrases at the bottom of the page to check that you understand the meanings. If necessary, ask your teacher about any of the phrases that you do not understand.

b) Complete the gaps in the following sentences with one of the phrases in the correct form (do **not** look back at the phrases). Do this as quickly as possible.

1 If you need to buy some new clothes, you ....
2 If children want to do well at school, they need to ....
3 If you don't want to eat at home, you can ....
4 If you walk round a strange town without a map, you might ....
5 When people grow up / get married, they normally ....
6 If you are rude or unkind to anyone, you should ....
7 If you're tired, it's a good idea to ....

Discussion point 2
• Were you able to use accurately all the phrases that you 'knew' at the beginning or not?
• If not, what kind of mistakes did you make? Why was this?
• How can you remind yourself of these points when you write down phrases and word combinations like these?
• What do you think is the best way to remember phrases like these?

---

have a rest   make up your mind   eat out   homework
get lost   go shopping   move house   leave school   tell the truth   say sorry   do your

Learner-training worksheet 5

Recording and remembering vocabulary

1 DIFFERENT WAYS OF RECORDING VOCABULARY

Look at the following ways that students use for recording new vocabulary and discuss the questions in the box below.

a

divorce rate — percentuale di divorzi

get married — sposarsi

average — medio

career — carriera

bother with — preoccuparsi di

b

do the housework

entertain friends

chat on the phone

c

A *acquaintance*
aunt
average

B *best friend*
blond hair
boss

C *career*
chat
classmate

d

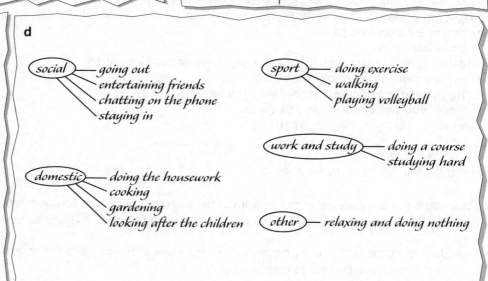

social — *going out*
entertaining friends
chatting on the phone
staying in

sport — *doing exercise*
walking
playing volleyball

work and study — *doing a course*
studying hard

domestic — *doing the housework*
cooking
gardening
looking after the children

other — *relaxing and doing nothing*

e

divorce rate –	dɪvɔːsreɪt	*number of divorces over a certain time*
acquaintance –	əkweɪntəns	*someone you know, but not a friend*
entertain (friends) –	entəteɪn	*invite people to your house and give them food and drink*
chat –	tʃæt	*have a conversation with a friend*

Discussion point 1
- Do you have a special notebook for recording new words and phrases?
- Which of the methods above do **you** use for recording new words and phrases?
- What do you think are the advantages and disadvantages of each one?
- How useful is it to copy out new words and phrases into your vocabulary notebook **after** the lesson?

2 DIFFERENT WAYS OF REMEMBERING VOCABULARY

a) Here are some different methods language students sometimes use for remembering new words and phrases. Read them, and then answer the questions in the box below.

- repeating the new words over and over again to yourself
- writing new words out three or four times
- inventing sentences / short dialogues in your head, using the new words
- testing yourself by covering up the words and using the definitions/translations to remind you of the word
- using cards with the new word on one side and the meaning on the other to test yourself
- making lists of related new words (for example, 'family vocabulary') and sticking it up on the wall in your house
- reading through your vocabulary notes for ten minutes every day
- selecting the new words that you personally find useful and only trying to learn these

Discussion point 2
- Have you ever tried any of these methods?
- Do you have any other methods for learning vocabulary not included on the list?
- Do you have any suggestions for your teacher about how he/she could help you to remember vocabulary (for example, by giving you vocabulary tests)?

b) Choose one of the methods of study listed above and try it out for the next week or two. Report back to the class on how useful you found it.

3 EXTENDING YOUR VOCABULARY BY YOURSELF

Here are some different ways that you can improve your vocabulary by yourself. Read them, and then answer the questions in the box below.

- reading books in English, including graded readers (such as the *Penguin–Longman Readers*)
- reading an English-language newspaper or magazine
- watching English-language films with subtitles
- finding out the words to English-language songs
- watching an English-language cable TV channel
- listening to the radio in English (the BBC World Service or local English-language radio programmes)
- getting an English penfriend

Discussion point 3
- Do you do any of these things already? How useful do you find them for improving your vocabulary?
- Do you have time to start doing any of these things? If so, which appeals to you most?
- If you do these things, how important do you think it is that you understand and study every new word that you meet?
- Can you tell the other students about any places or facilities that might be useful in your area (for example, a cinema that shows subtitled films, or a library that has English-language magazines)?

1A Get to know the *Students' Book*

A

How many **Language focus** sections are there in Module 1?

....

B

On what page is the **Language summary** for Module 6?

....

C

On what page is there a list of **irregular verbs**?

....

D

How many **Pronunciation** boxes are there in Module 2?

....

E

On what pages are the **tapescripts** for the listening exercises for Module 9?

....

F

What's the title of the **revision section** at the end of each module?

....

G

Where can you find a **pronunciation table**?

....

H

What colour is the **Useful language** box in Module 7?

....

I

How many **Consolidation** sections are there in the *Students' Book*?

....

J

On what page is the **Mini-check** for Module 3?

....

K

What colour are the **Analysis** boxes in Module 10?

....

L

What word is studied in the **Wordspot** in Module 4?

....

M

On what page is there a **map of Thailand**?

....

N

In which module do you study **past sentences with *if***?

....

O

Which module includes pictures from a ghost story called **The Guests**?

....

P

In which module do you decide how to spend **lottery money**?

....

1B Who am I?

Expressions of liking and disliking

Who am I?

Student number ☐

I really love .... ,

and I'm really into ....

I'm quite good .... ,

but I'm not very good ....

I don't spend much time .... ,

and I'm not really interested ....

I spend a lot of time .... ,

and I know quite a lot about ....

I spend too much time .... ,

and I don't have enough time for ....

I don't know anything about .... ,

and I absolutely hate .... !

1C Three-person snap

Short answers with *do*, *have*, *be*

Am I late? (**Answer:** *No, you're not.*)	Does your mother cook dinner every night? (**Answer:** *No, she doesn't.*)	Have your parents been to the United States? (**Answer:** *Yes, they have.*)
Are your parents very rich? (**Answer:** *No, they aren't.*)	Did you go abroad last year? (**Answer:** *No, I didn't.*)	Has your father got a new car? (**Answer:** *Yes, he has.*)
Have you got a dog? (**Answer:** *No, I haven't.*)	Is your brother older than you? (**Answer:** *Yes, he is.*)	Do you like getting up early? (**Answer:** *Yes, I do.*)
Has your sister lived in Germany for a long time? (**Answer:** *No, she hasn't.*)	Are we going out tonight? (**Answer:** *Yes, we are.*)	Do your relatives write to you very often? (**Answer:** *Yes, they do.*)
Have we been there before? (**Answer:** *No, we haven't.*)	Was I wrong to say that? (**Answer:** *Yes, you were.*)	Did your sister pass her exam? (**Answer:** *Yes, she did.*)

No, you're not.	No, she doesn't.	Yes, they have.
No, they aren't.	No, I didn't.	Yes, he has.
No, I haven't.	Yes, he is.	Yes, I do.
No, she hasn't.	Yes, we are.	Yes, they do.
No, we haven't.	Yes, you were.	Yes, she did.

1D Vocabulary extension

Phrases for talking about people around you

1 Read the conversation below and <u>underline</u> the following:

• a phrase which means:

   a colleague   b neighbour   c strangers   d classmates   e flatmate

• a verb which means:

   f   to start a conversation with someone you have not met before

   g   to have a friendly relationship with someone

   h   to develop a friendship with someone you have recently met, by talking and finding out about them

ANGELA: Hi, Mum, I just thought I'd ring and tell you that I've found a flat. It was just luck really – someone at work told me about it. It's got great views, it's on the top floor of a big block of flats.

MUM: Great – and have you met any of your neighbours?

ANGELA: Well, the woman who lives next door's really nice. I went to borrow some milk the other day and we got talking. There are lots of people I don't know, though!

MUM: Oh, I'm sure you'll meet them soon. So how's work going?

ANGELA: It's fine. I really like the job and I get on well with everyone in the office. Oh yes, and I'm taking an evening course – in flamenco dancing!

MUM: That sounds energetic!

ANGELA: Yes, it's great, and the other people on my course are really friendly. There are a couple of girls the same age as me – I'd like to get to know them better. Mike said we should have a party, and invite them.

MUM: Mike? Who's Mike?

ANGELA: Oh, he's just a guy ... Paula introduced me to him a few weeks ago.

MUM: Wait a minute – who's Paula?

ANGELA: Oh Mum, I'm sure I told you – Paula's the girl I share a flat with!

2 Match a question in column A with an answer in column B.

A	B
a Where did you first meet your best friend?	1 Someone who cooks well and doesn't forget to wash up!
b How many people on your course are older than you?	2 My aunt – she's really similar to me.
c How long did it take you to get to know the people next door?	3 At school, when we were ten.
d Do you ever get talking to someone you don't know on the bus?	4 Most of them – there's only one person I don't really like.
e Who do you get on best with in your family?	5 Actually, I think I'm the eldest.
f What kind of person would you like to share a flat with?	6 Sometimes, especially when it's really crowded.
g Do you get on well with the people you work with?	7 Not long at all – their children are the same age as ours so they play together.

3 Choose five of the questions to ask other students. (You can make changes if you want to, for example, 'Where did you first meet the girl you share a flat with?') Ask other questions to find out more details.

1E Something in common

Present simple and continuous

Role card 1

You live five minutes' walk from here.
You travel around the country selling computers.
You're writing a novel in your spare time.
You hate parties!

Role card 2

You live five minutes' walk from here.
You work for an international bank.
You're studying Chinese in the evenings.
You're really enjoying the party.

Role card 3

You live in a flat round the corner.
You're doing a course in journalism.
You're writing a novel in your spare time.
You know the host of the party very well.

Role card 4

You live in a flat round the corner.
You're working for a television company at the moment.
You're studying Chinese in the evenings.
You only know one person at the party.

Role card 5

You're staying in a hotel for a few days.
You travel around the country selling computers.
You go cycling every weekend.
You only know one person at the party.

Role card 6

You're staying in a hotel for a few days.
You work for an international bank.
You go to the cinema three times a week.
You know the host of the party very well.

Role card 7

You're staying with a friend in the centre of town.
You're doing a course in journalism.
You go cycling every weekend.
You're really enjoying the party.

Role card 8

You're staying with a friend in the centre of town.
You're working for a television company at the moment.
You go to the cinema three times a week.
You hate parties!

Role card 9

You live five minutes' walk from here.
You're doing a course in journalism.
You go to the cinema three times a week.
You only know one person at the party.

Role card 10

You live in a flat round the corner.
You work for an international bank.
You go cycling every weekend.
You hate parties.

Role card 11

You're staying in a hotel for a few days.
You're working for a television company at the moment.
You're writing a novel in your spare time.
You're really enjoying the party.

Role card 12

You're staying with a friend in the centre of town.
You travel around the country selling computers.
You're studying Chinese in the evenings.
You know the host of the party very well.

2A Past tense pelmanism / What about you?

Irregular Past simple forms

feel	felt	fall	fell
bring	brought	buy	bought
teach	taught	think	thought
sleep	slept	sing	sang
stand	stood	wear	wore
lose	lost	fly	flew
dream	dreamt	run	ran
spend	spent	read	read

What about you?

On a **separate** piece of paper, write down **short** answers to the following points. Write the answers wherever you want on the page, but **not** in the same order as below.

- something you brought to school today
- how you felt at the beginning of the lesson
- the last time you fell in love
- something you bought last week
- the last time you slept for less than six hours
- something your teacher taught you last lesson
- the last time you sang
- something you thought was frightening when you were a child

- the last time you stood somewhere for over an hour
- something you wore last weekend that you really like
- the last thing you lost
- how much money you spent yesterday
- the last time you flew somewhere
- the last time you ran more than 100 metres
- what you dreamt about last night
- the last book you read

2B Alibi

Past simple and continuous

Suspect A

You and your friend went to a **restaurant** yesterday evening.

Before you are interviewed by the police, you must decide what happened yesterday evening. You will be interviewed separately, so you must have exactly the same story – or you will be arrested! Remember, details are important.

Here are some things for you to decide:

- when and where you met
- what you did before the meal
- the name of the restaurant and where you sat
- why you chose that restaurant
- other people in the restaurant
- your waiter/waitress
- what you both ate and drank
- the bill and how you paid
- what you did after the meal
- transport during the evening
- anything else about the evening – you never know what the police might ask you!

Police officer A

You are going to interview a suspect who you think committed last night's robbery. The suspect says that he/she went to a **restaurant** last night with a friend.

With your partner(s), write down some questions to ask him/her. All police officers must write the questions, as you are going to interview the suspects separately, then compare your answers later. Remember – details are important in a police investigation! Make sure that you ask about **both** the suspects.

You can ask questions about the following:

- when and where the suspects met
- what they did before the meal
- the restaurant and where they sat
- why they chose that restaurant
- other people in the restaurant
- the waiter/waitress
- what they both ate and drank
- the bill and how they paid
- what they did after the meal
- transport during the evening
- any more questions that you can think of.

 PHOTOCOPIABLE

Suspect B

You and your friend went to the **cinema** yesterday evening.

Before you are interviewed by the police, you must decide what happened yesterday evening. You will be interviewed separately, so you must have exactly the same story – or you will be arrested! Remember, details are important.

Here are some things for you to decide:

- when and where you met
- what you did before the film
- which cinema you went to
- details of the film (actors, story, etc.)
- where you sat in the cinema
- other people in the cinema
- what you both ate and drank
- how much everything cost
- what you did after the film
- transport during the evening
- anything else about the evening – you never know what the police might ask you!

Police officer B

You are going to interview a suspect who you think committed last night's robbery. The suspect says that he/she went to the **cinema** last night with a friend.

With your partner(s), write down some questions to ask him/her. All police officers must write the questions, as you are going to interview the suspects separately, then compare your answers later. Remember – details are important in a police investigation! Make sure that you ask about **both** the suspects.

You can ask questions about the following:

- when and where the suspects met
- what they did before the film
- which cinema they went to
- details of the film (actors, story, etc.)
- where they sat in the cinema
- other people in the cinema
- what they both ate and drank
- how much everything cost
- what they did after the film
- transport during the evening
- any more questions you can think of.

 © Pearson Education Limited 2005

2C School reunion

used to, still, not ... any longer/more

Role card 1

When you were at Springfield High School, you used to play guitar in the school band. Now you are married and work in a bank, so you don't have any time for music. You sold your guitar ten years ago.

Role card 2

When you were at Springfield High School, you used to play tennis every afternoon. You were the best player in the school, and nobody ever beat you. You still play tennis occasionally, perhaps once or twice a month.

Role card 3

When you were at Springfield High School, you used to be brilliant at mathematics. You were always top of the class, and everyone else used to hate you! Now you are a top computer programmer and earn £100,000 a year.

Role card 4

When you were at Springfield High School, you used to get into fights after school. When you left school, you started boxing, and are now a famous boxer. You are fighting for the world title next week in Las Vegas!

Role card 5

When you were at Springfield High School, you used to go out with the English teacher's son/ daughter. Your classmates used to make fun of you because of this! You are now married to him/her, and have three beautiful children.

Role card 6

When you were at Springfield High School, you used to be very good at singing. As soon as you left school you made a record, which sold over a million copies. Now you are rich and famous, and have just started recording your fifth album.

Role card 7

When you were at Springfield High School, you used to arrive late for class every day! Your teachers used to punish you, but it didn't make any difference. Now you are an important lawyer, but you are still late for almost every meeting!

Role card 8

When you were at Springfield High School, you used to live next door to the school. Because of this you could stay in bed later than all your classmates! Your family moved away a few years ago, and you now live in New York.

 PHOTOCOPIABLE

Role card 9

When you were at Springfield High School, you used to play the piano in the school band. You are now married with two small children, so you don't have time to play in a band any more. You still play on your own when you have the time.

Role card 10

When you were at Springfield High School, you used to be captain of the school football team. When you left school, you tried to become a professional footballer, but you broke your leg and never played again.

Role card 11

When you were at Springfield High School, you used to be really good at mathematics. However, you haven't done any maths since you left school and have now forgotten everything you learnt. You need a calculator for everything now!

Role card 12

When you were at Springfield High School, you always used to fight with your brother, who was in the same class. Now your brother lives on the other side of the world, and you haven't seen him for years. You miss him a lot, because you have nobody to fight with!

Find someone who ...	Name(s)	Does he/she still do this?
used to play a musical instrument.		
used to be good at sport.		
used to fight a lot.		
used to be late all the time.		
used to live close to the school.		
used to be very good at singing.		
used to be good at mathematics.		
used to go out with one of the teacher's children.		

3A The best place in the world
Superlatives (and Present perfect)

GO FORWARD TWO SPACES!

YOUR OLDEST LIVING RELATIVE

THE MOST EMBARRASSING MOMENT OF YOUR LIFE

THE MOST FAMOUS PERSON YOU'VE EVER MET

YOUR MOST VALUABLE POSSESION

FINISH

MISS A TURN!

THE BEST BOOK YOU'VE EVER READ

THE HAPPIEST DAY OF YOUR LIFE

THE MOST EXPENSIVE ARTICLE OF CLOTHING YOU'VE EVER BOUGHT

THROW AGAIN!

THE BEST PARTY YOU'VE EVER BEEN TO

THE HOTTEST PLACE YOU'VE EVER VISITED

START

THE MOST EXCITING PLACE YOU'VE EVER VISITED

THE MOST EXPENSIVE RESTAURANT YOU'VE EVER BEEN TO

YOUR YOUNGEST RELATIVE

GO BACK TWO SPACES!

THE FUNNIEST TV PROGRAMME IN YOUR COUNTRY

THE WORST THING ABOUT LEARNING ENGLISH

THE LONGEST YOU'VE EVER GONE WITHOUT EATING

THE BIGGEST CROWD OF PEOPLE YOU'VE EVER SEEN

THE LONGEST YOU'VE EVER GONE WITHOUT SLEEPING

THE COLDEST PLACE YOU'VE EVER BEEN TO

GO BACK TWO SPACES!

THROW AGAIN!

THE MOST EXPENSIVE HOTEL YOU'VE EVER STAYED IN

THE MOST FAMOUS BUILDING IN YOUR COUNTRY

THE RICHEST PERSON YOU'VE EVER MET

THE BEST FILM YOU'VE EVER SEEN

GO BACK THREE SPACES!

THE THING YOU'RE MOST FRIGHTENED OF

THE MOST DIFFICULT EXAM YOU'VE EVER TAKEN

GO FORWARD ONE SPACE!

3B 100 places to visit before you die

Vocabulary extension (word building)

1 The following words all come from the text *100 places to visit before you die* on pages 28–29 of the *Students' Book*. Find the words in the text and <u>underline</u> them.

a careful *(Natural wonder, line 13)*   d difficult *(Ancient wonder, line 24)*   g beautiful *(Romantic city, line 14)*

b important *(Ancient wonder, line 7)*   e imagine *(Ancient wonder, line 24)*   h famous *(Romantic city, line 18)*

c historian *(Ancient wonder, line 18)*   f romantic *(Romantic city, line 1)*   i experience *(Romantic city, line 23)*

2 Are the words above nouns, adjectives or adverbs? Write them in the correct column of the table. (Make sure you keep the words in the same order as above.)

	noun	adjective	opposite adjective	adverb
a	care	careful	careless	carefully
b				
c	🧍			
d				
e				
f	🧍			
g				
h				
i				

🧍 = the person

3 Complete the rest of the table with the noun / adjective / opposite adjective / adverb forms of the words, as appropriate. Use an English–English dictionary to help you, if necessary. Mark where the stress is on each word, as in the example.

4 Complete the gaps in the following sentences with a word from the table. (Note that the sentences do not follow the same order as the words in the table.)

a The fall of the Berlin wall was a ......*historical*...... moment.

b If you want to write a novel, you need to have a very good ....

c Please drive .... – the weather is terrible and it's dangerous to go too fast.

d John's such a .... He's always buying Jenny flowers.

e Don't worry about all these small details – they're ....

f We saw lots of .... people at the restaurant – David Beckham, Tom Cruise, Madonna. Unfortunately, I didn't have my camera!

g Their daughter is really .... with long, blonde hair and big blue eyes. I'm sure she'll break lots of hearts when she grows up.

h The police are having a lot of .... finding the murderer because there aren't very many clues.

i My hairdresser is quite .... She only started work two months ago.

3C The City Language School
Recommending and advising

Learn English for life . . .

. . . at the City Language School!

Here at the *City Language School*, we offer you a wide range of courses:

• classes in the morning, afternoon or evening
• part-time English classes (6 hours a week)
• intensive English courses (15 hours a week)
• extra classes in – pronunciation
                – vocabulary
                – listening

The *City Language School* also offers you a variety of extra facilities:

• a **self-study centre** equipped with the latest computers
• a **language laboratory**
• a large **library** with over 1,000 books for you to borrow
• a **coffee bar** offering a variety of drinks and snacks.

We also offer a **Conversation Club** where you can talk to native English speakers in a relaxed and friendly environment.

So come and join us at the *City Language School* – where students come first!

New student

You have decided to go to the *City Language School* to study English, but you haven't decided which courses to do. You are going to talk to two students who have been studying there for two months. Look at the table and ask each student for their recommendations. Make brief notes about what they say.

You want advice on:	Student A	Student B
which course to do – part-time or intensive English.		
whether to study in the morning, afternoon or evening.		
which extra classes to do (you want to do at least one).		
the best place(s) to study in your free time.		
whether to join the Conversation Club.		
a good place to go for coffee, food, etc.		

© Pearson Education Limited 2005

Old student A

You have been studying at the *City Language School* for nearly two months. A new student is going to ask you for recommendations and advice about the school. Read the following information about your experience there before you talk to him/her.

This month you're doing ...
- the intensive English course (*great – you're improving fast; hard work – homework every night*)
- the afternoon class (*friendly students, good atmosphere*)
- extra classes – Vocabulary (*teacher, Laura, is great!*) and Listening (*boring – very difficult*)

Last month you did ...
- the part-time English course (*too slow – didn't improve much*)
- the evening class (*very quiet, only five students in class*)
- extra class – Pronunciation (*waste of time – teacher, Mark, worst in the school!*)

Free-time study
- self-study centre (*good – almost empty in the evening*)
- language laboratory (*okay – machines quite old*)
- library (*quite noisy at lunchtime*)
- Conversation Club (*boring – not enough native speakers*)

Food and drink
- school coffee bar (*excellent coffee, terrible food, good place to meet other students*)
- Happy Café (*opposite school; great pizza!*)

Old student B

You have been studying at the *City Language School* for nearly two months. A new student is going to ask you for recommendations and advice about the school. Read the following information about your experience there before you talk to him/her.

This month you're doing ...
- the part-time English course (*great – you talk a lot; teacher, Chris, is excellent!*)
- evening class (*friendly students – same age as you*)
- extra class – Vocabulary (*great – interesting topics*)

Last month you did ...
- the intensive English course (*didn't like it – too much grammar, homework every night, no fun*)
- morning class (*students mainly men*)
- extra classes – Pronunciation (*teacher, Mark, terrible!*) and Listening (*good – lots of videos*)

Free-time study
- self-study centre (*excellent, but crowded at lunchtime*)
- language laboratory (*very old – some machines don't work!*)
- library (*quiet – good place to do homework*)
- Conversation Club (*good fun – lots of speaking practice*)

Food and drink
- school coffee bar (*coffee okay, but expensive*)
- Moon Café (*next to school; wonderful coffee, great food – except for the disgusting pizza!*)

3D How do I get to ... ?

Asking for and giving directions

1 Look at the map below. Complete the directions from the station to the Grand Hotel using the words in the box.

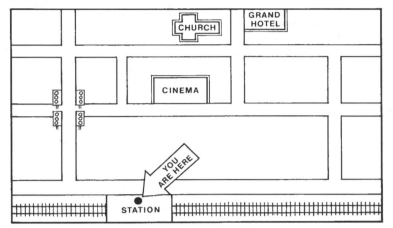

on	on	out	of
past	opposite	to	
at	keep	next	
turn	see	take	

You go (1) .... (2) .... the station and (3) .... left. (4) .... the first right, and (5) .... going until you come (6) .... some traffic lights. Turn right (7) .... the lights, and after a few minutes you'll (8) .... a cinema (9) .... your left. Go (10) .... the cinema and take the (11) .... left. Go straight (12) .... at the next crossroads, and the Grand Hotel is on the right, (13) .... a church.

2 Look at the map below and give your partner directions to one of the places. **Do not** tell your partner which place it is. When you have finished giving your directions, your partner must tell you where he/she is.

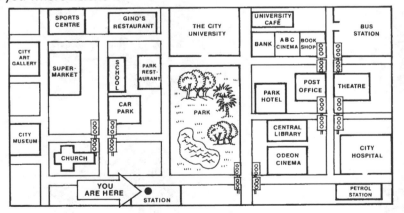

3 Choose a place on the map and ask your partner how to get there.

Useful language

Asking for directions
Excuse me, how do I get to ... ?
Excuse me, is there a ... near here?

Saying you don't know
I'm sorry, I've no idea.
I'm sorry, I don't live round here.

Giving directions
(You) go out of ... and turn left/right.
(You) take the first / second / next left / right.
(You) keep going until you come/get to a/the ...
After a few minutes you'll see a/the ... on your left / right.
(You) go past a/the ...
(You) go left / right / straight on at the crossroads.
It's on your left/right, next to / opposite the ...

4A Find someone who ... lied!

Present perfect simple (for experience)

Liar! question sheet

ride / a camel or an elephant?

see / a lion or a tiger in the wild?

go / to a casino?

win / a competition?

stay / in a five-star hotel?

meet / a famous person?

walk / into the wrong public toilets?

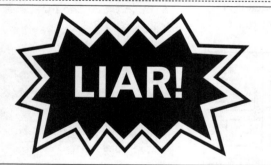

spend / over £500 in one day?

go / scuba-diving?

sleep / in the street?

go / parachuting?

climb / to the top of a mountain?

go / twenty-four hours without food?

spend / a whole day without talking to anybody?

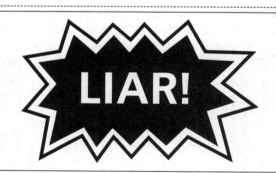

LIAR!

LIAR!

LIAR!

LIAR!

PHOTOCOPIABLE

4B How long have you had it?

Present perfect simple and continuous (for unfinished past)

How many students have a best friend?

Question: ....?

Who's known their best friend the longest?

Question: ....?

How many students support a football team?

Question: ....?

Who's been supporting their team the longest?

Question: ....?

How many students use a computer regularly?

Question: ....?

Who's been using a computer the longest?

Question: ....?

How many students are reading a book at the moment?

Question: ....?

Who's been reading their book the longest?

Question: ....?

How many students have got a pet?

Question: ....?

Who's had their pet the longest?

Question: ....?

How many students have got a favourite pair of shoes?

Question: ....?

Who's had their favourite pair of shoes the longest?

Question: ....?

How many students have a leather jacket?

Question: ....?

Who's had their leather jacket the longest?

Question: ....?

How many students own a car or bike?

Question: ....?

Who's had their car or bike the longest?

Question: ....?

How many students study another foreign language?

Question: ....?

Who's been studying another language the longest?

Question: ....?

How many students live in a flat?

Question: ....?

Who's been living in their flat the longest?

Question: ....?

How many students have a boyfriend/girlfriend?

Question: ....?

Who's been going out with their boyfriend/ girlfriend the longest?

Question: ....?

How many students have a favourite restaurant, bar or club?

Question: ....?

Who's been going to their favourite restaurant, bar or club the longest?

Question: ....?

© Pearson Education Limited 2005 **129**

4C What sort of person are you?

Vocabulary extension (word building)

1 Complete the table with the adjective forms of the nouns. Check your answers in *Vocabulary 2* on page 42 of the *Students' Book*. Then use an English–English dictionary to find the opposite adjectives. Mark the stress patterns on the words.

noun	adjective	opposite adjective
a courage	*courageous*	*cowardly*
b fairness		
c imagination		
d tolerance		
e determination		
f hard work		
g originality		
h talent		
i principle		
j self-confidence		

2 Complete the definitions with the adjectives from the table.

a A .... person believes in their own abilities and isn't shy in new situations.
b A .... person is very good at something such as art, music or sport.
c An .... person finds it easy to create stories or to think of new and interesting ideas.
d A .... person is brave and fearless in dangerous situations.
e A .... person is able to see both sides of a situation, and to decide what is right and reasonable.
f A .... person has strong beliefs which they have thought carefully about, and makes decisions and does things because of these.
g A .... person spends a lot of time and energy on their job or studies.
h A .... person does not give up easily and will not stop if they have a strong desire to do something.
i A .... person does not criticise people who believe, say or do something differently to them.
j An .... person thinks or behaves in a way which is unique and completely different from other people.

3 Walk around the classroom and ask the other students questions about the things below. When you find someone who answers yes, write their name in the column on the right. Try to find a different student for each question.

Find someone who ...	Name
is extremely good at music or sport.	
is shy and doesn't like new situations or meeting new people.	
enjoys creating new things.	
always arrives early at work or school, and always finishes late.	

 PHOTOCOPIABLE

5A *Have you got what it takes?*

Vocabulary extension (dependent prepositions)

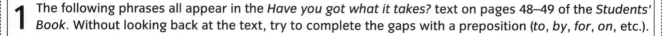

Which preposition?

1 The following phrases all appear in the *Have you got what it takes?* text on pages 48–49 of the *Students' Book*. Without looking back at the text, try to complete the gaps with a preposition (*to*, *by*, *for*, *on*, etc.).

a   to concentrate .... something
b   to think .... something or somebody
c   to distract someone .... something
d   to be interested .... something
e   to pay .... something
f   to intend .... do something
g   to talk .... something
h   to lead .... something
i   to be pleased .... someone
j   to believe .... something

2 Find the phrases in the text and check your answers. How many did you get right?

Student A

- Do you believe (1) .... ghosts?
- Are you interested (2) .... sports?
- What do you usually think (3) .... as you travel to work / school?
- When was the last time someone distracted you (4) .... your work?
- Do you believe that violence on TV leads (5) .... violent behaviour?

Student B

- Does listening to music help you to concentrate (1) .... your homework?
- How much would you pay (2) .... a pair of shoes if you really liked them?
- What do you intend (3) .... do after this lesson?
- What did you talk (4) .... this morning?
- When was the last time you were really pleased (5) .... someone in your family?

© Pearson Education Limited 2005   **131**

5B The great diamond robbery

Future clauses with *if*, *when*, etc.

The largest and most valuable diamond in the world, the Blue Ice Diamond, is on display at the National Museum. You are international jewel thieves, who are planning to steal the diamond! You are going to work out a plan – you must not get caught! Below is all the information you need to plan the robbery. First match the letters in brackets to an item on the map of the museum. Then plan your robbery and your escape!

1 The museum is open from 9:30 a.m. until 5:30 p.m. When the museum is open, four guards stand by the diamond at all times.

2 At 5:30 p.m. the front doors (F) are locked, and the keys are kept by one of the security guards. The two windows (W) are locked from the inside. There are two security cameras (S), one at the front of the building and the other in the Diamond Room.

3 When the museum is closed, there are two guards on duty. One guard (A) walks around the building, while the other guard (B) sits in the office watching the pictures from the security cameras on television screens (T). Every hour the two guards change places.

4 There is also an emergency phone (Ph). As soon as the guard picks up the phone, an alarm automatically rings in the police station next door.

5 The Blue Ice Diamond (X) is kept behind a locked glass door (G), which is connected to an alarm. If anyone breaks the glass, an alarm will go off in the police station next door.

6 The key which opens the glass door is kept in a cupboard in the security room (D).

7 Guard A keeps the key that turns off the alarm on the glass door in his pocket (P). (*Note:* you need **both** keys to open the glass door without the alarm going off.)

8 There is one extra guard's uniform in a cupboard in the security room (C).

9 The guards do not have guns, and you are not allowed to take **any** weapons into the museum.

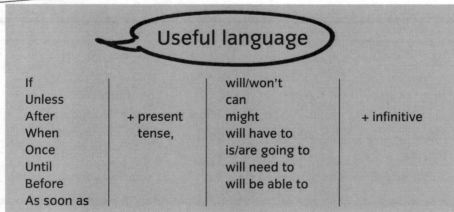

Useful language

If Unless After When Once Until Before As soon as	+ present tense,	will/won't can might will have to is/are going to will need to will be able to	+ infinitive

Once we're inside, we'll have to hide.

We'll have to get the keys before we steal the diamond.

When we get the keys, we'll be able to get the diamond.

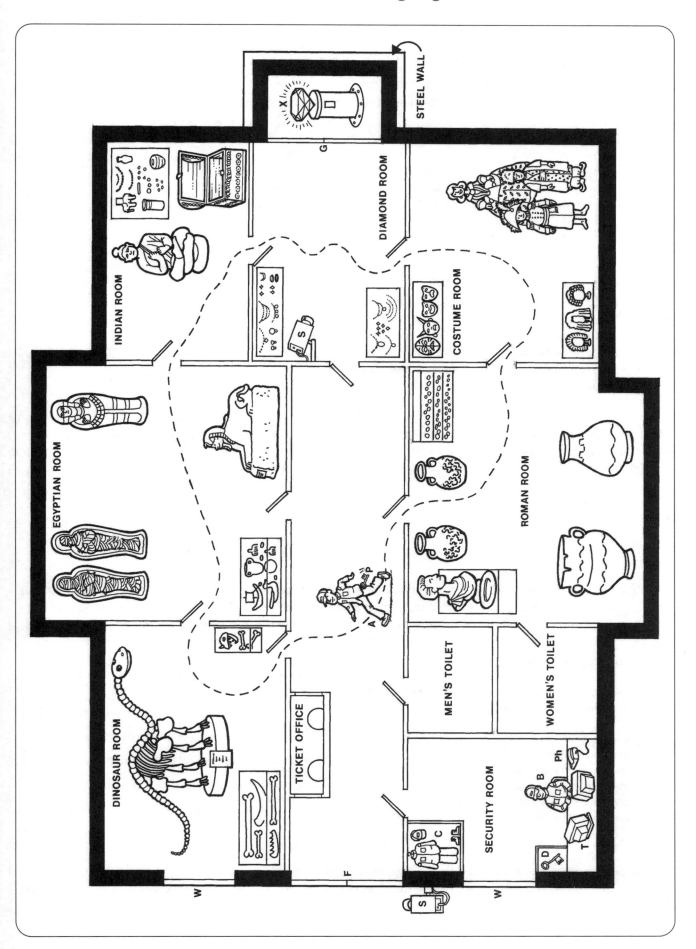

5C Vocabulary extension
Talking about work and training

1 Match the following questions with an answer below, paying attention to the words and phrases in **bold**.

a Do you earn a good salary working for the newspaper?
b What qualifications do you need for the job at the hospital?
c Does Anna have any **previous experience** of reception work?
d Are they going to give you any **training in** how to use the new computers?
e So when did you leave full-time education?
f Is Dr Clarkson **experienced in** doing this kind of operation?
g So you're **training to be** a language teacher, is that right?

1 Well, I graduated from university in 1995, then I took a **one-year diploma course** in computing, to get some more **practical skills**.
2 Yes, they're going to send everyone in the office on **a training course** next month.
3 Not yet, I'm still only **a trainee reporter**.
4 Well no, actually, I'm already **fully trained** – I finished my training course last month.
5 You need **a degree in** either Maths or Physics.
6 Not really, but she has good **secretarial skills** and a friendly telephone manner.
7 Yes, he's a very **skilled** surgeon – your husband's in safe hands.

2 a) Look at the job advertisement opposite. Who are they looking for? Do applicants need to have experience and qualifications?

We are looking for:
TRAINEE REPORTERS
for a popular radio station

No previous experience necessary
Applicants should have relevant qualifications
and good communication skills

Interested? Phone: 0114 234237

b) Work in pairs. Student A is the manager of the radio station and is going to interview applicants for the job of trainee reporter. Student B has sent in an application and has been asked for an interview. Look at the information on the cards below and spend a few minutes preparing what you are going to say.

STUDENT A: INTERVIEWER

Think about the questions you are going to ask student B. You need to find out about his/her:

• qualifications
• practical skills (for example, typing)
• relevant work experience
• ability to work in a team
• personality (for example, confident, lively)
• communication skills.

STUDENT B: APPLICANT

Think about what relevant qualifications, skills and experience you have. Use the following prompts and invent the details yourself.
• You have a degree in English (which university? / what did the course involve?).
• You have some experience of interviewing people (how did you get this experience?).
• You have some secretarial skills (what? / how did you get them?).
• You have trained people to use a computer (when? / why?).
• You speak two languages (which? / when did you learn them?).
• You think you have the right personality for the job (why?).

c) You are now ready to conduct your interview. Remember:
• Student A: you really want to find the right person for the job, so find out as much as you can about the applicant!
• Student B: you really want this job, so answer the interviewer's questions as fully as possible!

© Pearson Education Limited 2005 **PHOTOCOPIABLE**

6A Passive dominoes

Passive forms

... been described as the greatest actor ever.	In Britain, 28 million letters are ...	... delivered every day.	My car is ...
... being repaired at the moment.	*Hamlet* was ...	... written by William Shakespeare.	The tickets will all be ...
... sold before we get there.	Twenty-seven people were ...	... arrested after the match.	When we arrived, the children were ...
... being put to bed.	Dogs must be ...	... kept on a lead while in the park.	Three hundred people have been ...
... killed by an earthquake in China.	John's in hospital, but he's ...	... being looked after very well.	Quick, get a doctor! She's ...
... been shot!	The meeting will be ...	... held next Tuesday.	Fifteen people are ...
... known to have survived the explosion.	I don't believe it! My car has ...	... been stolen!	Old people shouldn't be ...
... left on their own.	If the police catch you, you'll ...	... be sent to prison.	The staff are going to be ...
... told about it at today's meeting.	I went inside although I had ...	... been told to wait in the corridor.	*Jurassic Park* was ...
... directed by Steven Spielberg.	All bags must be ...	... checked before entering the building.	A lot of coffee is ...
... produced in Brazil.	Purchases cannot be ...	... exchanged without a receipt.	I took some photos of him while he was ...
... being interviewed.	When I was a child, I used to be ...	... sent to bed early if I was naughty.	Marlon Brando has ...

6B Vocabulary extension

Passive verbs often in the news

1 The verbs in the box are often used in news stories. Organise them into groups which are similar in meaning. (Four of the groups should contain three verbs, one group should contain two verbs.) What is the difference between the verbs in each group?

to be damaged	to be murdered	to be burgled	to be arrested	to be killed	to be wounded
to be robbed	to be jailed	to be assassinated	to be injured	to be stolen	to be destroyed
to be hurt	to be held				

2 Circle the correct alternative in the following news stories.

a   'Several people were badly (1) *injured/wounded* and one was (2) *murdered/killed* when a bus crashed into a florist's this morning. The bus driver is being (3) *arrested / held* at a local police station for questioning. Witnesses say that he was driving at 60 miles an hour when the accident happened.'

b   'Eight houses in the same street were (4) *burgled/stolen* in the space of one hour yesterday while all the residents of the street were at a garden party. Police believe that more than £100,000 worth of valuables were (5) *robbed/stolen*.'

c   'The family of Geri Baines, who was (6) *assassinated/murdered* by her ex-husband a year ago, were angry today when they heard that he had only been (7) *arrested/jailed* for eight years, following a psychiatrist's report.'

d   'Over 80 paintings were completely (8) *damaged/destroyed* in a fire at the City Art Gallery last night. Another 120 paintings were quite badly (9) *damaged/destroyed* by smoke and will need very careful restoration.'

3 Match the following headlines with a newspaper article below. Then complete the gaps with the correct form of a verb from exercise 1.

- Wigs lead police to prisoners
- Hairdresser's final cut
- Pop star loses hair

1
Two people were slightly (1) .... and equipment was badly (2) .... when a hairdresser, Mari Clarke, 23, went 'crazy' with a pair of scissors in a high-street salon yesterday. Manageress Jacqui Reeves said: 'I feel sorry for Mari. She's been very depressed since her boyfriend was (3) .... for three years for armed robbery.' Ms Clarke is being (4) .... for questioning by police.

2
Multi-millionaire pop star Frankie Vale came home from a tour of Europe last night to find that his house had been (5) .... and his collection of valuable antique wigs had been (6) ....
Tapes of his new album, which comes out next week, were also (7) .... – pieces of plastic and tape were left all over the floor. 'This was done by someone who is jealous of me, and I know who it is,' said Frankie.

3
Two men who escaped from Winkfield prison last week dressed as women were (8) .... at Manchester Airport yesterday afternoon. Police were alerted when a nearby supermarket was (9) .... by two 'women' – as one of them was escaping, 'her' blonde wig came off. A shop assistant was slightly (10) .... when she was pushed to the floor by one of the escaped prisoners.

4 Write a news story using the passive verbs in exercise 1 for one of the following headlines.

- Flood chaos hits London
- Mass murderer dies
- Football fans in fight
- Burglars robbed

6C Adjective snap

'Extreme' adjectives

terrific	brilliant	appalling	terrible
ridiculous	furious	hilarious	tragic
fascinated	fascinating	astonished	astonishing
terrified	terrifying	boiling	freezing
good	good	bad	bad
silly	angry	funny	sad
interested	interesting	surprised	surprising
frightened	frightening	hot	cold

Questionnaire

1 Have you ever been somewhere which was really ....?

2 When was the last time you were absolutely ....?

3 Can you think of a very .... book you've read recently?

4 What was the last film you saw that was really ....?

5 Have you ever been really ....?

6 Have you seen anything very .... on the news lately?

7 Have you got any clothes that look absolutely .... on you?

8 Has anything really .... happened to you in the last few weeks?

© Pearson Education Limited 2005   **137**

7A Vocabulary extension

Informal words and phrases

1 The words and phrases in the box are 'neutral' – we can use them in any situation. Match each one with an informal word or phrase in **bold** in the sentences below.

man   doing   talk (to someone)   two or three   Wait!   unhappy   Don't worry
a long time   How are you?   friends   going   What's the matter?

a   **Hang on!** I'm not ready yet.

b   What are you **up to** next weekend?

c   There's a new **guy** in the accounts office – he's really nice.

d   You look terrible! **What's up?**

e   Can we **have a chat** with you about who to invite to the party?

f   Hi! Nice to see you! **How's it going?**

g   We had to wait **ages** for a bus this morning.

h   You've lost your dog? **Never mind** – I'll help you find him.

i   I'm going to see a film with some **mates** from college tonight.

j   You look **fed up**. Are you okay?

k   Nick and I are **off** to Paris tomorrow – I'm so excited!

l   Could you lend me **a couple of** pounds for a sandwich and a coffee?

2 The following dialogue is in the wrong order and the language is not informal enough. Put the lines in the correct order. Then replace the 'neutral' words and phrases with more informal ones so that the dialogue sounds more natural.

have a chat

a   Not too bad, thanks. I'm just phoning to ~~talk~~ really. ☐

b   Simon – that man you met on the plane? What's he done? ☐

c   No, not really. I went to the cinema with two or three friends from work last night. ☐

d   Well, he hasn't phoned for two weeks. ☐

e   Good! See you at the bus stop in an hour. ☐

f   Hi, Suzie! It's Ruth here. ☑1

g   Well ... okay, I'd like that. ☐

h   Did you? I haven't been to the cinema for a long time ... but, Ruth, you don't sound very happy. What's the matter? ☐

i   Oh hello, Ruth. How are you? ☐

j   Oh dear ... well, don't worry. Perhaps he'll phone tomorrow. Look, I'm going to the shops this afternoon – why don't you come? ☐

k   Okay. Wait a minute – I'm going to turn my music down ... so what have you been doing recently? Anything exciting? ☐

l   Oh, I suppose I'm unhappy because of Simon. ☐

3 Work in pairs. Write a dialogue using the informal words and phrases from exercise 1. Choose one of the following situations or invent one of your own. Act your dialogue out for the rest of the class.

• Student A telephones student B, a friend he/she has not seen for a long time, and tries to arrange to meet. Student B does not really want to meet and tries to make excuses.

• Student A has just failed his/her driving test. Student B is sympathetic, and tries to help him/her to forget about it.

     PHOTOCOPIABLE

7B Doonbogs!

Making generalisations

The creatures in the pictures below are called Doonbogs. They live on the planet Strackmuna, over eight billion kilometres from Earth. You are space scientists, and have just spent a year on Strackmuna living with these strange creatures. You've just returned home and now have to write a report on the Doonbogs' way of life for the Earth President.

Look at the letter you received from the Earth President before you left, and the photos you took on Strackmuna. Discuss your ideas with your partner(s), then write your report.

OFFICE OF THE EARTH PRESIDENT

Dear friends,

I wish you luck on your trip to Strackmuna to investigate the mysterious Doonbogs. While you are there, collect information on the following aspects of Doonbog culture:

- how they communicate
- their appearance
- their family systems
- their character
- how they travel
- leisure activities
- money and shopping
- what they eat
- their homes
- how long they live.

Also include in your report any other interesting facts you find out about Doonbogs.

Good luck, my brave travellers!

Chief Wiggum

Chief Wiggum,
Earth President

Useful language

Doonbogs generally/ usually …

It is quite common/ normal/usual for Doonbogs to …

Most/Some Doonbogs …

Doonbogs tend to / don't tend to …

7C What time shall we meet?

Making a social arrangement

Role card A1

You are going to ring an old friend to see if he/she would like to come to your house for a meal sometime next week. You would prefer him/her to come on Tuesday, because you finish work early then (see diary). You haven't seen him/her since he/she split up with his/her partner a few months ago. Make sure he/she knows how to get to your house, and what time to arrive.

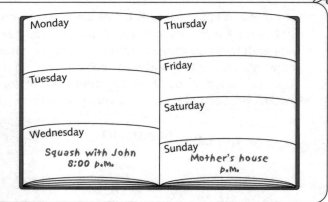

Monday

Tuesday

Wednesday
Squash with John
8:00 p.m.

Thursday

Friday

Saturday

Sunday
Mother's house
p.m.

Role card A2

You have recently met a wonderful man/woman, and are spending a lot of time with him/her. Next Tuesday, for example, he/she is taking you to the opera (see diary). You haven't seen a lot of your old friends for a while; you've just been too busy having fun! You are just about to go out to meet your new boyfriend/girlfriend when the telephone rings; it's an old friend of yours.

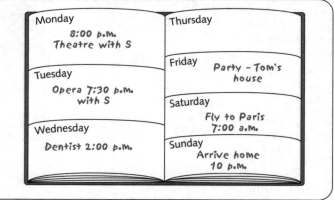

Monday
8:00 p.m.
Theatre with S

Tuesday
Opera 7:30 p.m.
with S

Wednesday
Dentist 2:00 p.m.

Thursday

Friday
Party – Tom's
house

Saturday
Fly to Paris
7:00 a.m.

Sunday
Arrive home
10 p.m.

Role card B1

You are going to phone an old colleague of yours. You both used to work at the same travel agent's until your friend left three months ago to start his/her own business. You would like to meet for a coffee or a drink after work, preferably next Friday. The rest of your week is quite busy (see diary). When you talk to your old colleague, make sure you arrange a time and a place to meet.

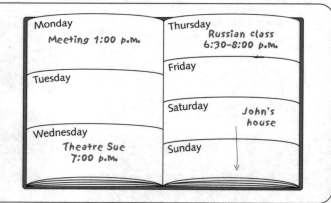

Monday
Meeting 1:00 p.m.

Tuesday

Wednesday
Theatre Sue
7:00 p.m.

Thursday
Russian class
6:30–8:00 p.m.

Friday

Saturday
John's
house

Sunday

Role card B2

You have recently left the travel agent's where you worked, and have started your own travel business. You've been working very hard to make it successful, and often work in the evenings. On Friday, for example, you are meeting a very important client (see diary). The telephone rings; it's one of your old colleagues from the travel agent's.

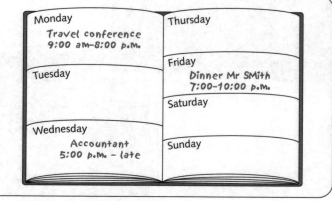

Monday
Travel conference
9:00 am–8:00 p.m.

Tuesday

Wednesday
Accountant
5:00 p.m. – late

Thursday

Friday
Dinner Mr Smith
7:00–10:00 p.m.

Saturday

Sunday

Role card C1

You are going to phone a friend and ask if he/she would like to go to the cinema with you sometime next week. You would prefer to go on Monday, as you're quite busy for the rest of the week (see diary). There are three films you'd like to see: *Terror house* (a horror film), *Love in the Afternoon* (a romantic film) or *Death Trap* (an action film). When you talk to your friend, make sure you arrange a time and a place to meet (see film times).

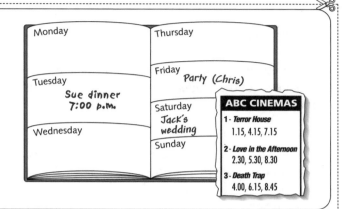

Role card C2

You have just started a new job in a restaurant, and often have to work in the evenings (see diary). At the moment you are having a coffee with a friend of yours. You've been talking about films you've seen recently. You saw a romantic film called *Love in the Afternoon* last week, and thought it was awful. You prefer horror films or action films. The phone rings; it's an old friend of yours.

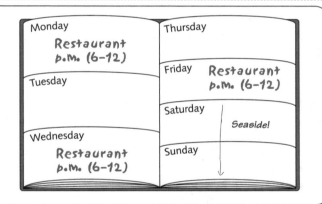

Role card D1

You are going to phone your son/daughter and invite him/her to visit you next weekend. Your sister Dorothy and her family are coming then (see calendar), and you'd really like your son/daughter to be there too. You haven't seen him/her since he/she started working in another city six weeks ago. If he/she can't come then, try to organise another date – you want to see him/her as soon as possible.

Today

JULY

Monday	Tuesday	Wednesday	Thursday	Friday	Saturday	Sunday
1	2	3	4	5	6 Dorothy +	7 family
8	9	10	11	12	13	14
15	16 Tom's birthday	17	18	19	20	21
22	23	24	25 Dentist 2:00 p.m.	26	27	28
	29	30	31			

Role card D2

You moved away from home six weeks ago to start a job in a different city. You haven't been home to see your parents since you started work. You would like to visit your parents soon, but you definitely don't want to go when your aunt Dorothy and her awful children are there – they drive you crazy! Your weekends are very busy (see calendar) – next weekend you are planning to go to the countryside with a few friends. The telephone rings; it's your mother/father.

Today

JULY

Monday	Tuesday	Wednesday	Thursday	Friday	Saturday	Sunday
1	2	3	4	5	6 Countryside with Phil, Anne	7
8 Meeting 9:00 a.m.	9	10	11	12	13 My party!	14
15	16	17 Doctor 7:00 p.m.	18	19	20 Jane to stay	21
22	23	24	25	26	27	28
	29	30	31			

8A *Machines behaving badly*
Vocabulary extension (verb–noun collocations)

Matching

1 The following phrases (verb–noun collocations) all appear in the *Machines behaving badly* text on page 81 of the *Students' Book*. Without looking back at the text, try to match a verb from A with a noun from B.

A
a   save   e   take
b   make   f   write
c   play   g   watch
d   answer

B
1   responsibility   5   a mistake
2   a TV programme   6   a computer game
3   the phone   7   an essay
4   time

2 Find the phrases in the text and check your answers. How many did you get right?

3 Cross out the noun which cannot be used with each verb. Use an English–English dictionary to help you.

a   save   a salary / money
b   make   a phone call / an e-mail
c   play   a laugh / a joke
d   take   the blame / the reason

e   answer   the door / the window
f   write   money / a cheque
g   watch   the clock / the picture

Student A

- When was the last time you (1) .... a joke on someone?
- When was the last time you (2) .... an essay?
- Have you (3) .... the blame for anything recently?
- How many phone calls have you (4) .... today?
- Do you often (5) .... the clock?
- Do you think that technology helps us to (6) .... time?
- What do you usually say when you (7) .... the phone?

Student B

- Do you like (1) .... computer games?
- Are you (2) .... money for anything special at the moment?
- Have you (3) .... a good TV programme recently?
- Do you often (4) .... cheques or do you prefer cash?
- Have you ever (5) .... a mistake at work?
- Would you (6) .... the door if someone knocked very early in the morning at the weekend?
- Do you like to (7) .... responsibility, or do you prefer it if somebody else is the leader?

8B Relative clauses crossword

Defining relative clauses

Student A

Student B

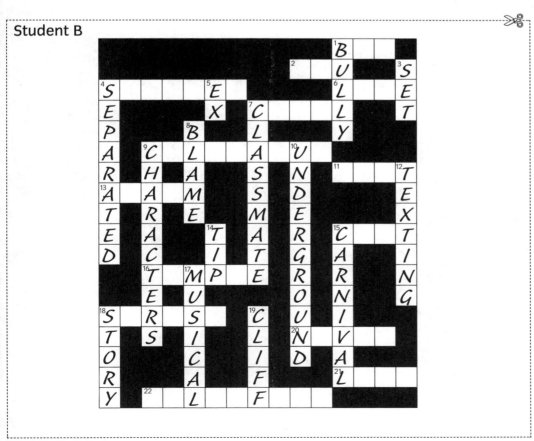

8C Camping holiday

Quantifiers (*a few*, *a lot of*, etc.)

Student A worksheet

Tomorrow you and a friend are going camping in the mountains for three days. Because you are going to camp in a very remote place, you have to carry everything you need with you (except water – there are lots of streams in the mountains).

Unfortunately, both you and your friend packed your rucksacks without talking to each other first. Tell your friend what's in your rucksack, and give your opinion of the things your partner has packed. Together you must **make a list** of what you decide to take with you.

Make sure that you have both got <u>plenty of everything</u>. You don't want to be cold, wet and hungry, and you need to be ready for emergencies!

In your rucksack you've got:

cooking equipment
- a portable gas stove
- four saucepans
- six plates
- four mugs
- ten boxes of matches
- eight spoons and knives

food
- twenty packets of soup
- 3 kg rice
- two big jars of coffee
- ten packets of biscuits
- 1 kg beans
- 1 kg chocolate
- three loaves of bread

clothes
- five T-shirts
- four jumpers
- three pairs of jeans
- six pairs of socks
- a pair of walking boots

other
- six novels
- ten packets of cigarettes
- a sleeping bag
- three tubes of toothpaste
- a camera
- six rolls of film
- washing powder

Useful language

We'll need	plenty of ...
We've got	a lot of ...
	lots of ...
	loads of ...

We/You've got	some ...
We/You have	several ...
	enough ...
	too much ...
	too many ...

We/You'll only need	one ...
	one or two ...
	a couple of ...
	a few ...
	a little ...

We/You haven't got	much ...
We/You won't need	many ...
	any ...
	enough ...

We've got no ...

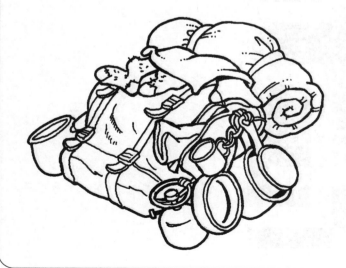

PHOTOCOPIABLE

Student B worksheet

Tomorrow you and a friend are going camping in the mountains for three days. Because you are going to camp in a very remote place, you have to carry everything you need with you (except water – there are lots of streams in the mountains).

Unfortunately, both you and your friend packed your rucksacks without talking to each other first. Tell your friend what's in your rucksack, and give your opinion of the things your partner has packed. Together you must **make a list** of what you decide to take with you.

You want to make sure that you both take <u>as little as possible</u> – it's very hard to walk with a heavy rucksack!

In your rucksack you've got:

cooking equipment
- two spoons
- one water container
- one big saucepan
- one plate
- one mug
- a lighter
- a small axe (for chopping wood)

food
- six packets of soup
- 2 kg pasta
- 1 kg rice
- a small jar of coffee

- four packets dried vegetables
- two packets of biscuits
- one loaf of bread

clothes
- two T-shirts
- one jumper
- one pair of jeans
- one pair of socks
- a pair of walking boots
- a raincoat

other
- a sleeping bag
- rope (50 metres)
- a torch with spare batteries
- a tent (with three tent pegs)
- soap
- a camera
- one roll of film

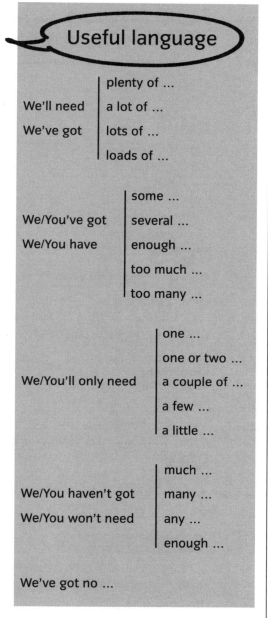

Useful language

We'll need	plenty of ...
We've got	a lot of ...
	lots of ...
	loads of ...

We/You've got	some ...
We/You have	several ...
	enough ...
	too much ...
	too many ...

We/You'll only need	one ...
	one or two ...
	a couple of ...
	a few ...
	a little ...

We/You haven't got	much ...
We/You won't need	many ...
	any ...
	enough ...

We've got no ...

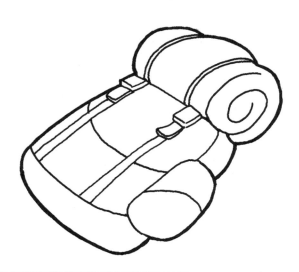

9A Election night special

Hypothetical possibilities with *if* ('second conditional')

Election manifesto for the .... party

Our slogan: ....

Tax

If we were elected, we would reduce taxes on .... and
...., which would mean that ....
....

We would also increase taxes on .... because it would stop people
....

Spending

If we became the next government, we would spend more money on ....
...., which would mean that more people would ....
....

We would reduce the amount of money spent on ...., because
....

Education

If .... became prime minister, he/she would ....
....
....

Health

The .... party's main health policy would be ....
....
....

Jobs and unemployment

If ...., unemployment would be reduced.

In order to create more jobs, we would also ....
....

The law

If .... was made illegal, ...
....

Other policies

....
....
....
....

9B How would your life be different?

Hypothetical possibilities with *if* ('second conditional')

How would your life be different if you .... (*have*) fifteen brothers and sisters?

How would your life be different if you .... (*have*) four arms?

How would your life be different if you .... (*can*) see the future?

How would your life be different if you .... (*know*) you only .... (*have*) a year to live?

How would your life be different if you .... (*can*) speak twelve languages?

How would your life be different if you .... (*be*) a famous Hollywood film star?

How would your life be different if you .... (*can*) talk to animals?

How would your life be different if you .... (*become*) the leader of your country?

How would your life be different if you .... (*be*) less than one metre tall?

How would your life be different if you .... (*be*) colour-blind?

How would your life be different if you .... (*not / need*) to sleep?

How would your life be different if you .... (*can't*) eat anything except grass?

How would your life be different if you .... (*be*) telepathic?

How would your life be different if you .... (*find out*) that your parents .... (*be*) aliens?

How would your life be different if you .... (*have*) ten children?

How would your life be different if you .... (*lose*) your memory completely?

 © Pearson Education Limited 2005

9C Hear ... Say!
Ways of saying numbers

Student A

Hear	Say
88	$75
236,000	59%
1.005	1,005
12.75	52,000,000
START ➡	15
2,000 m²	26,035
33.5	13.5
−13°C	99.99%
22.5	−75°C

Student B

Hear	Say
15	64
47.5 km per sec	12.75
13.5	1.005
$75	2,000 m²
26%	14.5
19	236,000
9,069,312	22.5
£27.50	4,444
33	88

Student C

Hear	Say
14.5	9,069,312
59%	**FINISH!**
1,005	26%
52,000,000	19
99.99%	47.5 km per sec
64	33.5
26,035	−13°C
4,444	33
−75°C	£27.50

9D Vocabulary extension

Talking about numbers, amounts and ages without being exact

1 Match a phrase in **bold** from column A with a phrase with the same meaning in column B.

A

a   I waited **a little less than a week** for a letter about the job.

b   Both my parents are **in their forties**.

c   Jake? He's **about fourteen or fifteen**.

d   The suspect says she left the building at **approximately 6:00 p.m.**

e   I waited **a little more than a week** for a phone call from Maria.

f   I can't remember exactly, but **I guess there were maybe** 50 people in the club.

g   My sister's boyfriend is **about the same age as me**.

h   The new guy at work is **in his late twenties**.

i   Danny's parents are both quite old – they're in their **late sixties or early seventies**.

j   There were **more or less** 50 people at Tom's wedding.

B

1   She says that she left **at around 6:00 p.m.**

2   I waited **a week or so**.

3   They're both **elderly**.

4   He's **about my age**.

5   He's **in his teens**.

6   They're both **middle-aged**.

7   There were **about** 50 people there.

8   I waited **almost a week**.

9   **There were roughly** 50 people there.

10 He's **about 27 or 28**.

2 How much do you know about the people and places around you? In pairs, ask and answer the following questions. If you don't know the exact answer, guess using the phrases from exercise 1.

Student A

a   How old is your sister's/brother's/mother's best friend?

b   How far is it from your English school to the nearest café or bar?

c   How many students are there in your English school?

d   How much does dinner for two cost in the most expensive restaurant in town?

e   What is the average age of the students in your class?

f   What time do the other people in your family get up in the morning?

Student B

a   What time do the other people in your family go to bed?

b   How many members of staff are there in your English school?

c   How old is the president of the United States?

d   How far is it from your English school to your house?

e   How much does a flight to the UK cost from your country?

f   How tall is the tallest person in your class?

How old is your mother's best friend?

Oh ... I don't know ... but she's definitely middle-aged!

© Pearson Education Limited 2005   **149**

10A Ralph and the guitar case

Past perfect, Past simple (Past continuous)

A Ralph woke up	**F** Ralph turned off the television and looked around the room.
B His head was aching	**G** He knew that it wasn't his
C He looked at the clock.	**H** Then he remembered
D It was raining outside	**I** Ralph stood up and walked over to the guitar case.
E He sat back down on the bed and turned on the television.	**J** When he looked inside, he couldn't believe his eyes.

EXTRA INFORMATION CARDS

1 and immediately knew something was wrong.	**2** It was five-thirty.	**3** what had happened the previous evening.	**4** A police officer was talking about a bank robbery.
5 He got out of bed and walked over to the window.	**6** and he was still wearing all his clothes.	**7** He had gone to a nightclub,	**8** He realised that he had been asleep for over twelve hours!
9 In the corner there was a guitar case leaning against the wall.	**10** Three hundred thousand dollars had been stolen	**11** where he had met a beautiful singer called Rosanna.	**12** because he had never played the guitar in his life.
13 and people were hurrying home from work.	**14** He quickly picked up the guitar case and ran out of the door.	**15** He laid it on the bed and opened it.	**16** After the show he'd bought her a drink, then another and another.
17 He realised he had drunk too much the previous night.	**18** and two people had been shot.	**19** He couldn't remember what they'd talked about, or how he'd got home.	**20** It was full of $100 bills!

© Pearson Education Limited 2005   PHOTOCOPIABLE

10B Jungle survivors
Reported speech

Back from the dead!

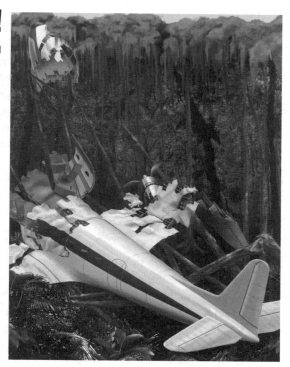

Three years ago a small passenger plane crashed in the middle of the Borneo jungle with twenty-seven people on board. Rescue teams arrived at the scene of the crash three days later. They searched the area, but found no survivors.

Two days ago, however, two people walked into a remote tribal village on the edge of the jungle and said that they were survivors of the plane crash. They told the astonished tribespeople that they had been living in the jungle by themselves since the day of the crash. We have sent two of our reporters to Borneo to interview these amazing people. Look out for an exclusive interview in next week's *Daily Planet*!

Reporter's role card

You are going to interview the survivors of the plane crash. With your partners, write down some of the questions you are going to ask. Try to write at least **twelve** questions.

Make sure you include questions to find out the following information:

- personal details
- how they know the other survivor(s)
- the crash and how they survived
- life in the jungle (food, shelter, etc.)
- the dangers they faced
- their health (now and in the past)
- the tribal village and its people
- plans for the future
- how they feel about flying
- how they are getting home.

Survivor's role card

You are going to be interviewed by a journalist about what happened to you. With your partner, decide what your story is. Make brief notes to help you in your interview. Use your imagination!

Here are some things you might be asked about:

- personal details (be imaginative!)
- how you know the other survivor
- why the plane crashed
- how you survived the crash
- life in the jungle (food, shelter, etc.)
- the dangers you faced
- your health (now and over the last three years)
- the tribal village and its people
- plans for the future
- how you feel about flying
- how you are getting home.

10C Vocabulary extension

Verbs to use instead of *say*

1 Match the verbs in bold in the following sentences with a definition below. Write the correct letter in the box.

a Anne told us that Tony was leaving the school, and **added** that she was very sad about it. ☐
b The doctor **repeated** that Dorothy must remember to take the pills twice a day. ☐
c The children **screamed** for help as the boat carried them further away from the beach. ☐
d The headteacher **announced** at the meeting that the exam results were excellent. ☐
e Martin **explained** that he always took the early train to get to work before eight. ☐
f 'This restaurant is terrible,' Fiona **muttered**, as the waiter took away the burnt steak. ☐
g 'Aren't you ready yet? It's nearly nine o'clock!' David **shouted** upstairs to Jane. ☐
h 'Are you coming with us?' asked Tricia. 'I can't,' Steve **answered**, 'I've got too much work to do.' ☐
i Just as the play was starting, Marie **whispered**, 'I've got to go outside – I feel really ill.' ☐
j 'Is that really the time?' John **exclaimed**, looking at his watch. 'I must go.' ☐

1 to say something again, because you want to make sure that someone heard or understood you
2 to say something very quietly, because you only want one person to hear you
3 to say something to several people in order to give them information
4 to say something in a very loud voice, because you are angry or want to warn someone of danger
5 to say something more, after the main thing you said
6 to say something loudly and suddenly, because of surprise or another strong feeling
7 to say something quietly and unclearly, when you are annoyed or complaining about something
8 to say something when someone asks you a question
9 to say something in a very loud, high voice, especially when you are frightened or in pain
10 to make something clear or easier to understand

2 Discuss with a partner why the following sentences are unlikely or impossible.

a 'Please don't tell anyone,' Denise whispered loudly.
b 'Sorry, can you mutter that again? I didn't hear you.'
c 'What would you like for breakfast?' his mum announced.
d Paul had to shout to his friend because they were in the library.
e 'Hello, everyone, I'm home!' added Sara.
f 'Leave me alone!' screamed the man in a low voice.

3 Complete the gaps in the following sentences with a verb from exercise 1 in the correct form.

a 'Ssh … I .... because I don't want to wake the children.'
b 'Please don't .... – I've got a headache,' said the teacher.
c 'How much?!' Rose .... when she saw the bill.
d 'No – I said that I would not answer any questions,' .... the minister.
e 'First you put the powder in and then you turn it on – okay?' Louis ....
f 'When did the judges .... that you had won first prize?'
g 'Get out or I'll call the police!' .... the terrified woman.
h Douglas has just left – he was .... something about the phone bill.

4 Work in pairs. Write an extract from a short story based on one of the following ideas, using the verbs given.
  • a terrible plane journey: *announce, explain, scream, repeat*
  • a terrible driving lesson: *explain, repeat, whisper, exclaim*

   PHOTOCOPIABLE

11A *To sue or not to sue?*
Vocabulary extension

---

1 a Find a **verb** in the title which means *to begin a legal process against someone.*
Write it here: ....
b Choose the **correct** alternative:
• to sue somebody *for/about* something

---

2 a Find a **verb** in the first paragraph which means *to hit something with your foot and fall or almost fall as a result.*
Write it here: *to* .... *on something.*
b Which of the following **prepositions** cannot be used with the verb?
over/up/on/down

---

3 a Find a **noun** in the first paragraph which means *damage or a wound to part of your body from an accident.*
Write it here: .... and mark the stress.
b What's the **verb** form?
Write it here: .... and mark the stress.
c What's the **adjective** form?
Write it here: .... and mark the stress.

---

4 a Which **preposition** is used with the adjective *responsible* in paragraph 3?
Write it here: *to be responsible* ....
b What's the **noun** from *responsible*?
Write it here: .... and mark the stress.

---

5 a Find a **noun** in paragraph 4 which means *money or other benefit paid to someone who has suffered an injury, a loss or a problem which was not their fault.*
Write it here: .... and mark the stress.
b What's the **verb** form?
Write it here: .... and mark the stress.

---

6 a Which **verb** in paragraph 5 means *to say that you are not satisfied with something*?
Write it here: .... and mark the stress.
b Which of these prepositions **cannot** be used with this verb?
of/to/about/at
c What's the **noun** form (it is also written in paragraph 5)?
Write it here: .... and mark the stress.

---

7 a Find a **phrasal verb** in the fifth paragraph which means *to have a good, friendly relationship with someone.*
Write it here: .... *(with someone).*
b The adverbs *well* and *badly* are often used with this phrasal verb. Complete the sentences below by putting *well* or *badly* into the **correct** place:
• *I get on with Carina because we have the same sense of humour.*
• *I'm getting on with Mike at the moment. We just seem to argue about everything.*

---

8 a In the final paragraph find two **nouns** which relate to the money people get or try to get, for example, when they have an accident.
Write them here: .... and
....
b Both of these words can also be **verbs**. Which one means *to ask for money or compensation*?
Write it here: ....
Which one means *to give money or compensation*?
Write it here: ....

© Pearson Education Limited 2005 **153**

11B In my opinion ...

Agreeing and disagreeing

COMPUTERS ARE BAD FOR SOCIETY

GO BACK TWO SPACES!

PEOPLE WORRY TOO MUCH ABOUT WHAT THEY WEAR

MEN TAKE SPORT TOO SERIOUSLY

BOXING SHOULD BE BANNED

THROW AGAIN!

SUMMER IS THE BEST SEASON

PEOPLE SHOULD LIVE TOGETHER BEFORE THEY GET MARRIED

THE WORLD WOULD BE A BETTER PLACE WITHOUT POLITICIANS

THERE IS TOO MUCH ADVERTISING IN SOCIETY

TRAINS ARE THE BEST WAY TO TRAVEL

VIOLENT TELEVISION PROGRAMMES MAKE PEOPLE MORE VIOLENT

START

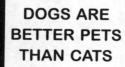 DOGS ARE BETTER PETS THAN CATS

ENGLISH IS THE EASIEST LANGUAGE IN THE WORLD

BLUE IS THE MOST BEAUTIFUL COLOUR

GO BACK TWO SPACES

PHOTOCOPIABLE

TEACHING IS THE MOST DIFFICULT JOB IN THE WORLD

FOOD IS THE GREATEST PLEASURE IN LIFE

GO FORWARD ONE SPACE

WOMEN ARE BETTER DRIVERS THAN MEN

OPINION CARDS

PARENTS SHOULD NOT BE ALLOWED TO HAVE MORE THAN TWO CHILDREN

THROW AGAIN!

THERE IS LIFE ON OTHER PLANETS

MISS A TURN

FINISH!

THIS COUNTRY IS THE BEST IN THE WORLD

YOUR SCHOOLDAYS ARE THE BEST DAYS OF YOUR LIFE

SMOKING SHOULD BE MADE ILLEGAL

PEOPLE WATCH TOO MUCH TELEVISION

GO FORWARD TWO SPACES

SPORT IS A WASTE OF TIME

 © Pearson Education Limited 2005

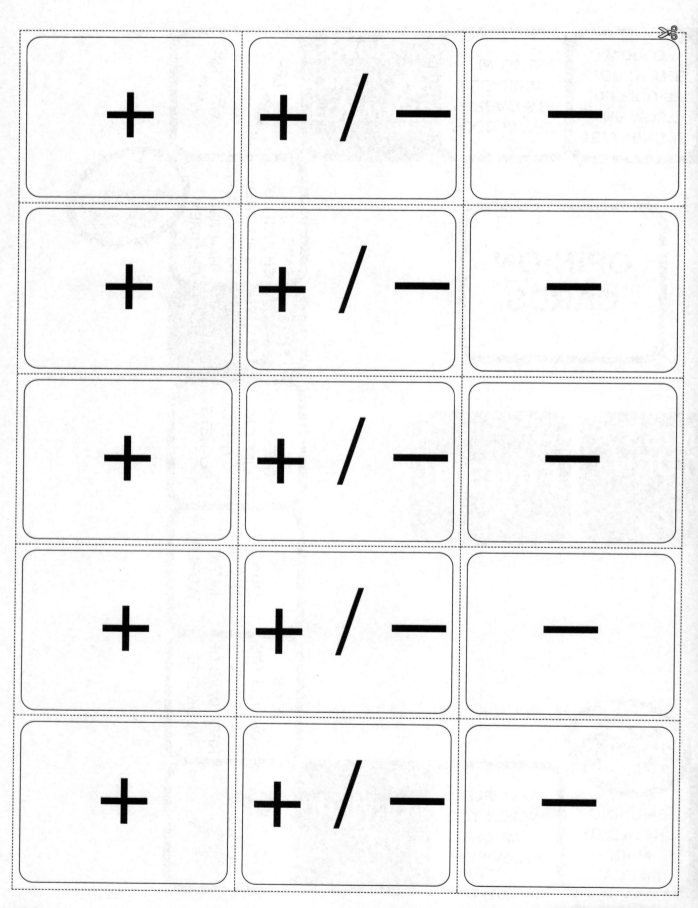

12A Suzie's story

Past sentences with *if* ('third conditional') and *should(n't) have*

I
Suzie wanted to be a musician, so her father gave her a bright pink guitar for her fifteenth birthday.

H
Natasha and Jo were musicians too, and so they all decided to form a band, which they called The Convicts.

E
She spent so much time practising in her bedroom that she didn't pass any of her exams at school.

L
Six months later The Convicts played their first concert. It was a disaster! They were so nervous they forgot all their songs and the audience laughed at them.

P
Her father was so angry that he took away her guitar and locked it in a cupboard.

B
Natasha and Jo were so upset after the concert that they left the band.

A
Suzie was so upset about losing her guitar that she ran away from home.

O
Suzie, however, didn't give up. She managed to borrow some money and made a record on her own.

N
She started living on the street, and was so hungry that she began stealing food from shops.

C
The record was a huge success, and Suzie became famous all over the world.

F
One day a policeman saw her shoplifting, and arrested her.

M
One day Suzie's father turned on the television to watch a football match and saw his daughter singing her latest song. He couldn't believe his eyes!

J
During the arrest Suzie hit the policeman, and was sent to prison for three months.

G
He found out that Suzie was playing a concert the following week, and went to buy a ticket.

D
While in prison she shared a cell with two women called Natasha and Jo, who became her best friends.

K
After the concert he went backstage and found his daughter. With tears in his eyes, he hugged her and gave her a present. It was her bright pink guitar.

 © Pearson Education Limited 2005

12B What should I do?

Giving advice

You're addicted to tomato ketchup. You eat three bottles of ketchup a day!

You've had hiccups for two weeks.

You can't stop watching television. Yesterday you watched television for eleven hours!

You are terrified of vegetables. If you see one, you feel ill.

You have a terrible memory. You forget absolutely everything.

You can't stop sneezing!

You think your cat can talk English. You want to make her famous.

You have terrible nightmares every night.

Your doctor has just told you that you only have twenty-four hours to live.

You can't get to sleep at night. You haven't slept for twelve days.

Your wife/husband believes that he/she is a dog.

You are a shopaholic – you can't stop buying clothes.

You have ghosts in your house.

You have an exam tomorrow and you haven't done any revision.

12C Preposition challenge

Revision of prepositions

Preposition cards

for	for	for	for
in	in	in	in
on	on	on	on
of	of	of	of
about	about	about	about
by	by	by	by

 © Pearson Education Limited 2005

Sentence cards

They've been living in that house .... ages.	I've applied .... lots of different jobs.
It's quite common .... people to worry about dying.	He was awarded first prize .... his beautiful painting of the sunset.
This is the best beach .... the world.	I'm really tired, so I think I'll stay .... tonight.
She was dressed .... a big baggy jumper and jeans.	I have a lot of confidence .... his ability.
My brother insisted .... coming with us.	It wasn't an accident! He did it .... purpose.
Don't leave me .... my own in this old house.	John's in hospital. He's being operated .... tomorrow morning.
Bill's absolutely terrified .... spiders!	I don't think he's capable .... looking after the children.
That woman reminds me .... my grandmother.	Those shoes are made .... plastic, not leather.
He was very angry .... what happened.	I don't know anything at all .... physics.
I'm really worried .... what will happen if they win the election.	He lay on the beach, thinking .... what had happened the previous evening.
I went to the wrong restaurant .... mistake.	I won't be lonely. I like being .... myself.
You can book tickets for the concert .... phone.	Inflation has gone up .... five percent this year.

Test one
TIME: 45 MINUTES

modules 1–4

Ⓐ Making questions

Look at the answer and write the question in the correct tense from the prompts given.

For example:

you / do your homework last night?

Did you do your homework last night ?

No, I forgot.

1 How much / the train to Edinburgh / cost?
.... ?
It depends. Do you want a single or a return?

2 Where / Sebastian / born?
.... ?
In Uruguay.

3 How long / you / know / your teacher?
.... ?
Since the beginning of September.

4 What / you / look for?
.... ?
My dictionary. I think I left it here yesterday.

5 all your classmates / go / to the party yesterday?
.... ?
Yes, and everyone was late for class today!

6 anyone / see / Mrs Pearson this morning?
.... ?
No, but she doesn't usually come in until 12.00.

7 you / use to speak / Japanese when you were young?
.... ?
Yes, but I've forgotten it all now.

8 it / rain / when you arrived?
.... ?
I don't think so.

9 How long / Sarah and Eduardo / be / married?
.... ?
Only for a few months before he died.

10 Paul / work / on anything special at the moment?
.... ?
Yes, he's got an idea for a new book.

[10]

Ⓑ Vocabulary: collocations

Cross out the word or phrase which is incorrect.

For example:

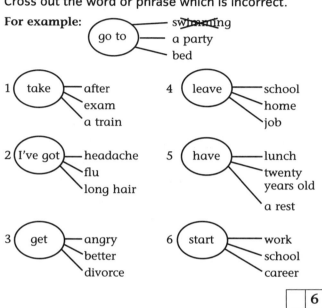

1 take — after / exam / a train

2 I've got — headache / flu / long hair

3 get — angry / better / divorce

4 leave — school / home / job

5 have — lunch / twenty years old / a rest

6 start — work / school / career

[6]

Ⓒ Prepositions

Complete the gaps in the following sentences with the correct preposition (*to*, *by*, etc.).

1 Juan's not very good .... spelling.

2 The supermarket's .... the centre of town.

3 Hi, Diane! I was thinking .... you yesterday.

4 The children's grandmother looked .... them while I was in France.

5 Does this photo remind you .... anyone?

6 Deborah brought her children .... as Buddhists.

7 Stratford-on-Avon is famous .... being Shakespeare's birthplace.

8 Tim's very interested .... motorcycles.

9 The new model's very similar .... the old one, but it goes much faster.

10 I like listening .... classical music when I drive.

[10]

D Tense review

Complete the gaps in the following sentences with the correct form of the verb in brackets.

1 Before you moved to Washington, how long .... (you / be) in Toronto?

2 'Dear Fernando, I .... (write) to say thank you for the present you sent me.'

3 Beth .... (have) her car for over eight years, and she's still very happy with it.

4 I'm sorry, I .... (not agree) with you.

5 Delgar .... (spend) his holiday in France when he produced his first great painting.

6 Kim and I .... (grow up) in the south of India in the 1950s.

7 My mother .... (get) much better now – the doctor says she can probably get up next week.

8 .... (you speak) to Liz this week? Jan told me she has decided to look for another job.

9 My grandfather's feeling very nervous because he .... (never fly) before.

10 I'm so tired. I couldn't sleep last night because our neighbour's baby .... (cry).

☐ **10**

E Short questions

Respond to the following statements with an appropriate short question.

For example:
A: I hate parties!
B: *Do you* .... ? I love them!

1 A: The children weren't very interested in the programme.
   B: .... ? Why not?

2 A: Bill Denton came to the office today.
   B: .... ? Why?

3 A: Oh no! There aren't any clean knives.
   B: .... ? Try looking in that cupboard.

4 A: My arm really hurts since I fell off my bike.
   B: .... ? Let me have a look.

5 A: Anna's got black hair.
   B: .... ? It was red last week!

6 A: I'm not going to Lorenzo's party tonight.
   B: .... ? Why not?

☐ **6**

F Vocabulary: word stress

Put the words below in the correct column of the table according to their word stress.

| famous recognise achieved travelled |
| retire courageous relative polluted parent |
| colleague arrived festival old-fashioned |

●o	o●	●oo	o●o
famous			

☐ **6**

G Comparatives and superlatives

Complete the gaps with the correct comparative/superlative form of the adjective in brackets.

1 My partner's cooking is far .... (bad) than mine.

2 This winter's definitely .... (wet) than last year.

3 Prague's one of the .... (pretty) cities I've ever been to.

4 Most of my classmates live a lot .... (far) away from school than I do.

5 The city centre is much .... (polluted) this winter than it used to be.

Complete the gaps with one word.

6 The exam was terrible! Everyone thought it was a .... more difficult than last year's.

7 A: These shoes are slightly too big.
   B: Try these. They're a .... smaller.

8 It's .... far the best house we've seen.

9 I've done some crazy things in my life, but going parachuting was the .... of all!

10 New York isn't as dangerous .... we thought it would be.

11 Maria found living alone was completely different .... living with her parents.

12 Lisa's job is very similar .... mine, but she gets paid more.

☐ **12**

© Pearson Education Limited 2005 **PHOTOCOPIABLE**

H Vocabulary: verbs to do with memory

Complete the sentences with the correct form of the verbs in the box.

remember   forget   remind   recognise   learn

1 I didn't .... Kate. She's got a completely different haircut.
2 I .... to tell David your address, so he won't know where the party is. I'll phone him.
3 I .... telling you about our holiday because we had an argument afterwards about how long the flight would be.
4 Have you .... your new phone number by heart yet?
5 When we get to the shops, can you .... me to buy coffee?

5

I *for/since/ago*

Complete the gaps in the following sentences with *for*, *since* or *ago*.

1 I've known my best friend Louise .... 1987.
2 My boss has had a bad cold .... a week.
3 Your mum and I used to play together years ....
4 I've been working here .... last summer.
5 Peter waited outside the cinema .... over an hour.
6 Jane's been doing aerobics classes .... she first came to Warsaw.
7 A: Would you like a sandwich?
    B: No, thank you. I only had lunch an hour ....
8 How long .... did we last see each other?
9 My flatmate's been living here .... a long time.
10 Tolstoy worked on *War and Peace* .... several years.

J Vocabulary: definitions

10

Write the missing word to complete the definitions.

For example:
A group of cars, buses, bicycles, taxis, etc. moving along a street is called ...... *traffic* ....

1 Your father has just married again. His new wife is your ....
2 Your sister's husband is your ....
3 You have never met or seen the woman who has just entered your office. She's a .... to you.

4 You used to go out with Maria, but you don't any longer. She's your ....
5 When you stop work, usually at about sixty-five, you ....

5

K Phrases

Complete the following sentences with *a*, *an*, *the* or — (no word).

1 Do you work .... full-time?
2 Dan's really funny. He's got .... great sense of humour.
3 Ukraine is .... second largest country in Europe.
4 I got a job as soon as I left .... school.
5 Sarah plays .... piano really badly.
6 Miss Stone's by far .... most popular teacher in the school.
7 You can have .... breakfast any time between 8:00 and 9:30.
8 Did you speak to Beryl .... last week?
9 Did you know that my stepbrother is .... actor?
10 When we were children, we all had blond hair and .... blue eyes.

10

L Verb patterns

Circle the correct form in the following sentences.

1 I spend a lot of time *sleeping / to sleep / sleep*.
2 Joseph wanted to learn how *playing / to play / play* the piano.
3 I really love *eating out / to eat out / eat out*.
4 My brother's really into *programming / to programme / programme* computers.
5 Mr Benson reminded us all *bringing / to bring / bring* sandwiches for the trip.
6 The Winter Palace is really worth *seeing / to see / see*.
7 Don't forget *inviting / to invite / invite* your husband to the office party.
8 Don't forget *setting / to set / set* your alarm clock. We've got to get up early tomorrow.
9 I don't have enough time *for reading / to read / read* much at the moment, unfortunately.
10 You should definitely *going / to go / go* to Lisbon – it's a great city!

10

TOTAL | 100 |

  © Pearson Education Limited 2005 **163**

Test two

TIME: 45 MINUTES

modules 5–8

A Talking about the future

Circle the correct form in the following sentences.

1 I'm sorry, I'm not free at 10:00. *I'll meet / I'm meeting* Tom for a drink then.

2 We'll phone you when we *get / will get* home.

3 Most people think Ireland *will win / is winning* the match next week.

4 Annie wants *that her boss gives her / her boss to give her* more money next year.

5 If *I remember / I'll remember* Gordon's address, I'll e-mail it to you.

6 When *the photos will be / will the photos be* ready?

7 I don't know if there's a flight at that time. *I look / I'll look* on the computer.

8 You won't get any coffee from that machine until the engineer *fixes / is going to fix* it.

9 I didn't realise Mr Cray needs the report now. *I'll do it / I'm doing it* straight away.

10 Do you think the printer *will work / is working* when we attach it to the new computer?

[ ] 10

B Vocabulary: collocations

Match a verb in column A with a noun in column B.

A	B
1 be	a a job
2 apply for	b a master's degree
3 do	c the army
4 join	d grey
5 go	e hands
6 make	f a trainee manager
7 go on	g an arrangement
8 shake	h holiday

[ ] 8

C Passives

In the following news stories, put the verb in brackets in the correct passive or active form. Make sure that you use the correct tense.

Three people (1) .... (take) to hospital last night after a fire in a house in Newcastle. Immediately afterwards police (2) .... (arrest) a young man.

Some children (3) .... (find) a bomb on a beach in South Wales yesterday. The bomb (4) .... (explode) and one of the children (5) .... (badly injure).

Ten people (6) .... (die) in an air crash in Chile. The accident (7)............................ (happen) last night when a plane carrying more than 250 passengers (8) .... (fly) into a mountain. It (9) .... (think) that the accident (10) .... (cause) by engine problems.

[ ] 10

D Vocabulary: word stress

Put the words below in the correct row of the table according to their word stress.

~~organise~~ satisfaction opportunity qualified amusing experienced interested ridiculous embarrassed challenging disappointed

○ ● ○	
● ○ ○	*organise*
○ ○ ● ○	
○ ● ○ ○	
○ ○ ● ○ ○	

[ ] 5

E Verb patterns

Complete the gaps in the following sentences with *to leave* or *leaving*.

For example:
Miss Sullivan intended .....*to leave*......... on the 4:30 train.

1 We're hoping .... next weekend.
2 In the UK people tend .... tips of about 10 percent for waiters.
3 Pete's thinking of .... his wife.
4 Hurry up! The train's about ....
5 I'm sorry, he's not here at the moment. Would you like .... a message?
6 I've decided .... my job.
7 I'm planning .... on the evening flight.
8 Would you mind .... your telephone number in case of an emergency?
9 Don't forget .... your keys.
10 It's not polite .... a party without saying thank you.

[10]

F Prepositions

Complete the gaps in the following sentences with the correct preposition (*to*, *by*, etc.).

1 I'll take this report home to finish. I really need to concentrate .... it.
2 .... my job there are lots of opportunities to work in different departments.
3 Just a moment – I'll put you .... to the manager's office.
4 In Japan it's common .... people to bow when they meet.
5 I gave up trying to book tickets because I waited .... hold for twenty minutes and nothing happened.
6 This dress belonged .... Stella's grandmother.
7 Would you like to go out .... a coffee?
8 Mr Woods hasn't got much experience .... office work.
9 Your mobile phone is so out .... date it should be in a museum!
10 It's based .... the story of *Romeo and Juliet*.

[10]

G Vocabulary: definitions

Write the missing word to complete the definitions.

For example:
Soap operas, sitcoms and national news are all examples of TV p.*rogrammes.* .

1 When you go shopping you are given a piece of paper to show how much you have paid and what you have paid for. This is called a r...................... .
2 In Europe, Saturday and Sunday are the weekend and Monday to Friday are the w...................... days.
3 The feeling of anger or unhappiness because someone has something which you want is called j...................... .
4 Another name for the words in a song is the l...................... .
5 Factual TV programmes about the science or the environment, for example, are called d...................... .
6 R...................... is an extreme adjective which means that something is very stupid.
7 I broke my leg in the bathroom and couldn't get out, but luckily my neighbour heard me shouting and came to r...................... me.
8 When something is not allowed by law or by a rule, it's b...................... .
9 Let's s...................... the bill and pay half each.
10 It's a long walk to your house from here. I'll give you a l...................... in my car if you like.

[10]

H Defining relative clauses

Complete the gaps in the following sentences with *who*, *which*, *that*, *whose* or *where*.

1 A daffodil is a yellow flower .... grows in the spring.
2 A reliable person is someone .... you can depend on.
3 A chemist's is a shop .... you can buy medicine and things like shampoo and soap.
4 A mobile phone is one .... you can carry around with you.
5 An orphan is a child .... parents are both dead.
6 A punctual person is someone .... is never late.

In two of the sentences above we can leave out the relative pronoun (*who*, *which*, etc.). Which sentences are they?

Sentence (7) .... and sentence (8) ....

[8]

I Social English: making requests

Make changes to these requests to make them sound more polite using the word in brackets.

For example:
I must speak to Mrs Kane. (like)
I'd like to speak to Mrs Kane, please.

1 I want to read your newspaper. (could)
.... ?

2 Give me some change for £5. (think)
.... ?

3 Look after my cat this weekend. (possibly)
.... ?

4 I want to watch television. (mind)
.... ?

5 Switch off the CD player when you go to bed. (mind)
.... ?

6 I want to have a bath. (all right)
.... ?

| 6 |

J Vocabulary

Circle the correct word or phrase in the following sentences.

1 Jenny was *shocking / upsetting / shocked* by the news.

2 I think you've forgotten to *plug on / plug up / plug in* the dishwasher.

3 Nick's *getting bald / going bald / losing his hairs.*

4 It's very *worrying / worried / terrific* that the doctors can't find what's wrong with Steve's baby.

5 Being a doctor is a *well-pay / good-paid / well-paid* job.

6 The president's decision is absolutely *surprised / surprising / astonishing.*

7 If you are going to that expensive restaurant, you should *dress up / dress down / dress good.*

| 7 |

K Quantifiers

Complete the gaps in the following sentences with a word or phrase from the box. (There may be more than one possibility.)

| a few   many   much   enough   too much   a lot of |
| too many   a little   plenty of   not many   several |
| not much   loads of |

1 There's .... traffic in the city centre – sometimes the cars don't move for up to an hour.

2 Have you got .... money for the ticket?

3 I usually see my father .... times a week.

4 Our maths teacher used to give us .... homework.

5 Don't worry. There are .... people who have the same problem as you.

6 Fortunately there isn't .... noise in the hostel after eleven o'clock.

7 Have you got .... minutes? I could show you my photographs.

8 I didn't enjoy the party because there were .... people there.

| 8 |

L Phrases

Complete the following phrases with *a, an, the* or — (no word).

1 What time did you go to .... bed last night?

2 .... good thing about this candidate is her previous experience in a similar job.

3 You didn't get the job? Oh, no! What .... shame!

4 I've never been good with .... money, so I never know how much is in my bank account or which bills I need to pay.

5 Would you like to go for .... walk?

6 My brother joined .... army when he was sixteen.

7 If your leg really hurts, you should go straight to .... hospital to have it checked.

8 My father used to be .... workaholic and we hardly ever saw him.

| 8 |

TOTAL | 100 |

Test three

modules 9–12

A Grammar: making predictions

Rewrite the following sentences using the words/ phrases in brackets. You are given the first word of each sentence.

For example:

I don't know if I'll see you tomorrow.

I *may not see you tomorrow* .... (may)

1   I think taxes will go up next year.
    Taxes .... (likely)

2   I think it'll snow tomorrow.
    It .... (may well)

3   I don't think Sylvia will be on the next train.
    Sylvia .... (almost certainly)

4   It's possible that Guy will pass his driving test.
    Guy .... (could)

5   I think Mary will move to Canada.
    Mary .... (probably)

6   I don't think the USA will win the Ryder Cup.
    The USA .... (definitely)

7   I don't think Max will telephone you until tomorrow.
    Max .... (likely)

8   I'm not sure if Andrea will like the present I've bought her.
    Andrea .... (might)

    [8]

B Vocabulary

Write the missing word. You are given the first letter of each word.

For example:

It means the opposite of *get better*: d*eteriorate* ....

1   It means the same as *regulations*: r..........................

2   It means the opposite of *liberal* (parents):
    s..........................

3   It means the same as *get better*: i..........................

4   It means the opposite of *borrow*: l..........................

5   It means the opposite of *increase*: d..........................

6   It means the opposite of *fall*: r..........................

7   It means the opposite of *refuse*: a..........................

8   It means the opposite of *guilty*: i..........................

C Grammar: sentences with *if*

Complete the gaps in the following sentences with a suitable form of the verb in brackets.

1   A: It's terribly late. What .... (you / do) if you .... (miss) the last train?
    B: I .... (get) a taxi. It isn't too expensive.

2   Our son lives in Florida, but it's very expensive to get there. If it .... (not / cost) so much, we .... (visit) him more often.

3   A: Do they know what caused the crash?
    B: They're saying that if the driver .... (not / be) drunk, the accident .... (not / happen).

4   A: Why don't you phone Angela?
    B: I .... (call) her straight away if I .... (know) her phone number.

5   Stephanie .... (become) an international athlete if she .... (train) harder when she was younger.

6   I'm going to the shops, so I can get you some aspirin. If the pharmacy .... (be / closed), I .... (go) to the supermarket.

7   I'm sorry Mrs Painter, but if James .... (not / work) much harder between now and June, he .... (not / pass) the exam.

8   A: What .... (you / do) if someone suddenly .... (leave) you loads of money?
    B: I don't know. I .... (probably / spend) it on travelling.

9   Why didn't you tell me about the problem yesterday? If you .... (tell) me immediately, I .... (do) something about it. Now it's too late.

10 I think that if Marcos .... (not / get) so angry that night, he and Ana-Maria .... (still / be) together today.

    [10]

PHOTOCOPIABLE   © Pearson Education Limited 2005   **167**

D Vocabulary: collocations

For each verb below, choose three words or phrases from the box that can go with it.

> ~~straight~~   somebody unhappy   your best   a lie
> sorry   yoga   ~~something over~~   a profit   well
> ~~back~~   goodbye   a prayer   sure   the truth
> someone   something

For example:

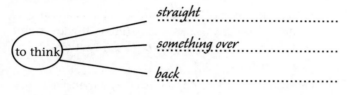

to think — straight ....
         — something over ....
         — back ....

1 to say

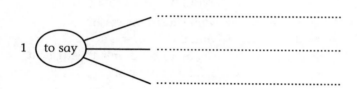

2 to make

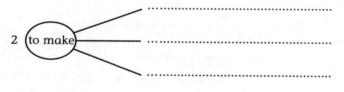

3 to do

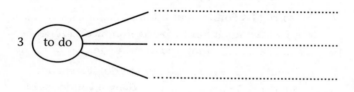

4 to tell

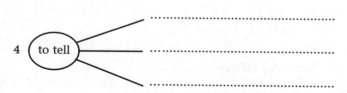

☐ 6

E Prepositions

Complete the gaps in the following sentences with the correct preposition (*to*, *by*, etc.).

1 George prefers to travel everywhere .... train.

2 Mrs Petrie told me .... for eating sweets in class.

3 I found a diamond ring outside the restaurant and handed it ....

4 James wants some time to talk it .... with his wife.

5 I bought a gorgeous new handbag made .... leather.

6 The suspected murderer appeared .... court this morning.

7 What percentage .... people smoke in your country?

8 It was lovely to see you. I'll be .... touch soon.

9 Would you phone the hotel and ask them to sort .... the problem?

☐ 9

F Grammar: reported speech

Write the following dialogue in reported speech, making any changes necessary to tenses, word order, etc.

JACK: Hello, Angela.
ANGELA: Why haven't you brought the money?
JACK: I didn't have time to arrange it.
ANGELA: I'll send your boss the photos if you don't give me the money.
JACK: Okay. I can get it by tomorrow. Where are the photos?
ANGELA: They're in a safe place. Don't worry.

Jack said hello to Angie, who ....
....
....
....
....
....
....
....
....
....
....

☐ 10

G Pronunciation: word stress

Put the words below in the correct column of the table according to their word stress.

pretend	disadvantage	necessary	persuade
science	obey	fortunately	economic	foreign
unemployment	obviously	promise	ignore

o ●	● o	o o ● o	● o o o
pretend			

| 6 |

H Grammar: verb forms

Complete the gaps in the following sentences with the correct Past simple or Past perfect form of the verb in brackets. Only use the Past perfect if it is necessary.

1 When I .... (telephone) my father last week, I .... (not / speak) to him for five years.

2 Eleanor .... (go) to university for four years before she .... (start) work at Microsoft.

3 All of the dinosaurs .... (die) millions of years ago.

4 I .... (got) home at five o'clock yesterday as usual and I .... (find) that someone .... (break into) my flat and .... (steal) my video recorder.

5 After I .... (leave) school, I .... (join) the army.

6 By the time he was twenty, Mozart .... (write) several of his most popular pieces of music.

| 6 |

I Numbers

Write the following numbers in words.

For example:
743,200
seven hundred and forty-three thousand, two hundred

1 –12°C
....

2 2001
....

3 87 km²
....

4 421,000 km per hr
....

5 72.5%
....

| 5 |

J Grammar: modal verbs

In each of the following sentences there is a mistake in either the meaning or the grammar of the modal verbs (*could*, *should*, etc.). Correct the mistakes.

For example:
We hadn't to wear school uniform at my school.
We didn't have to wear school uniform at my school.

1 You must to have a license to keep a dog.
....

2 I know I should have drunk so much beer last night! I feel terrible!
....

3 In the last century, women can't vote in our country.
....

4 Dr Grant told Sue she ought do more exercise.
....

5 You don't have to eat food in the library.
....

6 Students have to wear any clothes they like.
....

7 During the war, soldiers didn't allowed to write any letters to their families.
....

8 In many countries you haven't to drink and drive.
....

9 He shouldn't come to the disco if he didn't want to dance.
....

10 We've to solve this problem as soon as possible.
....

| 10 |

© Pearson Education Limited 2005

K Vocabulary: word building

Complete each sentence with the correct form of the word in capitals.

For example:
Everyone agreed he'd made the right ....*decision*........ .
DECIDE

1 Access to .... should be a basic human right. EDUCATE

2 Our .... for not doing our homework was to miss football. PUNISH

3 It wasn't very .... to go to the disco the night before the exam. SENSE

4 I want to study .... at university. ECONOMY

5 You need special .... to play ice hockey. EQUIP

6 The police .... someone, but they haven't got any evidence yet. SUSPICIOUS

7 There has been a lot of .... in this area recently. INVEST

☐ 7

L Linking words

Write a suitable linking word or phrase (*What's more*, *although*, etc.) in the gaps. Do not use a*nd*, *but* or *so*.

For example:
Many people use English on the Internet. ..*What's more*,.. more people have decided to study English.

1 English is very useful for travelling. .... , it can improve your chances of getting a better job.

2 Students who want to study in the USA have to pass an English listening test. .... , they often still find it difficult to understand what their teachers say.

3 English at the moment seems to be becoming the international language, ... in the future it is thought that Chinese may well become more important.

4 Spanish is also very important on the American continent. .... , more and more people in the United States are studying it as their second language.

☐ 4

M Verb patterns: infinitive or -ing

Complete the gaps in the following sentences with the infinitive or -*ing* form of the verb in brackets.

For example:
The shop promised ....*to give me*.......... (give me) my money back.

1 No one has ever persuaded Jo .... (eat) meat.

2 Everyone should be free .... (read) whatever they want.

3 It should be against the law .... (smoke) in all public places.

4 Mrs Ridley didn't know what .... (do) about the noise.

5 People shouldn't be allowed .... (take) their dogs into the park.

6 Paula suggested .... (go) to a film.

7 You shouldn't have refused .... (talk) to Paul.

8 I asked Pete .... (help) me with my homework.

9 I remember .... (see) a man go into the bank, but I'm not sure what happened after that.

10 The waiter could have denied .... (take) the money.

☐ 10

TOTAL ☐ 100

Resource bank key

Learner-training worksheet 2

1 *adj* – adjective; *adv* – adverb; *n* C – countable noun;
n U – uncountable noun; *v* T – transitive verb; *v* I –
intransitive verb

a *n* U   b *n* C   c *v* T   d *n* U   e *adv*
f *adj*   g *v* I   h *v* I

3 a 2   b 2   c 2   d 2   e 2

4 a found   b complain about   c looking forward
to going   d explain the homework to me

5 a a travel agency, an employment agency, a ticket
agency   b on the market   c boiling hot
d a sales clerk   e it is used in informal situations
f literary

6 cath<u>e</u>dral, <u>mean</u>while, per<u>cent</u>, <u>pop</u>ulated

Learner-training worksheet 3

1 does his homework   2a a series of actions
intended to persuade people to do something or
persuade the government to change laws and
plans   b (2 of the following) election campaign,
advertising campaign, a campaign for equal rights
3 On   4 prize   5 neighbor   6 in<u>crease</u>,
<u>increase</u>   7 on seeing   8 uncle, aunt
9 on   10 leapt, leapt

Learner-training worksheet 4

1
a Jack is jealous of his younger brother.
b I suggest that you take / I suggest taking the
   fast train at 9:45.
c Your school work is showing a big
   improvement.
d Last month a twenty-year-old man mugged an
   old lady/a man, etc.
e After his parents died, Pete's grandparents
   brought him up.

Discussion point 1

the preposition that follows *jealous*
the grammatical construction that follows *suggest*
the noun form of *improve*
when you can/cannot use the verb *assassinate*
the irregular Past simple form of *bring*

2 1 go shopping   2 do their homework
3 eat out   4 get lost   5 move house
6 say sorry   7 have a rest

1A Get to know the *Students' Book*

A two   B page 148   C page 155   D two
E pages 171 and 172   F *Study … Practise …
Remember!*   G on the inside cover of the *Mini-
dictionary*   H orange   I three   J page 156
K blue   L *take*   M page 74   N Module 12
O Module 10   P Module 9

1D Vocabulary extension

1 a someone at work   b the woman who lives
next door   c people I don't know
d people on my course   e the girl I share a flat
with   f got talking   g get on well with
h get to know

2 a 3   b 5   c 7   d 6   e 2   f 1   g 4

3B *100 places to visit before you die*

3

	noun	adjective	opposite adjective	adverb
a	care	careful	careless	carefully
b	importance	important	unimportant	importantly
c	historian history	historical		historically
d	difficulty	difficult	easy	
e	imagination	imaginative imaginary	unimaginative	imaginatively
f	romance romantic	romantic	unromantic	romantically
g	beauty	beautiful	ugly	beautifully
h	fame	famous	unknown	famously
i	experience	experienced	inexperienced	

4 b imagination   c carefully   d romantic
e unimportant   f famous   g beautiful
h difficulty   i inexperienced

3D How do I get to . . . ?

1 1 out   2 of   3 turn   4 Take   5 keep
6 to   7 at   8 see   9 on   10 past   11 next
12 on   13 opposite

4C Vocabulary extension

1

	noun	adjective	opposite adjective
a	courage	courageous	cowardly
b	fairness	fair	unfair
c	imagination	imaginative	unimaginative
d	tolerance	tolerant	intolerant
e	determination	determined	
f	hard work	hardworking	lazy
g	originality	original	unoriginal
h	talent	talented	untalented
i	principle	principled	unprincipled
j	self-confidence	self-confident	unconfident

2

a self-confident   b talented   c imaginative
d courageous   e fair   f principled
g hardworking   h determined   i tolerant
j original

5A Have you got what it takes?

1

a on   b about   c from   d in   e for   f to
g about   h to   i for   j in

Student A

1 in   2 in   3 about   4 from   5 to

Student B

1 on   2 for   3 to   4 about   5 for

5C Vocabulary extension

1

a 3   b 5   c 6   d 2   e 1   f 7   g 4

6B Vocabulary extension

1

to be damaged / to be destroyed – if something is
damaged, physical harm is done to it, but it can still
be repaired; if something is destroyed, it is harmed
so badly that it cannot be repaired or no longer
exists.
to be murdered / to be killed / to be assassinated – to
murder someone means that you kill them
deliberately and illegally; kill is the general word
meaning to make someone or something die; to
assassinate someone means to murder an
important, famous and usually political person.
to be burgled / to be robbed / to be stolen – burgle
means to get into a building and steal things from
inside; rob means to steal property or money from a
person, bank, etc.; if you steal something, you take
something that belongs to someone else.

to be arrested / to be held / to be jailed – if the police
arrest you, they take you to the police station
because they think that you have done something
illegal; they hold you at the police station for a
number of hours before charging you with the
crime or releasing you; if you are jailed, you are put
in jail after you have been found guilty of the crime.
to be wounded / to be injured / to be hurt – if you
wound someone, you hurt someone physically,
especially by making a cut or hole in their skin
with a knife or a gun (for example, in a battle); if
you are injured, you are physically hurt as a result
of an accident or attack (for example, in a car
accident); if you hurt someone, you cause physical
pain to them (for example: Don't hold my hand so
tight – it hurts!).

2

1 injured   2 killed   3 held   4 burgled
5 stolen   6 murdered   7 jailed   8 destroyed
9 damaged

3

1 Hairdresser's final cut   2 Pop star loses hair
3 Wigs lead police to prisoners

1 injured   2 damaged   3 jailed   4 held
5 burgled   6 stolen   7 destroyed   8 arrested
9 robbed   10 injured

7A Vocabulary extension

1

a Wait!   b doing   c man   d What's the matter?
e talk (to someone)   f How are you?
g a long time   h Don't worry   i friends
j unhappy   k going   l two or three

2

f, i, a, k, c, h, l, b, d, j, g, e

b that man – that guy
c two or three friends – two or three mates
d two weeks – a couple of weeks
h for a long time – for ages; What's the matter? –
What's up?
i How are you? – How's it going?
j don't worry – never mind; going to the shops – off
to the shops
k so what have you been doing recently? – so what
have you been up to recently?
l unhappy – fed up

8A Machines behaving badly

1

a 4   b 5   c 6   d 3   e 1   f 7   g 2

3

(incorrect nouns)
a a salary   b an e-mail   c a laugh
d the reason   e the window   f money
g the picture

Student A

1 played   2 wrote   3 taken   4 made
5 watch   6 save   7 answer

Student B

1 playing   2 saving   3 watched   4 write
5 made   6 answer   7 take

8B   Relative clauses crossword

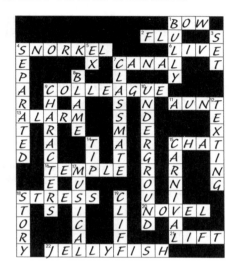

9D   Vocabulary extension

1 a 8   b 6   c 5   d 1   e 2   f 9   g 4   h 10
i 3   j 7

10A   Ralph and the guitar case

(There is more than one possible answer.)

A   Ralph woke up
1   and immediately knew something was wrong.
B   His head was aching
6   and he was still wearing all his clothes.
17   He realised he had drunk too much the previous night.
C   He looked at the clock.
2   It was five-thirty.
8   He realised that he had been asleep for over twelve hours!
5   He got out of bed and walked over to the window.
D   It was raining outside
13   and people were hurrying home from work.
E   He sat back down on the bed and turned on the television.
4   A police officer was talking about a bank robbery.
10   Three hundred thousand dollars had been stolen
18   and two people had been shot.
F   Ralph turned off the television and looked around the room.
9   In the corner there was a guitar case leaning against the wall.

G   He knew that it wasn't his
12   because he had never played the guitar in his life.
H   Then he remembered
3   what had happened the previous evening.
7   He had gone to a nightclub,
11   where he had met a beautiful singer called Rosanna.
16   After the show he'd bought her a drink, then another and another.
19   He couldn't remember what they'd talked about, or how he'd got home.
I   Ralph stood up and walked over to the guitar case.
15   He laid it on the bed and opened it.
J   When he looked inside, he couldn't believe his eyes.
20   It was full of $100 bills!
14   He quickly picked up the guitar case and ran out of the door.

10C   Vocabulary extension

1 a 5   b 1   c 9   d 3   e 10   f 7   g 4   h 8
i 2   j 6

2 a   It is unusual to whisper *loudly.*
b   You don't *ask* someone to mutter, because it means to speak unclearly.
c   To *announce* is to give information, not to ask a question.
d   It is more usual to *whisper* in a library, because you have to be quiet.
e   She is not *adding* anything, because this is the first thing she says.
f   It is very difficult to *scream* in a low voice.

3 a 'm whispering   b shout   c exclaimed
d repeated   e explained   f announce
g screamed   h muttering

11A   *To sue or not to sue?*

1   a to sue   b for

2   a trip   b down

3   a injury   b injure   c injured

4   a for   b responsibility

5   a compensation   b compensate

6   a to complain   b at   c complaint

7   a get on   b I get on well with Carina … ;
I'm getting on badly with Mike …

8   a payouts, claims   b to claim, to pay out

Test one (modules 1–4)

A
1 How much does the train to Edinburgh cost?
2 Where was Sebastian born?
3 How long have you known your teacher?
4 What are you looking for?
5 Did all your classmates go to the party yesterday?
6 Has anyone seen Mrs Pearson this morning?
7 Did you use to speak Japanese when you were young?
8 Was it raining when you arrived?
9 How long were Sarah and Eduardo married?
10 Is Paul working on anything special at the moment?

B
(incorrect words/phrases)
1 exam   2 headache   3 divorce   4 job
5 twenty years old   6 career

C
1 at   2 in   3 about   4 after   5 of   6 up   7 for
8 in   9 to   10 to

D
1 were you   2 am writing   3 has had
4 don't agree   5 was spending   6 grew up
7 is getting   8 Have you spoken   9 has never flown
10 was crying

E
1 Weren't they?   2 Did he?   3 Aren't there?
4 Does it?   5 Has she?   6 Aren't you?

F *(half a mark each)*
●○   travelled, parent, colleague
○●   achieved, retire, arrived
●○○   recognise, relative, festival
○●○   courageous, polluted, old-fashioned

G
1 worse   2 wetter   3 prettiest   4 further/farther
5 more polluted   6 lot   7 bit   8 by   9 craziest
10 as   11 from   12 to

H
1 recognise   2 forgot   3 remember   4 learnt
5 remind

I
1 since   2 for   3 ago   4 since   5 for   6 since
7 ago   8 ago   9 for   10 for

J
1 stepmother   2 brother-in-law   3 stranger
4 ex-girlfriend   5 retire

K
1 —   2 a   3 the   4 —   5 the   6 the   7 —
8 —   9 an   10 —

L
1 sleeping   2 to play   3 eating out
4 programming   5 to bring   6 seeing   7 to invite
8 to set   9 to read   10 go

Test two (modules 5–8)

A
1 I'm meeting   2 get   3 will win   4 her boss to give her   5 I remember   6 will the photos be   7 I'll look   8 fixes   9 I'll do it   10 will work

B
1 f   2 a   3 b   4 c   5 d   6 g   7 h   8 e

C
1 were taken   2 arrested   3 found
4 exploded   5 was badly injured   6 have died
7 happened   8 flew   9 is thought   10 was caused

D
○●○   amusing, embarrassed
●○○   qualified, interested, challenging
○○●○   satisfaction, disappointed
○●○○   ridiculous, experienced
○○●○○   opportunity

E
1 to leave   2 to leave   3 leaving   4 to leave
5 to leave   6 to leave   7 to leave   8 leaving
9 to leave   10 to leave

F
1 on   2 In   3 through   4 for   5 on   6 to
7 for   8 of   9 of   10 on

G
1 receipt   2 week   3 jealousy   4 lyrics
5 documentaries   6 Ridiculous   7 rescue
8 banned   9 split   10 lift

H
1 which/that   2 who/that   3 where   4 which/that
5 whose   6 who/   7 sentence 2   8 sentence 4

I
1 Could I possibly read your newspaper?
2 Do you think you could give me some change for £5?
3 Could you possibly look after my cat this weekend?
4 Do you mind if I watch television?
5 Would/Do you mind switching off the CD player when you go to bed?
6 Is it all right if I have a bath?

J
1 shocked   2 plug in   3 going bald   4 worrying
5 well-paid   6 astonishing   7 dress up

K
1 too much/a lot of   2 enough   3 a few/several
4 too much/a lot of/plenty of/loads of   5 a lot of/plenty of/several/loads of/many   6 much/too much/a lot of   7 a few   8 too many

L
1 —   2 The   3 a   4 —   5 a   6 the   7 —   8 a

Test three (modules 9–12)

A

1 Taxes are likely to go up next year.
2 It may well snow tomorrow.
3 Sylvia almost certainly won't be on the next train.
4 Guy could pass his driving test.
5 Mary will probably move to Canada.
6 The USA definitely won't win the Ryder Cup.
7 Max isn't likely to phone you until tomorrow.
8 Andrea might not like the present I've bought her.

B

1 rules   2 strict   3 improve   4 lend   5 decrease
6 rise   7 agree/accept   8 innocent

C

1 will you do; miss; 'll get
2 didn't cost; 'd (would)/could/might visit
3 hadn't been; wouldn't/mightn't have happened
4 'd (would) call; knew
5 could/would/might have become; 'd (had) trained
6 's (is) closed; 'll go
7 doesn't work; won't pass
8 would you do; left; 'd (would) probably spend
9 'd (had) told; could/would/might have done
10 hadn't got; 'd (would) still be / 'd (would) have still been

D

(half a mark each)
1 sorry, goodbye, a prayer
2 somebody unhappy, a profit, sure
3 your best, yoga, well
4 a lie, the truth, someone something

E

1 by   2 off   3 in   4 over   5 of   6 in   7 of
8 in   9 out

F *(1 mark for each phrase underlined)*

... <u>asked him why he hadn't brought</u> the money. Jack <u>said he hadn't had</u> time to arrange it. She <u>said she would send his boss</u>* the photos if <u>he didn't give her</u> the money. Jack <u>said okay</u>, he <u>could get</u> it by <u>the next day</u>. He <u>asked her where the photos were</u>. She <u>said they were</u> in a safe place and <u>told him not to worry</u>.

* also possible: She *threatened to send*

G

○●   persuade, obey, ignore
●○   science, foreign, promise
○○●○   disadvantage, economic, unemployment
●○○○   necessary, fortunately, obviously

H

1 telephoned; hadn't spoken   2 went; started   3 died
4 got; found; 'd (had) broken into; 'd (had) stolen
5 left; joined   6 had written

I

1 minus twelve degrees Celsius/centigrade
2 two thousand and one
3 eighty-seven square kilometres
4 four hundred and twenty-one thousand kilometres per/an hour
5 seventy-two point five percent / seventy-two and a half percent

J

1 you must have / you have to have / you've got to have
2 shouldn't have drunk
3 couldn't vote / weren't allowed to vote
4 ought to do / should do
5 mustn't eat / can't eat / aren't allowed to eat
6 can wear / are allowed to wear
7 weren't allowed to write
8 mustn't drink / can't drink / aren't allowed to drink
9 shouldn't have come / doesn't want to dance
10 We've got to solve / We have to solve / We must solve

K

1 education   2 punishment   3 sensible
4 economics   5 equipment   6 suspect   7 investment

L

1 What's more / Besides / Also,   2 However / Despite this   3 although   4 As a result / For this reason / Therefore

M

1 to eat   2 to read   3 to smoke   4 to do   5 to take
6 going   7 to talk   8 to help   9 seeing   10 taking

Pearson Education Limited
Edinburgh Gate
Harlow
Essex
CM20 2JE
England
and Associated Companies throughout the world

www.longman.com/cutting edge

Set in Congress Sans and Stone I formal

Printed in Spain by Mateu Cromo, S.A. Pinto (Madrid)

ISBN 0582 825180

Illustrated by Pavely Arts, Kathy Baxendale, Graham
Humphreys/The Art Market, Ed McLachlan, Graham Smith/The
Art Market.